Books of Daily Thoughts and Prayers

Books of Daily Thoughts and Prayers

BY

SWAMI PARAMANANDA

GYAN

Published by

GYAN

Gyan Publishing House
5, Ansari Road
Daryaganj, New Delhi-110002
Phone: 011-47034999, 9811692060
E-mail: books@gyanbooks.com

Distribution Network
gyanbooks.com
India, USA, Canada, UK, Australia

ISBN: 978-93-6433-122-7 (PB)
First Published, 1926

2nd Impression 2024

Printed at: Gyan Press, Delhi.

BOOKS OF DAILY THOUGHTS AND PRAYERS
Author: SWAMI PARAMANANDA

Book of Daily Thoughts and Prayers

By
SWAMI PARAMANANDA
Author of "Path of Devotion", "The Way of Peace of Blessedness", "Rhythm of Life", "The Vigil", "Soul's Secret Door", etc.

Onward, ever forward in the march of life—
Ever onward, ever forward, my soul,
March on! March on!

SREE
RAMAKRISHNA ANANDA ASHRAMA
1, NAKTALA LANE,
CALCUTTA-700047

Foreword

There are moments when the spirit is mute and powerless to give utterance to its interior yearning. It feels the need of a vibrant word to rouse it from its numbness and voice its voiceless aspiration. Hence attempts to provide, in one form or another, daily thoughts for the day's round are coincident with the rising of the religious consciousness. The ancient Forest-Books or Upanishads of the Vedic period were but the accumulated effort of great sages to help those who surrounded them in their woodland hermitage, to meet the daily problem with triumphant heart. The mediaeval breviaries and manuals of devotion were written or compiled to the same end. The present volume is another contribution to this daily sacrament of prayer and holy thought.

The idea of preparing it is not of recent conception. As far back as 1812 Swami Paramananda wrote me from Switzerland; "Other day I was thinking a little of the next book—(from your letters). Can't we call it 'A Book of Daily Thoughts and Prayers'? What do you think of it?" I had written to him that the idea had come to me to gather from his later letters and certain notes of his teaching material for a companion volume to the "Path of Devotion," made up from earlier letters. It was not possible, at the time, to carry out his new suggestion, as another book under preparation was practically ready for press when the suggestion came; but the intention remained with me and at last has assumed definite form.

The present volume has lost nothing through the delay, for now it has a much richer store to draw upon. From year to year I have garnered stray thoughts jotted down on scraps of paper lying on the Swami's desk or work table, or tucked in some book. I have noted vital sayings and set aside countless passages from letters. All the material used, except the lines taken from the Swami's poems, has been drawn from unpublished sources;—chiefly from familiar instructions given to his household at the morning or evening meal; or from fragments of conversation, written down with groping hand and unseeing eyes on the terrace of the Ashrama in the moonlight, or by the flicker of a hearth-fire, or by the dim flame of a far-away candle. The prayers were caught with the same stealthy silent pencil at the moment of their utterance. They sound in consequence the more living note of spoken supplication. The quotations from the Scriptures are from the Swami's translations.

Coming from such intimate sources, the words which follow possess special helpfulness in the intimate inward strivings of each day. They have been classified and arranged in consecutive and cumulative sequence. The thought is carried forward from day to day, so that at the end of a month a new and defined impression will be made on the character. Each day brings its salient thought to be held through the waking hours in continuous mindfulness; a brief lesson amplifies this and imbeds it more deeply in the consciousness; a prayer feeds and strengthens the natural upward-reaching devotional aspirations of the heart.

A few lines from the Swami's sacred and illumined poems are given as a daily exercise in memorizing. Memorizing is one of the most productive of spiritual practices. It provides a rich inner library to which one can turn in the moment of emptiness or distress. A single line called up in memory will sometimes turn the thought into an entirely fresh and wholesome channel. Thus on each page will be found food for all the faculties of the aspiring spirit.

The Swami's words lend themselves with peculiar aptitude to a work of this nature. His sentences have the focused, shining quality of a finely-cut gem which requires no embellishment of ornate setting. They stir the higher, holier impulses of the soul and impel to consecrated living. They carry forward by their inherent vitality and strength. The book calls for no other introduction than itself. With its tender counsel and ringing appeal it will find its way, by the force of its spiritual power, into the heart and sanctuary of every seeker whose hand it reaches.

DEVAMATA.

ANANDA-ASHRAMA,
APRIL, 1926.

Contents

Be not offended if my mortal hand
Lacketh grace to offer Thee oblation.
Yet this hand is Thy gift
Sanctified by Thy touch.
I will use it humbly
And lift this offering of love to Thy Feet.
I will cherish my mind
For it hath brought me thoughts of Thee;
I will cherish my heart
For it hath given me vision of Thee;
And I will crown this life with a crown of bliss
For it hath brought me to Thy gate.

January

LIVING CONSECRATION

He who is ever content and meditative, self-subjugated and possessed with firm conviction, with mind and heart dedicated to Me, he who is thus consecrated to Me is dear to Me.

Bhagavad-Gita

JANUARY FIRST

Salient Thought for the Day.

When we choose the spiritual life, we must make it real and vibrant.

Lines to Memorize.

We bring Thee our humble hearts.
No merit have we save our faith in Thine infinite compassion.
Do Thou make of us Thy tools that at all hours, in work and play,
We may revolve in Thy safe-keeping.

Lesson.

When we are imbued with the true spirit of consecration, all our activities are turned into worship. All tasks before us, small and big, become of deep significance. When our heart is thus filled with the consciousness of the ever-living and all-blissful Deity, we no longer feel the weary weight of life.

Prayer.

O Lord, help me to consecrate my whole life to Thee.
May I find all my joy in Thy blessed Presence.
Help me to fasten my heart to eternal Truth.
Fix my thought on Thee alone.
May I never fail to look up to Thee and seek Thy holy guidance.
Fill me and surround me with Thy Divine peace.
May Thy holy peace reign in my heart and life.

JANUARY SECOND

Salient Thought for the Day.

Represent the Ideal in your life. Let this always be your prayer.

Lines to Memorize.

Children of Light, walk in the light;
Let all darkness vanish from your path!
Children of Light, let your face shine with love and joy! . . .
Children of Light, dwell in the light!
Think of the light and live in the light!

Lesson.

The world is conquered by that one whose mind rests in his spiritual being. If a man keeps his thought fixed on his lower self, in spite of all his planning and calculating, he will give way to anger, hatred and jealousy, and his face will bear the mark of anger or hatred. If a man has love in his heart, his whole countenance will be shining. If we carry a sense of consecration with us in all we do or say, we become a channel for the Highest, and as a channel our power is unlimited.

Prayer.

O Thou All-effulgent Spirit,
I bring Thee my love and humble worship.
Awaken in me such wisdom that I may seek all my strength and safety in Thee.
Cleanse my mind from all alien thoughts
And make my heart so pure and shining
That it will ever reflect Thy Divine radiance and glory.

JANUARY THIRD

Salient Thought for the Day.

Hold fast to the Light, then all will come out right.

Lines to Memorize.

Let your life be a perpetual light;
Your words will scatter sparks of wisdom;
Your glance of love will penetrate desolate hearts;
Your song of bliss will rouse all downcast spirits. . . .
Children of Light, walk in the Light!
Let all darkness vanish from your path.

Lesson.

If we keep our mind free, clear and open, then there is no crisis in our life. We must never leave our inner house in darkness; we must ever keep the light of consecration burning there. Where there is light, God comes and no sense-robbers can enter. If we keep our life in harmony, evil will stay far from us. Some people pray only when in trouble. If we pray continually, then when trouble comes, our prayer will go on of itself.

Prayer.

O Thou Infinite Spirit,
Kindle my little lamp by Thy great Light
That I may never walk in darkness.
In my life may I ever have Thy holy Guidance.
May Thy Light ever shine upon my path.
Grant me Thy loving protection.

JANUARY FOURTH

Salient Thought for the Day.

We must order our whole life so that we may live close to God.

Lines to Memorize.

I walk before thee, and I watch over thee;
I dwell within thee
And I surround without thee;
In darkness I reveal thy path,
In sadness I lighten thy heart.
Fear not, nor be distressed;
I infill all space.
I am with thee always.

Lesson.

We must rest our life on the fundamental facts of being. If our life is empty, we must fill it; and more easily we are overthrown. But when we live in the material world, more we become bound and more easily we are overthrown. But when we live in Spirit, nothing can overthrow us. We should never fasten ourselves to the outer world.

Prayer.

O Lord, I lift my thought and prayer to Thee.
Reveal unto me Thy protecting and all-absorbing Presence.
Thou art the embodiment of all blessing.
Fill my life with holiness and peace.
Make it fruitful and wholly dedicated to Thy service,
And may I never forget Thee or turn my face away from Thee.

JANUARY FIFTH

Salient Thought for the Day.

We must always carry with us high and lofty ideals.

Lines to Memorize.

My life's lamp was dim and dying;
But Thou, unfailing Giver,
Didst fill it anew
With Thy fresh oil of life.
Now it burns again with fervent, steady and luminous glow.

Lesson.

Every day we can keep the light burning within; but when the light is burning we must not become so elated that we cease to be watchful. If we have something real and vital in our life, we cannot go astray. So long as we live in the spiritual depths of our being we are safe. When we live with an exalted spiritual Ideal constantly before us, our life will radiate power and the brightness of true joy.

Prayer.

O Thou Eternal Light of the Universe,
Fill my life with Thy Divine radiance.
Awaken in my heart the sense of Thy Holy Presence.
Abide with me at every hour in my work and play.
May I never fail to manifest Thee in all my thoughts, words and deeds.

JANUARY SIXTH

Salient Thought for the Day.

When we try to find our happiness from external conditions, every time we shall fail.

Lines to Memorize.

They call me again and again when I sit by Thy side;
They think I am lonely and unloved.
How they pity my state!
They offer me much, but I smile—
For they know not the secret of this unseen comradeship.

Lesson.

There is great joy, bliss and happiness in the life on spiritual consecration if we understand it. When our spiritual understanding deepens, spiritual truths become living for us. It is so sad when people close their door and deprive themselves of spiritual blessing.

Prayer.

O Tender Lord, Thou art the supreme Joy of my heart.
Thou art the One to be loved and sought after.
Thou art the Eternal among the changing.
Thou art an unfailing Light in the darkness of the world.
May I feel Thy great Life pervading my little life.
Thy mighty Love strengthening my lesser love.
Surround me with Thy holy protection
And grant unto me Thy peace.

JANUARY SEVENTH

Salient Thought for the Day.

All life is to teach us how we may bring the living presence of our Ideal into our consciousness.

Lines to Memorize.

Verily Thou art my life's fulfilment;
The cause of my joy and sorrow, laughter and grief;
My soul's sunshine and heart's raincloud.

Lesson.

When our life becomes empty, to fill this emptiness, we try to gather from outside and we gain emptiness. We try to find something permanent and we seek it in the fleeting. Consciousness of the presence of the Eternal within our soul alone will bring us peace and enduring satisfaction. There is no anarchy or accident in the cosmic universe. There is no uneven distribution of favor and disfavor. Only as we seek that which does not shift or change do we find our fulfilment.

Prayer.

O Thou Infinite and Ever-blessed One,
Thou art the conscious Being abiding in the hearts of all conscious beings.
Do Thou fill my heart with a living sense of consecration to Thee,
That I may learn to follow Thy path with unwavering faith and whole-hearted devotion.
Grant me spiritual insight that I may know and do Thy Will.

JANUARY EIGHTH

Salient Thought for the Day.

No man is cut off from the Divine Source.

Lines to Memorize.

My heart grows bold with faith as I know Thy protecting love.
I shall weep no more for sadness if Thou but stayest near me.
I know that Thy blessed Presence alone is life complete, unbroken peace, an island of eternal joy.

Lesson.

No one can have a monopoly of spirituality. No one can claim exclusive right to it. It is not something cut and dried. Spirituality means getting away from all that is calculating, cold and hard. No one can rob us of it except when we ourselves yield to our lower instincts.

Prayer.

Help me to give myself to complete spiritual union with the Source of strength and illumination.
Lift me above all bondage and weakness.
Make my mind so free and one-pointed that it may be full of strength.
May I turn towards the Light,
That Light which reveals, the Light that redeems;
To that Light which restores and replenishes.

Salient Thought for the Day.

If we keep ourselves ever close to the Great Eternal One, nothing can go wrong with us.

Lines to Memorize.

My soul is at peace since the dawn.
A cool breeze of new hope hath soothed my troubled heart—
Yea, the weight of life hath fallen from me.
I am bathed; I am refreshed in this new life
That Thou hast mercifully shed upon me, Thy undeserving child!

Lesson.

Spiritual life means renewal in everything, new ideas, new thoughts, new life. Even the body is renewed and sanctified. We have constant opportunity to prove that we are God's children. How? Not by works, but by our love, by our service, by our life.

Prayer.

May the Divine Mother give me spiritual joy
And make my heart free from all doubt and despair.
May my thoughts and prayers always be directed towards Her.
May She fill my heart more and more with selfless love, humility, patience, gentleness, and egolessness.
May holiness and peace reign in my life.

JANUARY TENTH

Salient Thought for the Day.

Think what it means to every man that, as he walks through life, he is eternally with God.

Lines to Memorize.

Thou art my life's consummation,
My abode of unbroken rest;
I lay at Thy transcendent Feet
My weary heart, for its peace.

Lesson.

In the midst of the crowd we can have quietude. There is a sense of aloneness in the spiritual life—not loneliness; because we never feel lonely when we have spiritual consciousness within us. We feel the Presence and that Presence seems to give us a sense of aloofness from the turbulence of the world. Loneliness is an interior condition. It does not come from being alone; one can be very lonely when surrounded by many people. That man is never lonely who lives close to God.

Prayer.

O Thou Unbounded Spirit of the Universe,
Make me to feel Thy nearness, that my mind may be freed from all doubt and fear.
May I find Thy Presence everywhere.
May I perceive Thy beauty and sublimity in all things.
Give unto me true devotion.
May I always feel that Thou art my Resting-place,
My Source of inspiration and joy.

Salient Thought for the Day.

Never fail to be watchful that you may be ready for the call.

Lines to Memorize.

I heard a voice call me at early dawn....
I stopped and listened;
I strained my hearing;
My mind stretched its wings but with no avail.
Now I have surrendered.
Come then, O mysterious One!
Tell me, why didst Thou call me?
I must know Thy will.

Lesson.

If we learn to do what is given us with an exalted spirit of consecration, then our actions will bear fruit in abundance. Our life becomes fruitful only when we do things with noble motive. The work itself is neither good nor bad, but the motive which actuates us determines the merit or demerit of every action. The highest motive in all action is when it is inspired by some spiritual Ideal.

Prayer.

O Supreme Spirit, who abides within all!
Awaken in my heart a living consciousness of Thee
That in the midst of all fleeting conditions I may ever remain watchful.
May I never fail to serve Thee with my whole heart and soul.
Grant unto me strength, steadfastness and firm faith.

Salient Thought for the Day.

Be faithful above everything.

Lines to Memorize.

My heart is Thy throne, ...
Humility is its pedestal;
Faith its cornerstone;
Prayers are its sweet frankincense.
The lamp of my life will burn day and night
If Thou wilt come and sit upon this lowly throne.

Lesson.

Our Ideal may seem very far, very unobtainable. That is the time for us to show courage and strength. Those who show courage and steadfast devotion to their Ideal are bound to succeed. We gain the highest by fulfilling our ordinary tasks and duties. Every duty is a privilege. Every task that comes our way is a blessing. Every time we have a chance to do something for God or His children it should be a great joy.

Prayer.

O Thou Eternal One! Infill my mind with the light of understanding.
Grant unto me firm resolution
That I may follow Thy path with courage that never fails.
Help me to draw Thee close in my heart.
Teach me to lean upon Thee wholly and never to seek my own will.
May Thy peace and blessing rest upon me and upon all living beings.

Salient Thought for the Day.

Stand like a sentinel guarding a Shrine.

Lines to Memorize.

Be brave; be true, and wait!
How long?
Who cares how long or how short!
Time is not our end;
Time is not our aim;
Nor waiting, our goal.
Yet wait and watch;
For time will bring ripening to thy soul.

Lesson.

To abide by one's Ideal necessitates undaunted courage, unfailing vigor, unwavering faith and selfless aspiration. One must be fearless in opposition; in failure one must be undepressed; and in moments of darkness one must have faith. Love of our task must make us forget ourselves and all sense of personal gain and loss.

Prayer.

O Thou All-compassionate One!
Grant unto me such a sense of Thy living Presence
That I shall never fail to consecrate all my thoughts, words and actions unto Thee.
Make my heart free from all blemish and unloveliness.
Make me ever loyal and true to Thy service.

Salient Thought for the Day.

When we reach the threshold of God, of Truth, then alone do we know true joy.

Lines to Memorize.

Love of the physical will pass
As all passing things must follow their course;
But love of the spiritual will never wane nor die.

Lesson.

Man is not satisfied; not even when he builds an empire. He is always longing for something deeper, more complete. This we do not find in the outer world. It is deep down in us. We never find any real happiness or the real source of strength until we are able to go down within our own soul. That is where we find God and Divinity. Our possessions, our friends, fail us often; but God who abides within us and who knows our heart, He never fails us. True joy cannot rest on material conditions; it is found only in Infinitude.

Prayer.

O Lord, Thou art the Goal of my existence,
Thou art the Refuge for all souls.
Arouse in me true yearning,
That through its force I may gain such power of penetration
That I may perceive Thee in the midst of all things.
Make my heart sincere, and my prayer simple and fervent.
Thou art the embodiment of all blessedness.
Grant unto me Thy loving protection.

JANUARY FIFTEENTH

Salient Thought for the Day.

Our real awakening in the spiritual sense takes place when we dedicate our life to an exalted Ideal.

Lines to Memorize.

My heart is Thy throne,
Yea, it is for Thee alone. . . .
It is love's own design
And built by life's unmixed devotion. . .
It is designed by love,
Encircled by love,
It is love's own creation.

Lesson.

The beginning of our regeneration takes place when we know our true nature through our connection with the Godhead. Real good comes to us when we find that we have the Divine spark within us. If we learn to unfold that, all we have to do is to remove the obstacles from its way, then it shines in its own glory. We must have a basis for our life which is dependable. Wise men make it their first duty to find their home in Truth.

Prayer.

O Thou Divine Essence!
Thou art one Absolute Being without a second.
Make me realize Thy Allness.
Enlighten my heart that I may always feel Thy Holy Presence.
Teach me ever to draw my strength through contact with Thee,
And surround me at all times with Thy blessing and peace.

Salient Thought for the Day.

Pray that you may learn to fill your heart with selfless love, humility and gentleness.

Lines to Memorize.

I give my peace unto thee, but thou must give up self.
Be not affrighted, my child,
There is no loss in giving up self.
Fear brings thee anguish and it brings thee doubt;
But doubt, anguish and fear will all leave thee
When thou hast given up self.

Lesson.

Love, humility and gentleness—these are the things which make us happy, these are the things we should crave for. Souls that are full of self and full of fear are always troubled. God will always make us happy and bless us when our heart is free from doubt, despair and harshness. Direct all your thoughts and prayers to Him, then you will be safe from pride and egotism.

Prayer.

O Thou All-abiding, All-loving One!
Manifest Thyself in all my thoughts, words and actions,
That I may transcend the limitation of the little self;
And draw nearer to Thee through selfless devotion.
Make my heart glad and peaceful and fearless.
May I always feel Thy Presence within my soul.

JANUARY SEVENTEENTH

Salient Thought for the Day.

God pleads tenderly with us, like a mother, to give up self.

Lines to Memorize.

I shall dwell in thee when thou hast given up self;
Nay, I shall possess thee, fill thee and own thee
When thou hast given up self.

Lesson.

Direct, simple, child-like method is the best. All great characters have exhibited simplicity and directness. This is a Divine gift. It is much easier to go by the direct path. Calculation, mental analysis and all such things entangle us and our mind becomes confused. When we have a true sense of consecration we are always simple, child-like and full of selfless devotion.

Prayer.

O Thou All compassionate Spirit
Reveal unto us Thy abiding love.
Destroy all selfishness in our hearts,
Fill us with strength and wisdom.
Make us worthy channels to express Thy power and do Thy Will,
And surround us ever with Thy protecting peace.

Salient Thought for the Day.

A common man always asserts his ego; a superior man is only conscious that God is manifesting through him.

Lines to Memorize.

Come thou [ego] no more into this house of mine, nor do thou bring thy companions;
This is now my King's dwelling.
Thou art no friend of mine.
Thou hast wrought me pain by thy harsh dissonant tone;
Henceforth enter thou no more this house of mine;
This is His dwelling;
This is a sacred shrine.

Lesson.

We must form the habit of spiritual consciousness. We must learn to look up to something higher. If we do this we minimize our sadness, our miseries and fears. In an ordinary person the opposite forces, good, evil, pleasure and pain, are constantly preying on his mind; but this need not be. When we establish rhythm, we have our fixed level and we are not preyed upon by the ego. We maintain our balance.

Prayer.

May the Supreme Spirit of the Universe protect me.
May His blessing abide with me.
May I always act in harmony with His Will
And give myself more wholly to Him.
May His peace fill my heart and life.

JANUARY NINETEENTH

Salient Thought for the Day.

He who has touched something higher, his sense of proportion is true.

Lines to Memorize.

Verily Thou art a transformer!
Thine unseen touch changes our blemish into beauty,
Our emptiness into fullness,
Our life's harshness into sweet tenderness.
The marvel of Thine infinite majesty
Fill my heart with wordless ecstasy.

Lesson.

We fight and we struggle to find a little peace of happiness, but we never find anything that is abiding on the outside. When we have joined our forces with our Maker, then only does there come upon us a sense of peace, a sense of security that none can shake. If we keep a light burning in our room, there is no access for darkness; so if we keep our mind filled with God, there can be no entry for evil or error.

Prayer.

O Thou All-seeing One, Thou knowest my inmost needs;
Do Thou manifest Thy loving Presence in my heart;
Teach me how I may place myself wholly in Thy keeping,
And trust with guileless faith in Thy Guidance.

Salient Thought for the Day.

We cannot be absorbed by the material and enjoy the spiritual.

Lines to Memorize.

Verily, Thou art self-luminous,—all is lighted up by Thy Presence!
The paths of my inner and outer life lie clear before me;
I need no other light to find my way out to Thee.
I shall carry no light save one—the lamp of Thy grace.

Lesson.

A person whose faculties are all active on the outside is ever bound. It indicates a great sense of poverty to go outside for everything. A wise man, when things go wrong, turns within himself. If a blow falls upon him, he does not take it; he withdraws himself from it. A man of small nature, who lives in the outside world, goes out to meet the blow and strikes back.

Prayer.

May I seek only that which is uplifting;
May all my thoughts, words and actions manifest Divinity.
Guard me from all selfishness and harshness.
Bless my life and give it power and strength for Thy service.
Fill my heart with Thy peace and Thy blessing.

JANUARY TWENTY-FIRST

Salient Thought for the Day.

It is better to look up and find our contact with something higher.

Lines to Memorize.

When life's perpetual spring is unsealed
Your stains will be washed,
Your thirst will be quenched,
And your parched spirit healed by its living waters.
In its miracle your barren heart will blossom with love, hope and joy.

Lesson.

If we are weak, we must look up to strength. If we are overwhelmed with despondency, we must look up to joy. If the darkness of gloom covers our mind, we must look up to the light. If we are in bodily pain, we must look up to health and holiness. If we are disheartened, we must strive for cheerfulness. Thus keeping our mind fixed on the higher, we transcend the lower.

Prayer.

O Thou All-abiding Spirit!
Help me to lift my thoughts from fleeting things
And fasten them to the Infinite.
Thou art the Giver of all joy and blessing.
Grant unto me thy peace and quietness of spirit.

Salient Thought for the Day.

Let your heart be fixed on Him; and whatever may be the outward change, remain undisturbed.

Lines to Memorize.

Perchance misfortune's hammering hand strikes its cruel blow.
Let it not harden thee.
Again when fortune gives thee her sweet caress,
Let it not make thee soft nor rob thee of thine aim.

Lesson.

No great success is ever accomplished without opposition. We must hold fast to our Ideal in all circumstances, especially when there are occasions for failure and depression, misunderstanding and criticism. This is the way we prove our strength—our deep spiritual strength and our devotion to our Ideal. The Divine Presence will always sustain us. It is never absent from us, in the forest, in the mountain-cave or in the world. When we have perceived the reality of God, we are freed from all fear, doubt and faltering.

Prayer.

O Thou Unchanging One!
Free my mind from all worldly cares.
Make it so pure and full of love that it may be a fitting altar unto Thee.
O Thou infinite Being! Reveal unto me Thy Reality
And grant that I may never lose sight of Thee.

JANUARY TWENTY-THIRD

Salient Thought for the Day.

Let your life be a constant sacrifice for your Ideal.

Lines to Memorize.

Lover, give thine all,—all thou hast and all thou art.
Give, give till thy hands and heart are free.
Dost thou fear?
Nay, perfect love knoweth not fear nor aught but joy in giving.

Lesson.

The thoughts we think steadily, create our atmosphere. People who are soaked with the world have occasional noble thoughts, but they do not think them often enough to produce an enduring effect on their atmosphere. It is only in living the life we create what endures. Spirituality becomes a vital factor only when we live and serve our Ideal faithfully. Our whole existence must be shaped by it. Then alone will our life be productive.

Prayer.

O Supreme Spirit, help me to forget myself,—all my grievances and struggles—
And lose myself wholly in selfless devotion unto Thee.
Guard me from pettiness and calculation.
Fill me with Divine love and the true spirit of self-sacrifice.

JANUARY TWENTY-FOURTH

Salient Thought for the Day.

Blessed are those who sacrifice their lives for God and his children.

Lines to Memorize.

Give thy life and give thy love:
Give all! Give all!
When thy hands and heart are free
Thou shalt receive Him who is all, yea, all in all.

Lesson.

We do our best part when we leave behind the element of self. It is not that we lack the power of love, we lack its application. We fail to find an avenue through which to express it. More we establish love in our heart and abide by it, more the vista of our usefulness expands. We never do anything noble without love. We must sever ourselves from selfish interest and fix our thought on loving self-forgetting service.

Prayer.

Infinite and All-loving Lord, I lay my heart at Thy Feet;
May it be cleansed of all stain of selfishness;
May it radiate a love that knows no hate;
May it find all its joy in willing service to Thee and Thy children.

Salient Thought for the Day.

It is easier to lay your life down than to live for the Ideal and humanity.

Lines to Memorize.

Since Thy asking I have emptied my heart of self.
Now it is full! Yea, it is full of the inexpressible.
At Thy will, I have cast off self, yet I am!
I have given up life, yet I live!
Yea, I live now, not separate
But in wholeness of Thy Life.

Lesson.

In this battle of life we must rise above all self-seeking and do our share for the love of it. Our motive should always be to turn out well whatever we undertake, rather than dwell on what personal gain or loss it may bring. When we are faithful to the Ideal we grow indifferent to success and failure, victory and defeat, good fortune and misfortune. That which affects the little self does not seem so vital to us. We find our rest and security in something higher.

Prayer.

O Thou Giver of all blessing, we cannot weigh or measure Thy gifts.
Give me a contented heart, free from self-interest and calculation.
Silence within me all rebellious thought
And awaken in me the spirit of consecration and joyous service.

JANUARY TWENTY-SIXTH

Salient Thought for the Day.

We cannot do our part unless we have unlocked the door and found something within.

Lines to Memorize.

Ever fresh life and joy well up in my soul
As I sit in Thy Presence with open heart.
Thou didst hold the key of this house in Thy hand;
And I, not knowing this secret,
Have wandered long and afar.

Lesson.

No man in this world can be productive or make his action far-reaching without entering deeper into his inner being. Unless he does this, his actions will all bear the mark of thoughtlessness. The existence offers us countless opportunities to serve the Ideal. If we carry unrest, depression, doubt and unhappiness in our heart, we cannot earn happiness for ourselves or bring it to others. Only as we carry joy, peace and spiritual faith do we serve God and the world.

Prayer.

O Thou Supreme One!
Fill me with Thyself.
Make Thy Presence felt in my heart.
Kindle within me the true fire of spiritual consecration
That all my impurities and unworthy feelings may be burned to ashes.

JANUARY TWENTY-SEVENTH

Salient Thought for the Day.

There must be aspiration in our hearts.

Lines to Memorize.

Wondrous Choir-master of the great universe!
I want to keep my gaze fixed on Thee.
Whene'er my eyes are turned away from Thee,
I fall out of rhythm.
My song apart from Thee lacks harmony—
Help me to keep my gaze fixed on Thee now
and always.

Lesson.

This world is like a symphony and we each have a part to play. We must so tune our instrument that whenever we strike a note, it will be a harmonious note. Some people are evil; not only so, they draw evil and produce only evil. Others see the whole world as a sanctuary of God.

Prayer.

All-loving One, bestow on me Thy Divine grace
That all my shortcomings may leave me;
That all my selfishness and egotism may be
removed;
That my heart may be sanctified
And tuned in perfect unison with Thy Divine
Heart.

JANUARY TWENTY-EIGHTH

Salient Thought for the Day.

Every man must go to God; every man must seek wisdom.

Lines to Memorize.

If thou wouldst have Divine grace,
Then crave not the favour of man.
If thou wouldst soar heaven's loftiest heights,
Then let not thy feet be chained to earth.
Bear no malice or envy in thy mind,
For these are heavy loads to carry.
He lifts those by His magic wand
Who come free of heart and hand.

Lesson.

Practical wisdom is something we radiate through our life. Everyone can acquire it. Great souls are anxious to give wisdom, but the one to whom they would impart it must have aptitude to receive. We cannot reach God unless we seek Him with childlike faith and devotion. We must have that higher wisdom which comes from surrender.

Prayer.

O Thou Effulgent Spirit, teach me how I may acquire true wisdom.
Destroy all darkness in me.
Grant unto me such childlike simplicity and openness of heart
That I may be able to reflect Thy Divine Light.
May that Light radiate through all my thoughts and actions.

JANUARY TWENTY-NINTH

Salient Thought for the Day.

People who wish to achieve something in the spiritual life must not wait for special occasions and conditions.

Lines to Memorize.

The stream of my life is ever flowing on,
Perchance checked by an impassable rock,
As if blocked for all time from its goal.
Yet the yearning soul with feeble stroke
Finds its course through adamantine walls.

Lesson.

We already possess all the higher qualities and we can possess them consciously. We can bring ourselves to such a state of mental evolution that we are always equipped for our task. Then after we have done a day's work, instead of being depleted, we shall feel strong. When we depend upon our inferior faculties we accomplish less and we are often tired. Our strength is replenished through simplicity, humility and trust.

Prayer.

May the All-abiding Spirit free me from anxiety and fear.
May He surround me with His protecting love.
May I learn to draw consciously on Him.
May I find my rest and peace in His abiding Presence.
May I fasten my life to that Unchanging One and depend on Him alone.

Salient Thought for the Day.

Life affords us endless opportunities for unfoldment.

Lines to Memorize.

The stream of my life is ever flowing on;
Perchance in swift current,
Again slow and still, as if stagnant,
But ever flowing on to find Thee, Thou ocean of life and bliss,
To join its little stream with Thine uncompassed waters,
To find its wholeness in Thy Being.

Lesson.

A person cannot begin to think and unfold his inner faculties without transforming everything. His speech, his thought, his action will all manifest it. His life of itself will be consecrated and steadfast in purpose. Egotism and aggressiveness often blind our vision and make us miss higher opportunities. Only as we learn to draw from within are we able to make the best use of the opportunities.

Prayer.

O thou Supreme Mother of the universe,
Reveal Thyself unto me that my mind be freed from all lethargy and doubt.
Lift my thoughts and prayers that I may have access to Thy Infinite Being.
Make my heart harmonious and peaceful
That I may be ready for Thy holy Spirit to come within me.

JANUARY THIRTY-FIRST

Salient Thought for the Day.

To convey our Ideal, it must first mingle with the life.

Lines to Memorize.

Alas, thy mortal mind holds thee captive by blinding thy sight
Break its distorting spell, and wake!
Awake and seek!
Look within and move within.
There thou shalt find thy true estate.

Lesson.

The outer life is an exact reproduction of the inner. The spiritual life plays a tremendous part in the world. We may be attracted by a flower and long to keep it always; but we cannot possess it if we sever it from its root. In the same way, we cannot be truly living, if our consciousness is cut off from its Source.

Prayer.

Let me offer up my heart with feeling of sacred consecration.
Let me give my life with humility and selfless devotion.
May all my thoughts, words and actions be dedicated unto Him from whom we are descended.

NOTES

Sail thy vessel on,—
Steady, friend, steadily sail along.
Water may be rough
Or water may be smooth,
But ever hold fast to thy compass.
The sky may smile
Or the sky may frown—
Hold fast to thy compass.
Wind may roar
Or wind may be still—
Hold fast, hold fast to thy compass and sail thy vessel on.
Steady, friend, steadily sail along.

February

RESOLUTION STEADFAST

He who is established and unshaken; he who is alike in pleasure and pain, who is the same in pleasant and unpleasant, in praise and blame, and steady; he who is alike in honor and dishonor, the same to friend and foe, giving up all selfish undertakings, he is said to have crossed beyond the qualities of Nature. And He who, crossing over these qualities, serves Me with unwavering devotion, becomes fit to attain oneness with the Supreme.

Bhagavad-Gita

FEBRUARY FIRST

Salient Thought for the Day.

Be like a rock, unshakable.

Lines to Memorize.

Hold fast to the end.
Goal can ne'er be far
If thy heart clings to Him with love,
With love hold fast to the end.

Lesson.

Discipline should not throw you down. When you take up spiritual life without any ulterior motive, not seeking ease or comfort, you seek tests and difficulties to prove your strength and endurance. You do not shrink from trial. Never pray to minimize your burden, but that you may be given wisdom to meet it. There are moments when we feel thwarted and when our spiritual vision seems blocked. These are the moments of greatest growth.

Prayer.

O Thou All-beneficent Spirit,
Make me firm and undaunted in my spiritual life.
May my mind rise above the ever changing objects of this world.
And be fixed always on Thee.
May my heart be unfaltering.
May it never turn away from Thee.
Make me strong in Thy strength.
May I never fall back or waver in my devotion to Thee.

FEBRUARY SECOND

Salient Thought for the Day.

Steadfastness is one of the basic virtues in life.

Lines to Memorize.

Be thou a lamp unto thy fellow-men, unfailing.
Let thy light of love burn at all hours without ceasing.
Be not downcast or depress thy heart if, perchance, it burneth dim.
Let it burn bright or let it be dim,
But be thou ever an unfailing lamp.

Lesson.

Be steadfast. When we hold steadfastly, then there comes a certain ripening within us. How long a man can hold, that is the measure of his merit. What is an hour or two when you are standing faithfully at your post? Realization comes when we endure. The spiritual life requires great steadiness and endurance. Hold to your faith and devotion. Never let them waver or grow weak.

Prayer.

May that Infinite One, who knows all my thoughts or feelings,
May He fill me with strength and wisdom.
May He remove from my heart all that is unworthy and alien.
May He make it free from all blemish
That in all my actions and in my words I may express His power and glory
And bring blessings to all His children.

FEBRUARY THIRD

Salient Thought for the Day.

Steadfastness is a quality of the soul. It is something which we unfold.

Lines to Memorize.

The light of the soul knoweth no boundary
lines;
If hath no east nor west, north nor south.
Yea, the light of the soul shineth everywhere,
Save when we keep our doors shut—
Alas, when we keep our doors shut!

Lesson.

We must acquire steady wisdom. We must not be fluctuating and changeable. People who are moody and unsteady afflict themselves and afflict others. If the light goes out, it is not through accident; it is through lack of care. We must never be neglectful. We must be steady; we must be vigilant. We need steadfastness and it comes when our thought is fixed on something which is abiding.

Prayer.

O Thou Effulgent Spirit!
May my heart and mind be filled with the light
which is divine.
Remove from me all darkness and unwisdom
And give me unshakable faith in eternal things.

FEBRUARY FOURTH

Salient Thought for the Day.

Never mind failures. Rise with fresh vigor. Everything is conquered by the giant force of will.

Lines to Memorize.

When man casts me down
God holds me up.
Seek thou not human aid
If thou wouldst be sustained by thy Lord.

Lesson.

It is a great blessing to meet with struggle and opposition; whatever fire there is in us is kindled by these. Life does not mean merely following the softest road, the path of least resistance; it is doing something vital. Hardships and difficulties bring out the best in us and make us strong. He who is the same in pleasure and pain, who is unshaken and steady, he alone lives a fruitful life. It is this which gives us balance and without balance we are always wavering and fitful.

Prayer.

O Thou Unbounded Spirit of the Universe,
Make Thy Presence felt in my soul
That I may realize Thy love and sustaining power.
Thou art the Giver of all blessing.
Grant unto me Thy blessing
That I may be ever conscious of Thy nearness
And transcend failure, grief and despair.

FEBRUARY FIFTH

Salient Thought for the Day.

Failure is not external. It means something is disordered within.

Lines to Memorize.

When Thou art near I am undaunted by fear;
Life nor death can crush my spirit.
But in Thine absence when my heart sinks in sadness
I know not even how to pray,
I lift my eyes to find Thee;
My soul suffers nightmares of anguish.

Lesson.

We are primarily of Spirit. Our real essence is in the Divine. To forget that becomes our greatest failure. Even mistakes are not evil. We learn through mistakes as much as through good deeds. It is not a misfortune to blunder, but it becomes a misfortune when a person broods over his blunder. When we live the life, we get rid of all brooding and despondency. It is when our heart is filled with ambition that we feel defeat and failure. We remain unmoved and undisturbed when it is wholly filled with the Ideal.

Prayer.

O Thou Mother Divine, make this heart glad.
Make it hopeful and strong.
May I go through difficulties and dangers with undaunted courage,
And may I never lose the sense of
Thy tender care and loving protection.

FEBRUARY SIXTH

Salient Thought for the Day.

To maintain our equilibrium is the greatest practical wisdom.

Lines to Memorize.

Covet not pleasure.
Shrink not from pain.
Stand firm on the balancing rod of life.
He who seeketh pleasure can ne'er escape pain:
For they are coupled,—the inseparable twins.
Let thy soul live in tranquil harmony
Amid pleasure and amid pain.

Lesson.

When we dwell in the body we are easily agitated. The balance is easily destroyed. But when we dwell in Spirit we maintain our poise. The small-minded man is easily disturbed, but the big man keeps his balance under all circumstances. When we are willing to live or die for our Ideal, we remain calm and poised in all the varying conditions of life.

Prayer.

O Thou Who art changeless and abiding,
Grant to me such trust in Thee that I may cross over all difficulties and trials,
And find absolute peace and quietude.
Help me to shake off all fear and anxiety
And rest in the consciousness of Thy protecting Presence.

Salient Thought for the Day.

It is a great blessing when we are struck. If there is anything in us, the blow will bring it out.

Lines to Memorize.

These dark shadow that fall upon the path of my life,
Causing me sadness, distress and pain:
I have learned to welcome these through Thy holy grace.
They show me how I lack wisdom;
How failing and faltering is my strength.

Lesson.

Be brave and hold fast. Patience conquers everything in the end. Our moods and feelings are only momentary—they come and go, being fleeting in nature; therefore we must try to endure them and look upon them as a witness. Never tear down your peace and happiness unnecessarily. Never lose faith in yourself. Pray that Mother may make your faith ever stronger and stronger and give you joy, selflessness and true devotion.

Prayer.

Do Thou, O Eternal One, awaken in me such wisdom
That I may find safety in Thee alone.
Grant unto me true fortitude and spiritual strength.
May I be enduring and unaffrighted by pain and trouble.
If I fail or stumble, may I always turn to Thee for help,
And find renewed courage and life in Thy Blessed Presence.

Salient Thought for the Day.

Stand as a tower of strength.

Lines to Memorize.

When I stand alone with Thee on this rock of refuge
I stand firm and unshakable.
Without fear or doubt of self
I gaze upon the valley of life.
My vision is clear;
Far and near, present and past
And all future in the bosom of time
Melt into one blending harmony.

Lesson.

Anyone can be good when things go smoothly; but when all goes wrong and a man can still go on bravely, he comes out triumphant. The real way is not to run away from one trouble to another, but to turn at once to the Supreme Source for help and guidance. More we are connected with that Source, more efficient we are and less we give way to weakness.

Prayer.

Infinite Spirit, hold me by Thy Compassionate Hand,
In my moments of pleasure and pain, success and failure, victory and defeat,
That I may never falter or be overcome by elation or depression.
Thou art the Divine Giver, grant unto me this blessing,
And keep me in peace and calmness of mind.

FEBRUARY NINTH

Salient Thought for the Day.

We never know when the hour of test will arise.

Lines to Memorize.

Awakener, I heard Thee call me in the stillness of night when all was in deep slumber.
Again I heard Thy voice;
But sleep was still upon me.
Since the light hath burst upon mine eyes and I see Thy Face,
My sleep is gone.

Lesson.

There come moments when we feel thwarted, when all spiritual avenues seem blocked. These are the moments for us to hold fast and wait. If we can learn to keep our mind in truth and in rhythm nothing can thwart us. As long as we cling to the reality of God, we shall remain fearless and unfaltering.

Prayer.

O Thou Infinite One, reveal Thyself unto me
That I may find my safety in Thy Divine Presence.
Help me always to be on guard and watchful
That I may overcome whatever may assail me.
Thou art the Giver of all strength.
Surround me with Thy loving protection
And grant that I may learn to look to Thee in the moments of joy and in the hour of darkness.

Salient Thought for the Day.

We must attain steadiness and balance through our own endeavour.

Lines to Memorize.

These shadows have taught me I am nothing
save when I walk in Thy Light.
With grateful heart I bless these ills that
teach me to love Thee and Thy Light.

Lesson.

A wise man, if he is struck, is not willing to stoop to striking back—not because he feels a sense of superiority, but because he wishes to prove his loyalty to his highest light. When we hear a harsh word, we let it grind into our consciousness. The remedy is to bring to another thought. The remedy for a weakening thought is to think the opposite thought; overcome evil by good.

Prayer.

May my thoughts and prayers turn to Thee,
O Lord!
Lift me above all confusion and wavering.
Grant unto me fixity of purpose and a determination that cannot be shaken.
Surround me with Thy loving blessing
And fill my heart with Thy Divine peace.

FEBRUARY ELEVENTH

Salient Thought for the Day.

The strength of life comes from finding the harmony of life.

Lines to Memorize.

Thy whisper hath filled my soul with an
  unending song.
In noise and stillness, in crowd and alone,
  Thy gentle tone is always in my ear.
Thy breath like sweet perfume hath soothed
  all my sense-cravings.
The touch of Thine immortal Hand is ever
  upon me.
I am filled! Filled am I from all sides!

Lesson.

Our vision is not always the same, but true vision is never lost. It may seem to grow less; but when it comes again it is stronger than ever. When we are in harmony, without calculation we say the right word, we do the right thing; we lose all thought of calculation. Whatever we have is the gift of the great Effulgent One. If we carry this thought ever with us, we cannot do anything wrong. When we connect ourselves with the Origin of life, we do not have to ask for the results of that connection; they come of themselves.

Prayer.

O Lord, help me to open my heart
That it may be filled with Thy divine harmony.
Free my mind from unruly restless thoughts.
Silence all doubt and despair within me.
Make me to realize Thy allness,
And tune my life in perfect unison with
  Thy all-encompassing Life.

FEBRUARY TWELFTH

Salient Thought for the Day.

Only when mind is steady it is possible to have true vision.

Lines to Memorize.

Out of the deep darkness of night
A light burst upon my soul,
Filling me with serene gladness.
All my inner chambers
Are opened at its touch;
All my inmost being
Is flooded by its radiance.

Lesson.

Do not close your door and brood in the darkness. When harshness and misery come, instead of going down under them, the awakened soul becomes triumphant. That is the way with saintly characters. When they meet with difficulties they always derive blessing from them. But how quickly we go down under the stress of life. Our sense of balance is increased or decreased according to our feeling for spiritual truth. As long as we have an unbroken consciousness of the Divine Presence, we shall feel secure and shall remain steadfast.

Prayer.

All-effulgent Spirit, Thou art the Light of the Universe.
Illumine my heart with Thy Divine Light.
Fill my mind with the light of understanding
And give me strength and devotion
That I may follow Thy path with firm resolution.

FEBRUARY THIRTEENTH

Salient Thought for the Day.

Without steadiness, nothing can be accomplished in the spiritual life.

Lines to Memorize.

Companion of my life,
Before I found Thee I was an aimless wanderer,
Roaming alone like a wanton child.
Thy divine beauty hath tamed my restless mind.

Lesson.

Everyone wants to be free from unhappiness, weakness and fear. But how can we, when we cling so tenaciously to the ephemeral? So long as we hold to changing things and go up and down with them, we can never find what we are seeking. Although we may have tremendous zeal for happiness and higher ideals, we miss our end.

Prayer.

All-loving Spirit draw my heart away from the fleeting objects of sense,
And fasten it to Thy abiding Reality.
Awaken in me spiritual yearning,
That through it I may perceive Thee in all things.
May I never yield to weakness
Or fail in my loyalty to Thee, who art the Source of my life and my strength.

Salient Thought for the Day.

We must be patient, we must be persevering, we must be steadfast, if we would develop our higher qualities.

Lines to Memorize.

Soul of the sanctified mystic is nurtured in the bosom of Divinity;
His rhythmic heart beats in unison with the unbroken harmony of life.
Blessed art thou who doth shed upon this discordant world
Thy sweet beneficence of love and peace.

Lesson.

When someone strikes you, glorify the pain; be grateful that you have a chance to prove your steadfastness and loyalty. A person's test of strength and wisdom rests on this,—how great is his sense of equilibrium under stress. A man must have so much balance, so much wisdom that he can withstand the onslaughts of life.

Prayer.

May I follow Thy path, O Lord, with unwavering faith and one-pointed devotion
Give me such spiritual insight that I may know my union with Thy Divine Being;
And may this so strengthen me
That I shall be unmoved by the hard experiences of life.

FEBRUARY FIFTEENTH

Salient Thought for the Day.

Our trials are a great blessing than the pleasant things which happen to us.

Lines to Memorize.

Brother, thy load is heavy and thou art weary;
But One who has placed the load upon thy head will also give thee strength to carry it. . .
He knows both thy strength and failing;
His gift is just and right-proportioned.
Bear thou then, with unruffled mind, joy and sorrow, loss and gain.

Lesson.

O blessed sorrow! you rend our heart with your sharp thrust, that we may be purged of self and delusion. You are truly our beneficent friend, but you come with fierce scorn of a foe. You are the awakener of our spoiled lethargic hearts. Come as oft as you think best.

Prayer.

Sweet Comforter, my soul's unfailing Refuge,
Thou art the embodiment of all that is blessed;
Bless me that I may find my sole comfort and joy in Thee.
Taking whatever Thou givest with trusting heart.
Make me a worthy channel to express Thy power and do Thy Will.

Salient Thought for the Day.

We eliminate weakness through our life. We can make ourselves like a fortress—invulnerable.

Lines to Memorize.

The ramparts of this dwelling where I live
Are built with faith, hope, courage and love.
These four walls stand all weather and storm.

Lesson.

If we can carry holy thoughts and hold a right sense of values, we can live our life without breaking under it, no matter how difficult it may be. We are hurting ourselves fundamentally when we lower our standard. If we hold to a fixed level of conduct, whatever the world does, we still maintain our standard. When we walk in the light of God, there is no darkness. The light of Truth always shines through our life when we have love in our heart.

Prayer.

Thou, O Lord, art the Source of my strength and sustenance.
Fill me with spiritual strength.
Make me steadfast and selfless and strong to endure.
May I rest in Thy Holy Presence
And feel secure in the consciousness of Thy protecting love.

Salient Thought for the Day.

We must keep our inner life orderly. We must keep it up. This cannot be done by someone else.

Lines to Memorize.

I sit in this garden of mine
Speechless and wonder-struck;
I walk in it gently with bare feet,
For it is now holy land.

Lesson.

A person neglecting his thoughts and feelings cannot suddenly get the blessing of the spiritual life. There are times when spiritual lethargy overpowers everyone, but the brave heart rises above it and overcomes it. If there is lack of fervor, increase it, double it, treble it, and the lack will be crowded out. The Supreme Being is never far away from us. It is because of our conception of Him that He seems far away. We hold Him aloof by our attitude of mind. We draw Him close through simple faith and purity of heart.

Prayer.

O Thou All-compassionate Being,
Free my thoughts and actions from all blemish
That they may manifest Thy Truth at every step.
May my life move in perfect rhythm with Thy Life.
May I never grow weary in Thy service
Or lack in ardor and devotion to Thee.

FEBRUARY EIGHTEENTH

Salient Thought for the Day.

It makes us stronger, to endure.

Lines to Memorize.

Brave heart, tired soul, remain awake awhile longer, awhile longer.
The hour of watching is almost over.
It will end,
And its end will bring thee gladness and rest.

Lesson.

We need to pass through times of darkness in order to learn the value of spiritual consciousness. When our life becomes blinded by despair, all our efforts seem unsuccessful; those are the moments when we need to hold fast. When we have a thing, we do not realize the lack of it. For instance when a person rolls in luxury, it is very difficult for him to imagine the misery of poverty. Same is it when we have great spiritual consciousness in us, we do not appreciate what misery, what unhappiness, its absence can create in a soul.

Prayer.

Supreme Spirit, Thou knowest my innermost being,
Thou knowest my strength and my weakness
Rouse in my heart such fortitude and firmness of faith
That nothing can throw me down or overwhelm me.
Help me to lift my thoughts above the distractions of this world
And fasten them to the stable and undying.

FEBRUARY NINETEENTH

Salient Thought for the Day.

We must never fall away. By steadfastness we surmount the greatest obstacles.

Lines to Memorize.

Fear not, nor be distressed,
I am with thee always.
There is no space before me:
I infill all space.
Yea, I am always with thee.
Fear not, nor be distressed.

Lesson.

If we are in tune, if we are fortified, we can go through the greatest misfortune without being crushed. If we are not in tune and thus fortified, we are in danger even in the midst of good fortune. There are obstacles in the spiritual path, but they only rise and overcome us when our life is out of rhythm. To remedy this we must find a proper basis for our action. When we find this, harmony is restored.

Prayer.

O Thou Inexhaustible Source of all blessedness,
Fill my mind with noble thoughts.
Strengthen and sanctify my life.
May I never give way to despondency or despair.
Make me undaunted in the face of every obstacle and difficulty.
And at all times may I look to Thee as my sole Support.

Salient Thought for the Day.

Nothing can withstand the power of the Unseen Presence.

Lines to Memorize.

The blessing of Thy Presence pervades my soul's sanctuary.
My slumbering mind, breathing its lingering perfume, is revived.
My heart, purified and gladdened, reacheth out to Thee in adoration.
Where Thou art, there abide joy and peace.

Lesson.

When one moves in perfect rhythm and harmony, for him there are no obstacles. There is a Power before whom nothing can hold. When light is brought into the room, darkness cannot resist it. Similarly when we bring the light of Truth into our inner life, no evil or sorrow can remain. We become invincible.

Prayer.

May the One Who has bestowed on me all my blessings,
May that One rouse in me the sense of His Holy Presence.
May I open my heart in guileless simplicity to His Divine influence.
May I lift my thought to Him in selfless aspiration.
May His peace rest upon me.

Salient Thought for the Day.

If you keep your gaze fixed steadfastly on the right course, no one can turn you back.

Lines to Memorize.

None shall hinder thy forward course
For I guide thy steps.
Place thy hand in Mine and walk with faith.
Where I am there is no ill.
Fear not, but walk forward with faith.
Light will come;
For where'er I am there is light.

Lesson.

As we learn to face our problems without being faint-hearted, we are sustained and helped in every way. Strength, inspiration, power to do, will come. We must always remember that however hard an experience may be, it always holds something for us. When these things come, we must not convert them into a tragedy by giving way to them.

Prayer.

O Thou Almighty One, wake me from my slumber of ignorance.
Help me to feel Thy unfailing protection and sustaining power.
May they make me invincible and resolute.
Bestow on me Thy abiding blessing.

Salient Thought for the Day.

The one who lacks in resolution and tranquillity, in vain does he seek knowledge.

Lines to Memorize.

My restless mind, wandering and tired,
Sitteth in Thy Presence in rapture.
Like a thirsty bird that drinketh the rain-drops
On a sultry mid-summer day.

Lesson.

We have no right to make ourselves so much a slave to circumstance that we lack resourcefulness. We should be so resourceful that constantly we have something to contribute to ourselves first, then to others. We should never give way to discouragement or to a sense of aloneness. We should be glad when circumstances offer us opportunities for aloneness. We should utilize these moments to cultivate the love of high ideals and learn to reflect them in our life.

Prayer.

Thou, All-wise One, art the Source of my life
and power;
Reveal Thyself unto me that my mind may be
freed from doubt and darkness.
May my thoughts and prayers be worthy
That I may gain access to Thy Infinite Light.
Through it all things are known.
Fill my heart with that Light, leaving no room
for aught else.

Salient Thought for the Day.

Steadiness and serenity go together.

Lines to Memorize.

Thy cool and consecrated blessing
Hath soothed all my inward being.
My fever of anguish is abated;
My restive mind is at peace.

Lesson.

Never let your mind grow turbulent or be shaken by agitation. When we limit ourselves to one-sided vision, everything becomes distorted and we are weakened. We are part of the great Immensity, we should not have any weakness or doubt. If we are part of that great Infinitude we should strive to express it in our life. We must learn to have a steadfast hold on the Supreme. Then we cannot be moved by the passing conditions of life. So long as we keep a firm grasp on Divinity, we shall always maintain our balance and be at peace.

Prayer.

Do Thou, O Lord, surround me with Thy protecting love.
May I direct my whole thought towards Thee
And find my rest and peace in Thee alone.
Take from me all anxiety and distress of mind,
Grant unto me quietness of spirit and a steadfast heart.

Salient Thought for the Day.

So long as we are at war with ourselves we cannot better ourselves.

Lines to Memorize.

Once I was a rebel and abhorred all subjection, even unto Thee;
My haughty heart would not bend:
Now I smile to think with what whole-souled surrender I lie at Thy blessed Feet.
Verily Thou art a transformer!
Thine unseen touch changes our blemish into beauty,
Our emptiness into fullness,
Our life's harshness into sweet tenderness.

Lesson.

Whenever there is any difficulty the wise man begins with himself, not outside. We find the remedy from within. The only way to prove our steadiness and our devotion to our Ideal, is to so order and organize our feelings and thoughts that they can never overcome us. Then we are able to be so steadfast that we never fall away from our higher Principle. Only by remaining faithful do we attain ripening.

Prayer.

Thou art the one eternally abiding Source of my life.
Thou knowest my innermost needs.
Make me worthy of Thy blessing.
Make me worthy of Thy kingdom.

Salient Thought for the Day.

We deepen our misfortunes by dwelling on them.

Lines to Memorize.

I worship Thee in forms of infinite vastness.
In Thy unfathomed glory the atom of my life is magnified.
In this unfolded vision my soul is expanded;
And knowing how my finite life is contained in Thine Infinite Majesty,
My soul is at peace.

Lesson.

We must not throw away our light. If we are carrying a lantern, we do not throw it away when we come across a well-lighted place, because we think we may need it again. Similarly when our mind is bright, we must hold on to that brightness. We must hold to the light of such moments that they may sustain us in the dark hours.

Prayer.

O Thou Infinite Being, Thou art the Goal of my existence.
Thou art my one safe Guide; my one safe Shelter.
Nothing can overwhelm me as long as I depend wholly on Thy care.
Teach me to be vigilant and tireless in Thy service.
And unfaltering in my daily living.

Salient Thought for the Day.

Those who are careful in little things, nothing can thwart them.

Lines to Memorize.

When the Fire of Truth burns in the heart,
It furifies the heart.
When its spark comes out of the tongue,
It is vibrant with light.
Lo, it falls upon the ear that is not closed to the subtle, spiritual sound like far-distant music,
Rousing the soul to a new world.

Lesson.

Unless we have true vision and are watchful, when difficulties come, we shall not be able to meet them. We must safeguard ourselves by acquiring wisdom. Wisdom is abiding and always sustains. Even our mistakes are not evil; we learn as much through our mistakes as through our good deeds, But when we have learned, we must be careful not to repeat them.

Prayer.

All-pervading Spirit of the Universe!
Help me to find my union with Thy Infinitude.
From Thee alone do I draw strength and life.
By Thy light alone can I kindle my little light.
Contact with Thy Being alone can cleanse my impurities,
And bring me peace and bliss.

Salient Thought for the Day.

Never raise voice or hand when adverse things come. Try to endure all for the sake of God. This will bring true strength.

Lines to Memorize.

When Thou dost stand behind me, my whole being is vibrant with strength;
Life's upheavals vanish and world's onslaughts touch me not.
Teach me how I may keep Thee with me always.
I am ever with thee, but thou knowest it not;
Thou dost not look toward Me with Thy inner eye.

Lesson.

From the lack of fortitude and self-control we bring misfortune on ourselves. When people thwart us, what a consolation to know that we still have our place in God's arms. No matter what may befall us, it is wonderful to know that we have our union with God. We are partakers of a divine heritage.

Prayer.

Supreme Lord, I pray to Thee with yearning heart,
Do Thou fasten my life to the Path of Truth.
Thou only canst make me firm and enduring.
Make Thy way known
And grant that I may walk in it, looking always to Thee for guidance.
May I never turn my gaze away from Thee.

FEBRUARY TWENTY-EIGHTH

Salient Thought for the Day.

We should never indulge in thoughts that disturb our mind, distort our vision or shake our resolution.

Lines to Memorize.

No hurt nor strife there can be when thine heart is free.
Sadness and gloom, envy and fear,
Depression and pride jealousy and life's countless cares :
These will never enter thy home
When thine heart is free and filled with love.

Lesson.

We overcome the lower by the higher. Evil does exist, but we do not have to accept it as an inevitable fact of life. We can always counteract it. We all have a common heritage. God's blessings are showered upon us, but we deprive ourselves of them. We do not know how to retain them. We cannot think petty thoughts and receive the highest blessing.

Prayer.

All-merciful Spirit, bestow upon me Thy Grace.
Throw Thy light of wisdom upon my path.
Free me from petty thoughts and fears.
Give me understanding that I may come to Thee
And serve Thee with steadfast devotion and selfless consecration.
Grant me Thy peace.

FEBRUARY TWENTY-NINTH

Salient Thought for the Day.

Spirit always conquers. Never be frightened over anything, but hold fast in faith. Nothing can harm us when God is watching.

Lines to Memorize.

With Thy strength
Will I break these fetters
That bind my ever-free soul.
If Thou dost grant me strength,
Thy strength I want, not mine.
Nay, never my strength I want
But only Thine—only Thine.

Lesson.

If you will keep your heart open and steadfast, the great Spirit will not fail you. Life brings discipline to make you nobler and stronger. Nothing is too much for the devotee who looks to God for his strength and protection. Be brave and enduring. The brave heart is invincible.

Prayer.

Supreme Spirit of the Universe,
Help me never to forget my Divine nature.
May I meet all dangers and difficulties with undaunted heart,
Looking to Thee for guidance and safety.
Without Thee no victory is possible
With Thee there can be no failure or defeat.

NOTES

Behold the sweet blossom of life, revealing beauty
uncreate by mortal hand,
Not seen by these, our eyes,
Unsensed by senses;
Yet seen and felt by the sense of sanctity.
Holy sanctity, Light of heaven,
Fill my life with Thy divine radiance.
Transform my body, my senses and all that is
senseless in me.
Make me Thine own!

March

POWER OF HOLINESS

Fill thy mind with Me, be thou My devotee, worship Me and bow down to Me; thus steadfastly uniting thy heart with Me alone and regarding Me as thy Supreme Goal, thou shalt come unto Me.

Bhagavad-Gita

MARCH FIRST

Salient Thought for the Day.

Is your heart ready to respond to the call of your Ideal ?

Lines to Memorize.

Hast thou courage to travel alone you invisible path ?
Then carry this lamp in thy hand and walk with steadfast gaze—
Look not back ; the past will melt in the dark—
Follow, follow, follow on by its glow.

Lesson.

We must pave our way to God. We must strive for a point of contact. We must be possessed of the Great Power before we can do anything worthwhile. We cannot afford to neglect our soul attributes for the sake of the flesh. If, however, we keep our heart full of exalted ideas, we shall not fail to find a point of contact. When we are truly sanctified, our ear is never deaf to the higher call.

Prayer.

All--beneficent Spirit of the Universe,
Make me free from all blemish and unworthiness
That I may feel Thy Presence everywhere.
Thou alone canst give me strength to lift my feet and move freely along the way of life.
Give me sight that I may perceive Thee in all things.
May I so tune my heart that I may feel perfect surrender unto Thee.

MARCH SECOND

Salient Thought for the Day.

The biggest, the best thing you can do is to unfold your higher qualities.

Lines to Memorize.

Cast off from thy mind all base thoughts, and plunge—
Plunge in the ocean of love!
Fear not drowning, nor death,—
Love is life,
Yea, it is eternal and endless bliss.

Lesson.

People who lack in fineness of feeling also lack in sense of sanctity. We have great power. It is not ours, but we are a channel for power. It flows through us in a mighty current when conditions are right. We make them right by sanctity and self-effacement. Our thoughts must be lighted up. We must shine with the light of holiness, light of faith, light of devotion.

Prayer.

May I think only on those things that give freedom to the soul,
That I may be a truer instrument in the hands of the Infinite.
May I aspire always after the highest.
Help me lift the evil of selfishness.
Help me lift the evil of worldliness.
Help me purify my mind and heart.

MARCH THIRD

Salient Thought for the Day.

Manifest spiritual magnitude.

Lines to Memorize.

In this world of dream, my soul, dream a truer dream,
Whose mighty pulse will lift thee to a high pinnacle and make thy body vibrant with new life . . .
Stop not dreaming this great dream till its image speaketh to thy soul with a living tongue.

Lesson.

There is a finer type of spiritual instinct. If you can manifest that, you will always glorify whatever you do. People who fasten themselves to small things deprive themselves of bigger things. Those who lose their life for the sake of Truth find life. They become more living. Human beings become bigger or smaller according to the use they make of their opportunities.

Prayer.

May my mind be so cleansed and strengthened
That it may respond to the Great Mind of the Universe.
May my heart be in tune with the Heart of the Universe.
May His power and glory be manifest in my life.
May His grace surround me and inspire me in all my actions.
May I be shielded from all pettiness and littleness
And made worthy of His love and blessing.

Salient Thought for the Day.

We all have the instinct of heroism within us.

Lines to Memorize.

It is never too much to lay down one's life for a holy cause.
If it is His Will, I am willing;
If it is for the good of many, I am willing;
If it is for the happiness of many, I am willing;
If it is for the salvation of many, I am ready and willing.

Lesson.

Only when we are ready to give up without calculation or fear of results, are we able to do big things. Renunciation always brings freedom from self-limitation. It removes something that is alien to our true nature. When the bigger thing comes the lesser thing is wiped out. The wiping out of the lesser leaves room for the larger, more heroic impulses of the heart.

Prayer.

Let me open my heart that I may feel His divine inspiration.
May I make my thought free from all distractions.
That my sight may become clear
And I may perceive His Holy Presence.
Rouse my mind and soul and spiritual consciousness,
That I may manifest nobility and strength in all my actions.

Salient Thought for the Day.

A man can transform himself by changing his consciousness and cultivating the spirit of holiness.

Lines to Memorize.

This, my house, grows dark and cold when Thou art absent from it.
The light of my soul it lusterless without Thee;
The pulse of my life is silent when Thou, Life of my life, art not in my dwelling.
I pray unto Thee with all the powers Thou hast bestowed upon me.
That Thou will never abandon me.

Lesson.

As we learn the art of upbuilding, our heart blends with the Divine Heart. We cannot have happiness or give happiness until we have learned to blend our heart with the Heart of God. We must have a sense of kinship, more than that, a sense of true relationship with the Supreme. There is no use for us to have religion unless it becomes dominant in our life. A man must stand up and show that he has an Ideal and that he is loyal to it.

Prayer.

Awaken in me spiritual yearning.
May I be earnest and tireless in my search for Truth.
May I serve God with my whole heart and soul.
May I learn to work, worship and aspire without striking any discordant note.

MARCH SIXTH

Salient Thought for the Day.

The world is in need of the healing balm that holiness brings.

Lines to Memorize.

My touch will kindle hope in thy heart
I shall reside in thy soul as peace.
My love will fill thee with bliss.
Fear not, but walk forward with faith.
My Hand is thy safety.

Lesson.

A man may not profess any faith, yet he may be the embodiment of all faith. Holiness comes from the practice of religion. We must live in such a way that we may convey the living quality of religion to the heart of the world. There is one way to reach the hearts of men and that is first by reaching our own depths. We must be willing to die for our Ideal or to live for it without a whimper, whatever may happen.

Prayer.

I lift my heart and thought to the Infinite, All-loving, All-seeing One.
He alone can grant my prayers.
He alone can quicken my spirit and give up spiritual understanding.
May He rouse in my soul true yearning for such understanding.
And bestow on me His ever-living, ever-abiding protection and blessing.

Salient Thought for the Day.

Our first duty is to God.

Lines to Memorize.

The strength of my life art Thou;
The vigor of my spirit is ever in Thee.
In Thee I live a perpetual life;
Without Thee the weight of death is ever upon me.

Lesson.

Great men call upon us to know our true nature that we may know our kinship with the Supreme. The practice of holiness gives us this knowledge. Holiness is the best of all good. Holiness is happiness. Happiness belongs to him who is strongest in holiness. The world has never been enriched because we have evolved dogmas and creeds. In holiness lies the strength of religion.

Prayer.

O Thou All-beneficent Power,
Lead me by Thy compassionate Hand
That I may walk always in the path of holiness;
That I may think only holy thoughts
And speak only holy words.
Keep a protecting hold upon me
That I may not go astray or fall in the struggle of life.

Salient Thought for the Day.

We charge ourselves with a great blessing when we embody holiness in all our actions.

Lines to Memorize.

It is not enough for man to be God-fearing;
But let him be God-loving and God-abiding.

Lesson.

Every man betrays himself when he neglects his inner life. If man has lower instincts uppermost, despite him they will betray him. If higher—that too will show itself. We lift ourselves higher and higher as we think of Divine things. The great universe is open to us, but we are not always open to it, to its blessings, its inspirations, its lessons.

Prayer.

May my supplications rise up from my inner depths
That I may truly lay everything on the Divine altar,
And feel that self-importance, joy and sorrow, success or failure, count as nothing.
Grant unto me inner awakening
And may I ever walk by the inward light.

MARCH NINTH

Salient Thought for the Day.

We must know Truth through its radiation in our life.

Lines to Memorize.

Good deeds and misdeeds are like the white and dusky clouds:
One reflects the Sun of Truth, the other veils Its face.
But there is a hidden, inner course: a clear cloudless sky.
It is the Spirit's Way,—
The mystic realm of light.

Lesson.

Man's duty, first and foremost, is to bring blossoming. Idle curiosity is worse than ignorance. To run here and there out of idle curiosity can have but one reaction: it reacts as a great hindrance to our spiritual progress. We must make our ideals living within us. We must strengthen our life with these ideals. We must fasten our heart and our mind to the unshakable rock of Truth.

Prayer.

Through the Grace of the Supreme Being may I realize that I am a part of Infinitude.
May I realize that it is He who acts through me in all that I do;
That if I yield all things unto Him, I shall be freed from weakness and blundering,
And find perfect peace and joy in His Holy Guidance.

Salient Thought for the Day.

Pray that you may be saved from the onslaughts of ego.

Lines to Memorize.

Good and ill, pleasure and pain,
And all the conflict of dual life
Fade before the constant Sun—
This Sun of Truth, life of the mystic soul,
His unending joy and unfailing peace!

Lesson.

When a person yields to selfish impulses, it shatters his moral fibre and weakens him; then the ego overcomes him. Great power is working. Each one can be a pure channel for it, a clear ready channel, if the spirit is right. Also if the spirit is not right and the ego is uppermost, you can hinder that mighty power. The first act is to cleanse your heart of vanity, pride and selfishness. You must keep your inner atmosphere fragrant with holy thought.

Prayer.

I lift my inmost thoughts and feelings to That One from whom comes all my strength and all my blessing.
May my heart and mind be single and one-pointed in their aspiration and service to Him.
May I never yield to selfishness or harshness.
May the blessing of the Supreme infill my life.

Salient Thought for the Day.

Detachment from self-assertion brings fullness of life.

Lines to Memorize.

Think not of self,
But let thy love encompass other hearts.
True love hath no boundary lines;
Like the infinite sky it covers all space.

Lesson.

Forget yourself as much and as often as you can. One cannot conceive a holy life without self-forgetfulness. As long as we think of ourselves, we cannot think of God. We should be able to lay down the little self without any sense of loss. This becomes easy when a holy cause is born in the mind or when a holy purpose rises in the heart, which blesses and sanctifies.

Prayer.

O Thou All-compassionate Spirit!
May I have such love and gentleness that I shall never hurt any living being.
May I hold such thoughts as will uplift my heart and mind.
May I always remember that Thou art the only Doer.
May I speak and act and think as Thou makest me.
May I ever remain as a tool in Thy Hand.

Salient Thought for the Day.

We must pour out our higher instincts through our life.

Lines to Memorize.

You bubbling brook,
Behold its clear, sparkling drops
It is a symbol of holy life,
Ever new, ever flowing, ever fresh.
For it springeth from an unfailing Source, ever fresh and ever new.

Lesson.

When we first try to walk in the spiritual path, we find only obscurity; but the awakened soul finds it bright and full of God. It is obscure because we create our own obscurity. It is bright for the one who is awake, because he carries with him a light that is unfailing. When we see only darkness all about us, if we can get a sense of Divine protection, light will come.

Prayer.

Thou art so near, O Eternal Spirit, yet I do not see Thee.
Thou speakest, yet I do not hear Thee.
Uncover my eyes, that I may perceive Thy holy Presence.
Open my ears that I may hear Thy divine Voice.
Make me untiring and one-pointed in my search for Thee.
May I dwell ever in Thy Light
And find my joy and peace in Thee.

MARCH THIRTEENTH

Salient Thought for the Day.

It is only by living a life of holiness we create what endures.

Lines to Memorize.

To show us the way of light
Thou art come to this plane of life
As love and wisdom incarnate in flesh.
Free of ego, free of stain art Thou.

Lesson.

One may speak a word and it becomes vibrant, ringing, living ; it brings new life. Another may speak the same word and it carries no weight. A great personality, what does it mean ? It means that certain forces are embodied. It is a light which we cannot help seeing. Whatever that person does is sanctified ; and what can sanctify but wisdom, knowledge of the Source ? If a man is able to feel the realities of life, he becomes so sensitive, so full of feeling that it makes him a lover of God and a lover of humanity. This comes only through wisdom and wisdom comes only through living the life.

Prayer.

O Thou Holy One, may Thy beneficent power flow through me, making my life pure and holy.
May I consecrate every thought and deed to Thee.
May I open myself to Thy blessing.
May I be willing to give all, that I may receive all from Thee.

Salient Thought for the Day.

Our mind is too outward.

Lines to Memorize.

I think these thoughts when I am alone with Thee in my inmost sanctuary,
Where no noise of mortal sound disturbs the rapture of communion
That ever fills my soul in Thy holy Presence.

Lesson.

We are constantly reaching out; and we cannot move away from the centre of our being without exhausting ourselves spiritually, physically and mentally, because we cut ourselves off from the Source of supply. It is the outgoing man who blunders. The one who looks for help from outside nearly always meets with disappointment. Our real help comes from an inner source. We do not go to heaven in a crowd. We do not seek the crowd when our mind is filled with holy spiritual thoughts.

Prayer.

All-abiding Spirit, help me to assimilate Thy holy word in stillness.
Free my mind from ignorance and outwardness.
May I look to Thee for all guidance and inspiration.
Do Thou protect and lead me in all I say and think and do.

MARCH FIFTEENTH

Salient Thought for the Day.

The world cannot hinder us, if we do not allow ourselves to be hindered.

Lines to Memorize.

Amid world's confusion who will show me the way,
If Thou dost not come?
Thou art the way
And Thou art the One that leadeth the way.
I cannot find the way or follow the way
Save when Thou dost lead me by Thy Hand.
Then I follow Thee,
Yea, and I follow Thy way.

Lesson.

We are given freedom to choose our path. We are free to shape our destiny. We are our own enemy. If we absorb the world too much, it weights us down. If we have once established our contact with God, we cease to see evil and it cannot overcome us. There must be an objective in our life. The objective of the soul is to find a clear connection with Divinity.

Prayer.

O Thou All-wise Being, I offer Thee my humble prayers.
Thou knowest my needs,
Thou knowest my innermost feelings;
Do Thou fulfil my needs and make me worthy,
That I may live a holy life and spread Thy blessing.

Salient Thought for the Day.

In seeking the lesser we often lose the greater.

Lines to Memorize.

Holy Eternity, boundless Glory,
I crave to invoke Thee,
But my tongue hath no utterance!
I long to follow Thee,
But my feet are fastened to the ground in wonderment.
Wilt Thou not remove my fetter of self
That I may follow Thee always without hindrance?

Lesson.

A person who looks from a low point, his judgment is always erroneous. A majesty comes when we look from a high point. A person who identifies himself with the wrong end of life loses his spiritual grandeur. Have a lofty point to think upon. Build around that, cling to that, and your life will be renewed. If you keep a stream flowing, the water is continually fresh. In the same way if we keep that higher channel open, a perpetual renewal takes place.

Prayer.

O Thou who art the Light of the Universe,
Grant that I may have access to Thy Infinite Light.
All things shine after Thee.
It is Thy Light which reveals all things.
Reveal Thyself unto me that I may be renewed and filled with Thy Divine wisdom.

MARCH SEVENTEENTH

Salient Thought for the Day.

Man never loses anything when he reaches out for the larger life.

Lines to Memorize.

The strange and mysterious drama of life, enacted in unspoken words,
Makes us dumb with wonder,
And our mind still with unfathomed thoughts.
Our soul cries in dumb ecstasy :
O wonder of wonders !
O beauty of creation !
O boundless life !
I, a part of Thee,
And Thou, my origin !

Lesson.

In the realm of religion it is not outward splendor or what is dazzling, it is holiness, it is guilelessness that heal and redeem. We must learn to live in the world without being swept by its glamour. When our fulfilment depends on the Eternal, we grow vast and majestic in our thought and in our life.

Prayer.

O Thou Supreme Being, give unto me such holy inspiration
That at the hours of the day my spirit may be wholly fixed on Thee.
May my work, my play and my worship, all be dedicated to Thee.
May the outer glamour never turn my thought away from Thee.
May I never sacrifice Thy blessing for the fleeting things of the world.

Salient Thought for the Day.

We must seek the path of holiness, the path of strength, the path of consecrated action.

Lines to Memorize.

These thoughts of my inmost soul that I sing,
It mattereth not whether they be in rhyme, rhapsody or prayer.
The songs of the soul are not made of words.
The singers that are true sing not with their voice or tongue
But with feelings which are beyond utterance.

Lesson.

The finer qualities can never be monopolized by anyone. We can sing the same song as the great saints and Saviours. We may remember only fragments of it, but we can gather all these parts and sing the whole song as they have sung it. When we partake of the inward life, we become sanctified and all things assume their proper value in our outer life.

Prayer.

O Thou Eternal, Infinite Deity,
Grant unto me a serene heart.
Grant unto me a peaceful heart.
Fill my heart full of love for Thee and Thy children.
Cleanse it of all weak and narrow feelings.
Make it joyous and selfless and all-embracing.

MARCH NINETEENTH

Salient Thought for the Day.

Wise ones find their peace through renunciation.

Lines to Memorize.

I can speak no more, for all sounds, are harsh and dissonant since I heard Thy unbroken harmony. . . .
Thy gentle note was drowned in this world's gross tumult;
But now my ears have grown deaf to all other sounds save Thine.

Lesson.

The light of wisdom teaches self-detachment—detachment from the petty details of life. This is true renunciation. We must never forget our connection with Divinity. We all want something that will make our life more complete, but this does not mean the acquisition of things. The wise pray: "Make my life more beautiful, more fruitful, more productive of good." The man who gives up always finds something of greater value.

Prayer.

O Thou Giver of all good, open my mind, my heart, my whole being to Thy higher gift.
Thou alone canst bestow what I need to make my life complete.
Thou art the embodiment of all loveliness and blessedness.
Thou art the beginning, Thou art the end;
Thou art all there is.
May I rest my life in Thy Divine Life.

Salient Thought for the Day.

We must learn the art of always carrying the inner light of holiness.

Lines to Memorize.

This flame that burns in my heart was lighted by Thy Hand.
Thy servant keeps watch.
Thou alone canst give him power to conquer sleep
That his eyes may keep watchful vigil in the dark hours of night
Which so oft rob our inward sight.

Lesson.

We feel the Presence of the Great Spirit of the Universe in silence. The silence is not so much external silence, it is the silence of our inner being. As long as there is turbulence and unrest within us we can never reflect the Spirit of Holiness, nor can we penetrate to the innermost depths of our being. Only when there is a cessation of all unrest within our heart do we feel the Divine Presence and at once arise within us a new sense of sanctity.

Prayer.

O Thou Effulgent Spirit, shed Thy radiance in my heart and mind;
Fill my being with Thy divine light
That it may shine in all my thoughts and actions
And bring brightness in other lives.
Surround me with Thy protecting love and Thy abiding peace.

Salient Thought for the Day.

When we constantly unite our heart with our Ideal, it becomes an uplifting and redeeming factor in our life.

Lines to Memorize.

In the hour of silent communion
I taste sweet ecstasy of bliss.
Thou art the Light of my soul,
This body is only its shade.

Lesson.

When we plant a seed it has no apparent sign of life, but we know it contains the germ of life. We care for it, we water it, then it sprouts; very soon we see a little plant and hopefulness comes. We are able to care for it more because we see a sign of life. Same is it with our life. A very small understanding may be there, a small capacity for feeling; but if we foster these, we strengthen them and through our aspiration they become larger every day.

Prayer.

O Thou All-pervading Deity,
May I find my refuge in Thy all-abiding, all-tender Heart.
Fill my life with fresh inspiration, that it may be full of spiritual fruition.
My own strength is not sufficing;
My real strength lies in Thy strength.
May I ever follow Thy path and unite my will with Thy Will.

MARCH TWENTY-SECOND

Salient Thought for the Day.

We are never safe until we have found our foundation in Truth.

Lines to Memorize.

The shower of Thy blessing
Fell on this parched ground
Which was barren as a desert.
At first I did not believe
That aught could soften it,
But Thy miracle hath changed
This waste to a flower land.

Lesson.

If we only learn to have a steadfast hold on the Supreme, all our outer actions can be easily regulated and sanctified and be made a part of the inner consciousness. True devotees hold fast to Divinity and because of that they are always able to maintain their balance. They feel secure, no matter how many times they are whirled round and round by the outer circumstances of life. This is a secret we learn through the practice of holiness.

Prayer.

May the Infinite All-abiding Spirit give me inspiration, strength and courage that will sustain me in all my thoughts, words and actions.
May I lean on Him and depend on Him alone.
May I look up to Him alone for protection and safety.
May I find all my peace in Him.

MARCH TWENTY-THIRD

Salient Thought for the Day.

We must first seek the blessing of the Divine.

Lines to Memorize.

I ask for naught
Save what Thou placest in my hand at Thy pleasure.
World's treasure is empty and sordid to my soul;
It only burdens my mind and heart.
Even a grain of Thy blessing fills my whole life with true joy and peace.
I crave naught but Thy grace.

Lesson.

When God blesses us, everything that we do, everything we touch, is tinged with His blessing. If we have found this in our consciousness, we carry it everywhere. It is not only sometimes we have it, we have it all the time. Even in our blunders, when we fall down and make mistakes, we know even then we cannot be crushed, we cannot be lost; because we have something which is entirely ours.

Prayer.

May my heart be freed from all doubt and despair.
May it find peace through Thy grace.
Through Thy grace all things are possible unto man:
Even the lame can cross the mountain and the dumb become eloquent.
Open my heart to Thy blessing that my life may find its fullness in Thee.

Salient Thought for the Day.

Even a little spark of holy aspiration will transform the heart and mind and make them capable of higher thought and feeling.

Lines to Memorize.

When pure Spirit shines who sees it?
Few; yea, only a very few
For not many have the seeing eye.
Many see the light of the sun, the moon, the far-distant stars
And the light of yon road-side lamp;
But only the pure heart with the eye of love
Can see the light that shineth from pure Spirit.

Lesson.

A man who is spiritual cannot be less capable in any direction. He has greater capacity for loving God, he is able to love his fellow-beings more; he has clear vision and greater power. Too often we are afraid to take interest in big things because we do not wish to let go of the small; yet in that bigger thing we find the smaller included. Our life is never impoverished by higher aspiration, it is always enriched.

Prayer.

O Thou all-radiant One—
Out of Thy Compassion, kindle in my heart a new fire of holy aspiration.
Clarify my sight, that I may gain new vision.
Cleanse my mind, that I may perceive Thy Presence in all things.
And dedicate myself with new ardor to Thy service.

Salient Thought for the Day.

Our prayers are more effective and beautiful when we carry holy thoughts in our mind at other times.

Lines to Memorize.

In my prayer I knew not what to ask of Thee,
For my mind was rent with many desires,
And my heart was torn with longing,
So I could not pray with a single heart;
But a sudden dawning hath come upon me with a lightning flash.
Now I sit with but one prayer in my heart:
That Thou fillest we with Thy love first and last.
Only this I ask with all my heart and soul.

Lesson.

So long as there is much noise on the outer plane, we cannot hear the voice of the subtler spiritual plane; nor can we hope to gain access into the higher realm. When day after day we strive to cultivate the consciousness of our inner being, our prayers grow more fervent and God hears our least call; but our heart must be one-pointed and we must feel that our being is a part of His Being.

Prayer.

Make me so humble and free from self-consciousness,
That my life may be filled with holy inspiration.
May I learn to be refreshed through the sanctity of my thought.
Thou alone canst sanctify my life.
Make it holy and pure and full of ardent devotion.

Salient Thought for the Day.

It is sincerity of purpose that makes us realize unity with the Divine.

Lines to Memorize.

There are many ways to sing:
Song of the mind, song of the senses, song of the heart, song of the soul.
It goes ever deeper and deeper.

Lesson.

Holy thought and aspiration take away all hatred, envy and jealousy and we become gentle, beloved children of God. But this unity cannot be reached by calculation or pretense, or by intellect alone. It requires more than mere intellectual grasp. It requires the Spirit of Sanctity. This unity is found in silent communion, when we lose all sense of the importance of the outer and feel the importance of the inner. There is no such thing as imitation in the spiritual life.

Prayer.

Thou, Supreme One, art the Eternal among non-eternal things,
Thou art the Light of all light,
Thou art the Substance of all life.
Sanctify my thought and lift my aspirations.
Grant me access to Thy Holy Being,
Make me Thine own.

MARCH TWENTY-SEVENTH

Salient Thought for the Day.

How fervent and watchful we are depends on our attitude of mind.

Lines to Memorize.

Playmate of my soul, once Thou didst teach me a dance
And we both clapped our hands with a joyous song in our hearts.
Today my whole life floats in its rhythm
And my body sways with its beat.

Lesson.

Sanctity never enters into a lazy life. If the mind becomes saturated with worldly thoughts and feelings it grows dense, heavy, unresponsive. Even in the hour of devotion, our spiritual aspiration when we try to awaken it, does not respond, of our mind is dull and heavy. But this does not happen with people who live carefully and thoughtfully. They do not slacken in their ardor. They do not leave their spiritual practice for the last moment. All through the day in everything they do, they are preparing themselves. When we do this, even our ordinary tasks can be full of lofty inspiration.

Prayer.

Help me to lift my thoughts and manifest true holiness of life in God.
Fill me with His blessed Being.
May I learn to live close to His Divine Heart
And be unmoved by the voice of the world.

Salient Thought for the Day.

We must be genuine and earnest. We cannot play the hypocrite in the realm of sanctity.

Lines to Memorize.

None can hear His footsteps save those whose sanctuary-door is open;
His noiseless tread is heard only by those whose outer ears are closed.

Lesson.

In order to practise the sense of the Divine Presence within us we must get rid of all insincerity and complexity. That is why singleness of purpose is preached so insistently; our thought must be unmixed and simple. Until our heart is simplified, it is difficult to feel the Presence of the Divine. To make the heart simple we must not listen to the voice of the world, we must not yield to sights and sounds. Then our perceptions become keen and we perceive the Presence.

Prayer.

O Thou who art eternally abiding in my soul,
I lift my heart in worship unto Thee.
Do Thou nurture within me the true spirit of sanctity.
May insincerity or doubt or scepticism never overwhelm me.
May my mind be free from unrest and distraction.
May I remain firm in my devotion and faithful in my life.

MARCH TWENTY-NINTH

Salient Thought for the Day.

When we are impatient, we throw away our opportunities.

Lines to Memorize.

Far have I travelled,
Long have I struggled,
Following the impulse of my restless will.
Seeking! Seeking! Seeking!
In quest of happiness I sought through life's mansion,....
But happiness I found not there.
I found happiness nowhere till my self-will was lost in His Will.

Lesson.

The real sign of a spiritually-minded person is his silent, tolerant, patient attitude. He attains his end because he does not interfere with the higher plan. He moves with the higher forces. He is always in harmony with the Divine Will. Anger, impatience, calculation, quarrelling and disputes: this is what we find in the world. Those who have taken up the spiritual life cannot afford to indulge in such things.

Prayer.

O Lord, grant unto me calmness of spirit and serenity of heart,
Shield me from the entanglements of my lower nature.
Help me to seek Thee with perseverance and unswerving consecration.
May I never tire in my search after Thee
Or turn aside and forget Thee.

Salient Thought for the Day.

Ardent devotion sanctifies everything.

Lines to Memorize.

My life's broken harmony is restored,
The unfinished song is complete
Since I have found my place at Thy sacred Feet.
Thy beckoning hath saved me from falling into the snare of deception;
Contact with Thy holy Being hath refilled my ebbing life.

Lesson.

It is not the aggressor, it is not the scheming, calculating man, who does most for the world; it is the man who has a true sense of consecration and sanctity. When man learn the higher order of life, when he learns the higher law of love, he brings healing and happiness to himself and to others. We are all children of God; but in our practical life we do not always express those qualities which show us to be children of God. We must manifest it through our daily living.

Prayer.

May I feel uplifted and inspired and free from all that is sordid and sad for my soul.
May I hear with my ears what is holy and sublime;
May I see with my eyes that which is spiritual, pure and exalting.

Salient Thought for the Day.

Only one who is sanctified can live, aspire and serve truly.

Lines to Memorize.

Rhythm of life, I feel thy beating pulse
In the still depth of my soul,
Where sensuous sounds melt into oblivion.
Thy ceaseless music drowns all discord,
Blending chaos of life in eternal harmony.

Lesson.

The sanctified soul never wants to rule, he never wishes to make his voice heard and for that reason he becomes the mouthpiece for the outpouring of Truth. The man who is sanctified is devoid of all self seekng. He feels that his first obligation is to his spiritual being. If he does anything to weaken his spiritual fibre, he suffers. His mind seeks naturally the high, the holy, the Divine. His inner being is like fertile soil ; when a spiritual seed is dropped into it, it becomes fruitful.

Prayer.

O Thou Great Eternal One, keep me close to Thee ;
May I find my whole happiness in Thy Divine Being.
Enfold me with Thy beneficent love
And make me one with Thee.
Still all discord in my heart.
Fill my mind with harmonious thoughts.
Rouse in me holy aspirations.

NOTES

Man of vision, stand firm!
Hold fast to thy faith!
These blinking lights that come at the dark hours of night,
These thick clouds that gather round the sun to veil its face,
Are but passing phantoms.
They are unreal—fleeting illusions to distract our minds form high vision.
Be thou steadfast,—unwavering like yon mountain.
The light above, that once shed its glow upon thy path,
Is yet watching over thee from beyond the clouds.
Stand firm in faith :—and never lower thy gaze!

April

BLISS OF HIGHER VISION

He who is satisfied with wisdom and direct vision of Truth, who has conquered the senses and is ever undisturbed, to whom a lump of earth, a stone and gold are the same, that one is said to be a saint of established wisdom.

Bhagavad-Gita

APRIL FIRST

Salient Thought for the Day.

Knowledge of God destroys anguish, it destroys doubt, it destroys weakness.

Lines to Memorize.

When Thou art with me I feel lack of nothing.
Love, joy, wisdom and strength,
Faith and prayer, surge in my soul.
All will I forsake to have Thee as mine.

Lesson.

Where is our highest security? Not in wealth or outer material resources. It is in the living connection with our Source. Our real safety lies in a spiritual principle. Only one who has made spiritual practices his habit will gain this connection. Our life, our hands and feet, our mind and heart, are wholly changed as we have bigger, loftier understanding. Now we see Infinitude only here and there, casually, but we must create our contact with it.

Prayer.

O Thou Infinite Spirit, help me to know Thee,
That I may rest my life and strength and happiness in Thee.
Free my mind from doubt and ignorance,
That I may grow more and more conscious of Thy tender love and unceasing protection.
May I ever seek Thee and depend on Thee in all undertakings.
May I find my peace in Thy Divine Being.

Salient Thought for the Day.

When we live in the thought of Eternity, we find a cure for all our material ailments and distresses.

Lines to Memorize.

I have found a perennial spring hidden in my inner garden.
I have bathed in it; I am drunk with its ethereal, sparkling drops.
Come, friend, I will show thee this spring of unfailing waters;
It will quench thy soul's thirst and heal thy body's wounds.

Lesson.

As long as life goes on expressing itself through outer avenues, we are handicapped. We can make our life more productive if we are not cut off from our Source. We do not survive long when we lose our connection with that Source. Only when we find the great Eternal Presence does life become complete. Then we lack for nothing.

Prayer.

O Thou Eternal Being, I offer unto Thee my inmost thoughts and prayers.
Cleanse them of all that is small and unworthy.
Remove from my mind all alien desires,
That my whole life may be in tune with Thy Divine Life;
And may I express Thy radiance in every hour of my existence.
May all the activity of my body, mind and heart be directed wholly unto Thee.

Salient Thought for the Day.

Always point the mind to that which is unlimited and vast.

Lines to Memorize.

In the glow of my sacred lamp
I caught a glimpse of Thy countenance,
Which hath roused in me
An all-consuming longing
To see Thee again.
I keep vigil,—
My altar light burns day and night with the hope of Thy coming.

Lesson.

There are those who even when they hear the voices of the world, take their stand and say: "I must know God, however difficult it may be." They dwell upon this thought and they carry it with them wherever they go, and out of this comes realization.

Prayer.

May the all-pervading Spirit of the Universe fill my heart with His light
That I may have no doubt or darkness within me.
May I realize His majesty and glory
And learn that only as I trust in His protecting power am I safe and peaceful.
May He bestow on me His blessing that my life may be noble and fruitful.

APRIL FOURTH

Salient Thought for the Day.

When we consult our inner being in everything, we begin to hear the voice of God and perceive His Presence.

Lines to Memorize.

Lo! a perfect cave in the utmost depths of my heart was awaiting, ever ready and ever still.
It was afar, yea, out of reach of all our ills.
Now I sit with Thee in unbroken peace—in rain, storm and wind.
They come and beat against my outer life, but have no access to where my heart's treasure lies.

Lesson.

The ultimate vision of Reality far surpasses all that we can picture. When we attain it, we no longer think whether we are worthy or unworthy, rich or poor, happy or unhapy. We gain a new spirit. We seem to breathe the real oxygen of life, we find fresh hope and courage. As we have certain hours for our outer duties, so we must have a time which we devote to our soul culture. When day after day we strive to cultivate this inward sight, we cannot fail to unfold it.

Prayer.

O Thou in-dwelling Spirit,
May I learn that my own strength is never sufficient,
But that my strength lies always in Thy strength.
May I so offer up my life that all my thoughts and actions may have their source in Thee.

APRIL FIFTH

Salient Thought for the Day.

We cannot lay our finger on all-encircling Infinitude, yet It is everywhere.

Lines to Memorize.

I know in my inmost depth
That no mortal light
Can reveal Thy immortal Face :
Thou art seen only in Thine own effulgence.
Yet with yearning hope in my heart,
I keep my little altar lamp
Day and night, burning—burning !

Lesson.

It is a sacrilege to believe that we have no part in God's life. The power of God is within us and all about us. Unbroken and undivided Oneness pervades the universe. We all partake of it. As long as the realm of Divinity remains distant from us, we can have no access to it and true knowledge will not come. It must be brought close through sincere yearning and living the life.

Prayer.

O Thou Infinite All-encompassing Deity
Clarify my vision that through Thy grace I may perceive Thy abiding Presence
And never again lose sight of Thee.
Teach me to seek Thee always and look to Thee wholly for protection.

APRIL SIXTH

Salient Thought for the Day.

Great things are near, but we must have a certain unfoldment to be able to partake of them.

Lines to Memorize.

The reascnance of Thy voice aroused me
Who was slumbering in idle dreams.
My waking was only for a moment,
But Thou hast wrought a strange miracle within my soul.
Now even in sleep I find something in me always awake and watching.
That which Thou hast roused in me can sleep no more.

Lesson.

Nature holds for us a rich treasure. She has lessons for us; but we must have spiritual vision to perceive what she offers. We take layer after layer off and things unfold themselves; this is the real secret of revelation. When it comes, man realizes he has a mighty spiritual heritage, that he has the power of Divinity within him. But no one can force this realization on us, we must acquire it ourselves.

Prayer.

O Thou who dwellest in my heart!
Help me to withdraw my mind from all mundane glamour
And it will reflect the Spirit of Truth.
Awaken me from the sleep of ignorance and delusion,
And grant me understanding of my divine nature.

APRIL SEVENTH

Salient Thought for the Day.

We must not cut ourselves off from the basic Reality of our life.

Lines to Memorize.

Soul art Thou in our life;
Life art Thou in our body.
Who can know Thee, Thou subtlest of subtle?
How can we ever know Thee,
Save when Thou dost come to us in Thy glory
And grant unto us our sight?

Lesson.

It is never too late to come to the Centre of our being. We may be tired, we may be worn and weary, but we can still turn to that Centre. Time is always ripe for that. When we make our contact there, we find protection. If we do not make this contact, our actions are never productive. When we touch that one basic Principle, we find the solution for all problems. Why is a man restless? It is because he has lost touch with the centre of his being.

Prayer.

O Supreme Deity, lift my heart from the mire of delusion,
That I may ever rejoice in Thy benign Presence.
Make my search after Thee steadfast and unfaltering.
Thou art the storehouse of all light and inspiration;
Shed Thy light upon my path.

Salient Thought for the Day.

God is in the abyss of our soul and is waiting for us to return to Him.

Lines to Memorize.

O Light! Thou art my life!
My strength, my inspiration and action,
My vigor and joy—
All are contained in Thee.
Shine forth! Shine forth!
Shed Thy beneficence!
Let thy healing radiance warm my ebbing life.

Lesson.

There is a yearning in every earnest soul to kindle the fire of Truth. It dwells in all, but we do not know it. Often we brood in wretchedness thinking we have it not, but it is always there and when the spiritual eye opens, we recognize our connection. We have our redemption, we have our happiness through this connection. Brooding does not take us onward. The only danger-point is when we lose our vision.

Prayer.

O Thou All-loving Lord, may I never forget Thee.
May I ever remember that Thou art my Friend and Companion,
My Spiritual Guide and Refuge from all onslaughts of the world.
Thou art the Giver of all sight:
Give me vision of Thee.
Illumine my heart with Thy Effulgence
That I may never turn my gaze away from Thee.

Salient Thought for the Day.

To attain realization we must maintain a lofty standard of consecration in our daily life.

Lines to Memorize.

The paths of my inner and outer life lie clear before me :
I need no other light to find my way out to Thee.
I shall carry no light save one—the lamp of Thy Grace.
This I can never part with ;
I see by its white radiance, even when mine eyes are closed.

Lesson.

When our yearning for Truth is genuine and our heart is single, we come into the presence of the Supreme. We converse with Him and we realize that our being is a part of His Being. Then all the little things of life, all its petty details, do not bind us. We breathe freely in this higher sphere of consciousness. We are renewed and become imbued with the Spirit of God.

Prayer.

Infinite Spirit, make my heart free from all stain and selfishness,
That I may have the desire to follow Thy path with whole-hearted consecration and devotion.
May I learn to live ever in contact with Thy Divine Being and find my true happiness in communion with Thee.
Bestow upon me Thy sacred blessing,
Infill me with Thy Divine peace.

Salient Thought for the Day.

As soon as we find a larger happiness, we cease to cling to the lesser one.

Lines to Memorize.

Noble thoughts are like sweet perfume,
Ever refreshing to our mind and heart,
While impure thoughts rise as noxious vapors to poison our soul and paralyze our mind's truer sense.

Lesson.

We hold ourselves down by our own thought and action. There is a power which excels worldly wisdom. Yet the world of higher aspirations is not separate from this world; it can be found here and now. We fail to sense it because we do not open the right avenues. There is not a single person who has found happiness, peace or lasting contentment in the finite world; but after they have found it within, they can carry it to the outside.

Prayer.

O Thou inexhaustible Source of all blessedness,
Make my heart serene and glad,
Kindle in me a burning fire of aspiration,
May no unworthy thought find access to my mind,
And may my heart always remain a fitting altar unto Thee.

APRIL ELEVENTH

Salient Thought for the Day.

Great Truth can never rise in the mind of the thoughtless or in him who is enslaved by selfishness.

Lines to Memorize.

What avails quarrelling for thy freedom if thy heart remains selfish and vain?
Cast off the chain from thy neck, thou freeman,
And be free as the air of heaven!

Lesson.

All these fragments, all these disjointed fibres of our mind, if we can bring them together in one-pointed devotion, it will remove every blemish from our heart and give us sight. Our eyes are blurred now because we are looking here and looking there. Our eye is not single, that is why we cannot see. By meditation we clarify our sight. In meditation we do not become inactive; but the channels, through which our usual activity flows, become blocked and our higher facilities force open other avenues of activity.

Prayer.

O Thou All-compassionate Being, awaken in me a more yearning spirit and a deeper longing for the Truth.
Grant unto me greater wisdom
That I may be able to discern the real and forsake the unreal.
Reveal Thy true nature unto me
And may it free me from all bondage and blindness.
May I never weary in my search for Thee.

Salient Thought for the Day.

Outer clarified vision comes as a result of inner clarified vision.

Lines to Memorize.

Wert Thou always so near and I hunted for Thee so far?
Verily when I ran out to find Thee
I was going away from Thee.
Faith have I none in my own wisdom or vision.

Lesson.

Only those who have clarified vision can see, feel and touch the Infinite. We seem to perceive subtler things more clearly when we close our eyes. This does not mean that we must become blind, but these channels of the outer senses become barriers to our inner sight. When a mystic goes before the altar, he closes his eyes to all sights, he closes his ears to all sounds; not that he must assume blindness or deafness, but that he blocks the outer senses in order that his inward sight and hearing may become more vivid.

Prayer.

O Thou All-seeing One, may I never forget that vision of Thee gives life;
Vision of Thee gives exaltation.
Bestow upon me this deeper sight.
The Truth is always shining;
Help me to find It,
That I may never stray away from Thee.

APRIL THIRTEENTH

Salient Thought for the Day.

Understanding is born from within.

Lines to Memorize.

Thou art born of Spirit,
Not created by thought,
Nor moulded by fancies,
Thou Divine spark of unfathomed origin!
As vision Thou enterest in the heart of the prophet;
In the soul of the poet Thou dwellest as raptures of inspiration;
And in the throat of the singer as music.

Lesson.

Our whole nature will be washed clean by the water of pure spiritual understanding. It must be true understanding, however, not mere theory. It comes as the fruit of realization. When it comes we feel it, our whole life is filled with it. There is no more doubt or questioning. We do not hesitate, we do not calculate. A new consciousness rises in us and we yield ourselves to that undying Reality which abides in our soul.

Prayer.

O Supreme Spirit, lift my thought from all unrealities
And grant me perfect tranquillity of mind.
Thou art the One to be realized.
Destroy in me all delusion
And bestow on me the blessing of Thy abiding wisdom.

Salient Thought for the Day.

We have innate introspection and divine inspiration.

Lines to Memorize.

When all is covered by the blank sheet of darkness and naught is seen,
Thou enterest unaware with Thy all-filling light,
Transforming gloom into brightness.

Lesson.

When man awakens, he finds that he is part of one great Reality and he realizes his union with all things. People come in contact with something high and beautiful, but if they keep their doors closed, it hinders instead of helping them. All men have a hunger for everlasting happiness, for everlasting peace; but that which is everlasting cannot be acquired suddenly. We must first realize from what source it comes.

Prayer.

May the Divine Spirit who is ever within me,
Who knows my hidden thoughts and feelings,
May He open my sight that I may perceive His glory
And feel new and more fervent devotion unto Him.
May He inspire within me nobler thoughts
And more selfless aspirations,
That I may ever seek the Highest.

APRIL FIFTEENTH

Salient Thought for the Day.

If we learn to depend on our higher faculties, we shall not fail to reach our goal.

Lines to Memorize.

I sailed on the wing of thought,
Crossing many deep streams where
My feet would have sunk in weight.
But the wing of thought carried me to the unwonted shores of life where I found Thee,
And in Thee I found my rest.

Lesson.

We always find great joy and satisfaction in the spiritual. In the light of Spirit there cannot be any darkness. We learn this through meditation. We cannot lose that light. It may be obscured, but it cannot be extinguished. Realization of that light brings a sense of Presence. No one can force on you this sense of a higher Presence. It is a quality of the soul.

Prayer.

O Thou Giver of all light, illumine my mind and heart with Thy divine radiance.
Bestow upon me divine vision,
That my life may be productive of the highest good.
Make my steps steadfast and unfaltering;
And though many times I may fail and stumble blindly,
Still may I never doubt Thy loving guidance.

Salient Thought for the Day.

No price is too great to pay for inspiration and higher vision.

Lines to Memorize.

Thou art the might of the mighty,
Sanctity of the saint,
Melody of the musician!
Thou all-glorious Spirit of transcendent loveliness,
In awe and dumb wonderment
I adore Thee!

Lesson.

Scientific knowledge alone is never sufficing. It may be a starting point, but we must look for something deeper. We must reach the storehouse of learning. Science plus union with God makes up the Yoga system. The term *Yoga* is a sacred word—so sacred that there is a hush of silence when it is uttered. It signifies "union"—union with That, union with the Supreme. We have to find our access to the within and Yoga gives us the methods by which we can do this.

Prayer.

Thou Gracious Lord, I seek Thy Grace and blessing.
Do Thou bestow upon me Thy Grace
And make my life more worthy of Thy blessing.
Fasten my heart to Thee with steadfast devotion and faith.
May I never fall away or lose Thy Grace.
May my thought ever be fixed on Thee.

APRIL SEVENTEENTH

Salient Thought for the Day.

Through the practice of silence we gain knowledge of our spiritual nature and bring our outer nature into harmony with it.

Lines to Memorize.

Hush! This is the hour of silence
When soul seeks its refreshment.
Turbulent mind, thou art ever restive for sport and gain;
Thou art ever mad for new sensation and art in feverish plight.
Wouldst thou rob me of my true happiness?
Be still, that thou mayest not miss this new and blessed joy.

Lesson.

Stillness is not negative, it is not lack of life; it is control of life. Silent power is always constructive. The practice of silence helps us gain a glimpse of our inherent nature. That is why wise men spend so much time in silence. Unless we have quietness of mind, unless we have learned to control our restless thought, we cannot remain unmoved in all the experiences of life.

Prayer.

O Thou Supreme One, in this hour of silence lift my prayer to Thee
Sanctify me by Thy touch,
That I may feel a nearness that destroys all doubt and heaviness.
May I rest in Thy Divine Presence and protection
And open my heart, my thought and feeling to Thy Divine inspiration.

APRIL EIGHTEENTH

Salient Thought for the Day.

In meditation our Ideal does not grow greater but our relation with it grows more fundamental.

Lines to Memorize.

How long I waited for Thee I cannot say,
For time was not in my thought.
When I watch for Thee my mind is merged
in Thee.
Time exists not for me when Thou art near.

Lesson.

Meditation means a finer province of thought. Thought can break through everything. The reason why our thought does not reveal to us is because somethnig is constantly cutting in on it. Only when our whole nature becomes silent, free from pretense, free from demand and discontent, can we have the steadiness of mind necessary for communion with the Ideal. We must express God-like qualities in our daily actions, if we would recognize His voice and perceive His Presence.

Prayer.

O Thou who abidest in all things,
I lift my prayers and aspirations unto Thee.
Open Thou all avenues to Thee
That I may reach Thy Divine Spirit
And find rest in Thy great Presence.
Help me to realize that thou art everywhere;
And make my heart so fervent in devotion
That I shall not fail to reach Thee.

APRIL NINETEENTH

Salient Thought for the Day.

When our mind grows still, we find within us an unfailing source of supply.

Lines to Memorize.

"Be still! Strain thou thy mind no more",
spake a voice from an unseen depth:
"Close thine eyes, they see not the true; come
thou with me."
Thus a gentle hand led me to a noiseless land.
Its cooling, scented breeze soothed all my inner
anguish.
Lo! I stood before a crystal lake in whose
limpid waters
I saw—and I knew.

Lesson.

We must be indrawn, we must learn a deeper mode of thinking, if we would establish connection with our inner Source. When we touch It, we experience a new fullness of life, a new and vivid, sense of realization. People imagine that the contemplative life makes us passive and negative; but this shows that they have never had access to It. When one finds the realm to which contemplation leads, all dullness vanishes and life is filled with abundant joy—enough to give to others.

Prayer.

May He who watches over this universe
May He quiet my mind and heart,
And make my whole being so harmonious and
peaceful
That His glory may be manifest within me.
May I never break my connection with that
Source of all bliss.

APRIL TWENTIETH

Salient Thought for the Day.

The light of the soul sheds its radiance everywhere.

Lines to Memorize.

The light that I see yonder
And the light that shineth near
Is but the same light.
It is soul's light:
It is God's light;
It is the light of love.
This lamp of life may burn dim or it may burn bright;
But ever is it undying in dying.

Lesson.

We all have that majestic soul within us. We can all grow with its expansion, or we can stay in a narrow little circle and contract. The greatest misfortune that can come to a soul is to lose its spiritual vision. No one can rob us of it. Only the things that rise within ourselves can rob us of it. They are our real enemies, they cheat us of our rightful heritage.

Prayer.

O Thou All-radiant Being, shed Thine infinite light on my life,
That it may radiate only brightness and joy.
Thou shinest through all things.
Do Thou shine through my every thought and action,
And reveal Thy blessed Presence to others.

Salient Thought for the Day.

It is because of that Supreme Light that we are able to think, to move, to work.

Lines to Memorize.

Hail to Thee, Thou who dost light in our heart
The flame of all-consuming love!
Hail to Thee, Thou who dost rouse in our soul
Adoration for all this, Thy creation!
In speechless thought I marvel at Thy boundless blessing.

Lesson.

In order to bring that living Reality into our life, we must become vibrant with spiritual aspiration, we must open every avenue to God. If we start with negative thought, it becomes a great drawback. That which is first, we must give that first place. Life is a question of unfoldment. It holds a special lesson for each one of us. No one can escape from that lesson or break away from connection with that basic Reality.

Prayer.

O Thou Infinite Spirit, reveal Thyself unto me
That I may feel Thee near.
Help me to contemplate Thy infinite Essence within my heart.
Thou art the source of all my power;
Thou art the origin of my life.
May I never forget that Thou art Consciousness abiding within my consciousness,
That Thou art the Support and Sustenance of my being.

APRIL TWENTY-SECOND

Salient Thought for the Day.

God has given us reason. He has given us a higher sense of values. We need both to attain union with our Source.

Lines to Memorize.

Wake, awake!
A new light hath come into this house that was once so dark.
Rise, my spirit!
Arise, my mind, my body and all ye sense-slumberers!
Behold the glory of light, dispelling all darkness!

Lesson.

We learn balance through our union with the Supreme Source and man is stronger as he gains this union. The richest experience of life comes when we find our inner Refuge, where we can retire and feel security. Buddha calls it an island. The thing is to find it through our thought and aspiration. Only when we find this inner point of contact, can we take our place in the world and fill it wisely.

Prayer.

O Thou Supreme One, bestow upon me a true understanding,
That I may come to Thee with a sincere spirit of consecration.
Thou art the Storehouse of all light and wisdom,
Thou alone can strengthen and inspire me.
May I rest my life in Thine
And find my peace in thee.

APRIL TWENTY-THIRD

Salient Thought for the Day.

All the faculties we have can be freed from limitation by connecting them with their Source through meditation.

Lines to Memorize.

Let all doors and windows of this house be open to the sanctity of sun.
Leave nothing unopened, nothing hidden from the beneficent light.
Gloomy thoughts shall never enter this house again;
Doubt and despair will vanish;
Yea, they will all vanish from this house before the light.

Lesson.

In meditation you drop contact with the world, which weights you down. A little meditation done each day, if you do not fail, will change your whole life. Life of meditation is life of peace; life of meditation is life of happiness; life of meditation is life of spiritual grandeur in the soul of man.

Prayer.

In this hour of silence may I lift my heart and thought and fix them on the All-abiding Spirit.
May He bestow upon me His Grace and throw light upon my path.
He is my only Guide and Protector,
My one Friend and Companion.
May I realize oneness with Him
And yield myself up wholly to His protecting love.

APRIL TWENTY-FOURTH

Salient Thought for the Day.

The sign of life's fulfilment is in softness and mellowness.

Lines to Memorize.

Soul in search is never at rest.
Soul in slumber knoweth not the precious peace.
Soul in wakeful communion is at rest and hath found its peace.

Lesson.

One feels suffocated within the boundary line of dogmatic religion. We must avoid fanaticism. A fanatic never has clear vision. We need a balanced attitude of mind. The greatest mellowness and gentleness are to be found in those who have realized most. A man has nothing to give until he has learned to shut the door and commune with his own soul.

Prayer.

O Thou All-knowing One, free me from the anguish of doubt and calculation.
May I never close my being to Thee.
May I open every channel to receive Thy Divine inspiration.
May I find my home in Truth
And rest my life and happiness in Truth alone.

APRIL TWENTY-FIFTH

Salient Thought for the Day.

Differences are wiped out when we have direct illumination.

Lines to Memorize.

I see naught else but Thee;
I feel naught else but Thee;
I crave no other knowledge.
I only know that Thou art mine,
And I am for ever Thine.

Lesson.

Universal vision gives us a conception of Divine Being. Through universal vision we approach nearer and nearer to the Supreme. We cannot have freedom of life, if we have any crookedness or narrowness in our thought or habit. We cannot have access to God without sincerity and directness. Only absolute dependence and absolute trust—such trust as a child has in his mother—will enable us to establish a living relationship with Godhead.

Prayer.

May the All-embracing Spirit of the Universe waken in my soul a sense of His Presence.
May that living Presence fill my whole being.
May it kindle in me a new fire of love and sympathy for all men.
May I express that love in all words and actions.
May He grant me sincerity of heart and openness of mind.

APRIL TWENTY-SIXTH

Salient Thought for the Day.

Commune with Thy Spirit in silence.

Lines to Memorize.

It is not death that robs our life,
Nor is it the dark of night that bars our inward sight;
Nay, it is the Veil of Unknowing.

Lesson.

We cannot live on borrowed knowledge. Borrowed knowledge is fluctuating and shifting. We must make it our own, based on our own experience. Whenever we have to go elsewhere to learn about something, it does not belong to us. That is true knowledge which accompanies us. It is like carrying a light. That one light makes all things plain. This is what we call wisdom.

Prayer.

O Thou Source of all knowledge,
May I learn to know Thee as Thou art in Truth.
Grant me constant inward contact with Thy Spirit,
May my mind be uplifted and my heart purified;
May my sight be turned within
That I may gain true vision of Thee
And become peaceful and full of joy.

APRIL TWENTY-SEVENTH

Salient Thought for the Day.

Who is the wiser, the one who revels in the small details of life or he who enjoys the fruit of life?

Lines to Memorize.

My heart sings a strange, unknown song,
But never can I hear the words.
Its music soothes my soul to rest
Yet the words remain ever unheard.
My heart sings it alone in stillness—
this, the wordless song.

Lesson.

We have great difficulty in holding our mind on the larger view of things, but it can be done. We can bring ourselves to a stable, high point of equilibrium. It is wise to open all the avenues of our being to the Universal. It gives us access to a larger life and a higher vision. There are certain things which have universal attributes, like music. Something of greater magnitude is conveyed by them. They connect us with the universal storehouse of life and knowledge.

Prayer.

O Lord, make my life full of Divine inspiration,
That it may become productive only of good.
Free me from all pettiness and narrowness.
Help me to keep my thought fixed on That
which is vast and majestic.
Expand my heart and enlarge my mind
That I may be able to contain Thee
And give myself up wholly to Thee.

APRIL TWENTY-EIGHTH

Salient Thought for the Day.

Wisdom does not consist in gathering information. It consists in finding a clear access to the Highest.

Lines to Memorize.

Since Thou hast come of Thine own great compassion for me,
Who am devoid of all merit,
Wilt Thou not vouchsafe a little boon to me?
Then place Thy saving Hand upon mine eyes.
And cure me of my blindness
That it may never again hide Thee from me.

Lesson.

That which enshrounds our vision is ignorance. The way out of it is through wisdom. Wisdom is that which keeps us from blundering. It is like carrying a light. We can all unfold it. It rests with us whether we will walk in darkness or whether we will kindle the torch of wisdom in our mind and heart and walk by its light. It alone can show us the way to God.

Prayer.

O Thou Infinite Being, show me the way to Thee
That I may gain access to Thy Presence
And bathe in Thy light.
May I never fail to see Thee.
May I never turn my face away from Thee,
And may I seek Thee always with steadfastness and fervent faith.

APRIL TWENTY-NINTH

Salient Thought for the Day.

When the little rays of light in our mind are focused, our mind becomes like a search-light and reveals Truth.

Lines to Memorize.

Thine eyes stretched beyond the pale light of mortal world,
For what vision art thou lost in thought?
Thy motionless gaze,
Thy fervent ecstasy
Thy illumined face,
All these unearthly marks...
Have given me sight for seeking the unseen.

Lesson.

Our body, mind and heart, instead of working in unison, go in opposite directions; that is why we accomplish so little. When we unite all our faculties, we gain the power of penetration. Unless man possesses the power of penetration, he has not fineness of vision to perceive Reality. Knowledge is really image-making. The individual derives great benefit from this image-making, but it can also make us visionary. There must be action with it. They go together.

Prayer.

O Thou All-compassionate One,
Bestow upon me power to show forth Thy Truth in my life.
May I center my mind and heart in Thee alone.
Help me to gather up my scattered thoughts
And turn them on Thee in whole-hearted aspiration.

Salient Thought for the Day.

Truth is the richest thing we can acquire in life. We must recognize its vital importance and be loyal to it.

Lines to Memorize.

Enter Thou my inmost being;
Leave nothing in dark.
Fill my heart, my soul, and all my soul's hiddenmost parts,
Unknown to my mortal mind.
Come Thou!
I invoke Thee with my soul's yearning voice.

Lesson.

Not a particle of Truth can ever be lost, not a single effort to realize the Truth can be unfruitful. Only thing required of us is to have patience and perseverance and unshaken trust in the Divine. What else is needed? Life should be lived just for the sake of itself. I mean for expansion, for vision of That, but never for the opinion of any creature, rich or poor, learned or ignorant. Worship of Truth brings great strength of conviction and absolute fearlessness.

Prayer.

O Thou Effulgent Light,
Thou who art ever unchanging, without beginning or end,
Make Thy effulgence felt in my heart.
Fill my whole being with it, leaving room for naught else.
May Thy Light of Truth illumine my path;
May I follow it, faithfully and with fervor of Spirit.

Merit? Merit? Brother, who told thee I had merit?
Merit have I none, nor ever did I have.
What merit hath the straw?
The weaver shapes a basket with it.
If the basket be fair it is not merit of the straw;
It is his skill who maketh it.
I am that straw which once lay at the great Weaver's feet.
But He, the Compassionate, took it in His hand and fashioned it.
Now I cherish this basket of His fashioning
To gather His blessing.

May

HUMILITY, SIMPLICITY, PURITY OF HEART

Humility, unostentatiousness, non-injuring, forgiveness, simplicity, purity, steadfastness, self-control; this is declared to be wisdom; what is opposed to this is ingorance.

Bhagavad-Gita

Salient Thought for the Day.

Keep your heart free and clean and humble, then God will enter.

Lines to Memorize.

Since Thou hast told me Thou wouldst enter my home, I have cleansed it and decked it with wild flowers.
My house was bare—Oh, how full it is now!
My flowers were unscented—now they are fragrant.
I would not exchange this cottage of mine for all the palaces of the world!

Lesson.

Service, humility and purity are the foundation of character. Without them no spiritual growth is possible. So one must practise these qualities with earnestness and sincerity, and God will come. When we know that great Spirit, whom we call Father or Mother, as our own, all pride, fear and turbulence vanish and we find peace. As our heart becomes free from blemish, we feel the presence of the Divine within us and we are able to reflect it in our outer life; but we do not keep it to enjoy selfishly, we give it to others in every word, act and thought.

Prayer.

May the All-compassionate One purify my mind and cleanse my thought;
May He fill my whole being with His Divine love and strength.
May He fulfil my one desire and prayer.
And make me a worthy dwelling-place for His holy Spirit.

MAY SECOND

Salient Thought for the Day.

Humility is the richest jewel you can wear.

Lines to Memorize.

Wouldst thou worship the High, the Holy?
Then strip thyself of this garment of self and put on a fresh vestment of humility.

Lesson.

Humility it the greatest ornament in life. If you place your hand in the Divine Hand with real humility, no one can take you away from Divinity. If you come with truly humble heart, no one can cast you off from the Divine. Some people when they receive a blessing are able to retain it, because they are humble and receptive. Among those who aspire are many different types, some must express their devotion through austerity; they are unbending and critical of others in the spiritual life. There is another type which employs only mildness, gentleness and humility in every task. Great souls belong to the second type.

Prayer.

O Thou Giver of all gifts,
Bestow on me the gift of true humility.
Free me from all pride, vanity and self-assertion.
Grant unto me a lowly heart
That I may do all things simply and without aggressiveness.
May my mind dwell ever on Thy vastness and glory
And feel itself nothing apart from Thee.

Salient Thought for the Day.

A man who has gained his access to Divinity, he has simplified his whole life.

Lines to Memorize.

I want no playmate but Thee.
They do not understand my simple games;
They have no need of me, for they have many others.
I have no other than Thee; yea, I am lonely and sad;
But I await Thy pleasure with humble submission.

Lesson.

God sees our actions. Loud prayers cannot deceive Him. To reach Him we need to be pure-hearted and genuine. Too much calculation defeats our purpose in the spiritual life. It is simplicity and guilelessness which carry us forward. It is not enough to take up the spirtiual life as a fad. It can never benefit us. To profit by it, we must get its true import.

Prayer.

May the All-abiding Spirit, to whom I look for help in every hour,
May He purify my heart and make it so free from stain
That it may be a worthy dwelling-place for Him.
May He make me simple and guileless,
That I may trust wholly in His loving care and protection.
May I draw all my strength from His inexhaustible store-house
And live in unbroken contact with His Divine Being.

Salient Thought for the Day.

We get rid of our problems by a process of emptying.

Lines to Memorize.

Bathe thyself in the water of life.
The earth water cannot cleanse thy stains.
Adorn thyself with the garb of simplicity,
Anoint thy heart with selfless love:
Thus do thou enter the shrine with soft and gentle tread.

Lesson.

The mind must be emptied before it can be filled. In this way we free ourselves from our cares and worries and troubles. We go round and round our problems, but it is not through calculation that they can be solved. The only way we can be rid of them is to drop them like a dead weight. If we form the habit of gazing on something that is pure Light, doubt, misery or despondency may come, but the Light will never fail us.

Prayer.

O Thou All-loving Deity, help me to direct my whole thought to Thee.
Thou art the Consciousness of my consciousness;
Thou art the Life of my life;
Fill my whole heart with Thy Divine Presence,
That there may remain naught else beside Thee.
May I turn with childlike simplicity to Thee in time of trouble
And find my peace in Thee alone.

MAY FIFTH

Salient Thought for the Day.

A little sacrifice of the flesh does not count for anything.

Lines to Memorize.

I will sing to Thee now with my whole voice and lose myself utterly.
When Thou didst ask me first, I was shy and self-conscious ;
But now, through Thy patient and unchanging love, my heart is open.

Lesson.

We are happiest when we have a sense of spiritual values awakened in us. We get this sense through purity. We must try to touch the heart of our blessing. We must give ourselves the chance to be imbued with these higher feelings. These hands, this heart and mind can produce what is lovely and far-reaching ; or they can be detrimental to us. Every act of ours should produce something of worth and beauty.

Prayer.

O Thou Supreme Spirit, accept the fruits of this day's labor and make them worthy.
I offer them unto Thee with lowliness and devotion.
Thou art the Giver of all good ;
Grant unto me a sincere heart and a humble spirit.
Guide me in all things by thy gentle Hand,
And bestow upon me the blessing of Thy Divine peace.

MAY SIXTH

Salient Thought for the Day.

When is one's mind pure? When it is simple, when it does not hold anything but Truth.

Lines to Memorize.

Wouldst Thou dwell in this house of mine,
O Thou King of the great universe?
If this be Thy pleasure, I shall keep it clean, untouched and apart.

Lesson.

When your mind is simple and your heart one-pointed, then you see only light. "When thine eye is single, thy whole body is also full of light." This is not only a spiritual fact, it is a practical fact. A man who scatters his thought over many things, he is always weak and his mind is confused. Man must find out how to maintain connection with his Source. The calculating mind never finds it; the selfish mind never finds it. That mind which is pure, cleansed and shining—that mind alone finds it.

Prayer.

O Thou, who art the nearest of all beings,
Grant that I may move in Thee and live in Thee alone,
That my whole existence may rest in Thee.
Bestow upon me this blessing,
That I may never for a moment forget Thee.
Thou art my eternal Home and Resting-place.
Reveal Thy true nature unto me, that I may manifest it in my daily life.

Salient Thought for the Day.

Human life is a sacred thing.

Lines to Memorize.

My adoration to Thee, Thou heroic, compassionate heart,
Who dost lift the distressed from their woeful state !
Thou Giver of superabundant life,
My soul's adoration to Thee alone,
Thou incarnate Spirit of light and love.

Lesson.

Our sacred obligation is not much to the outside world as to ourselves. We must prove our Divine heritage ; we must show by our life that we are descendants of God, that we have a mission from Him, that we live for Him, that we spread His love and the sense of His living Presence. It is not a question of mere preaching. Everyone does not have to be a preacher, but everyone must live the life with humility and purity of purpose.

Prayer.

May the unbounded Spirit, who directs all our thoughts and actions,
May He help me to live so worthily
That my life may gain new majesty and sanctity.
May I be free from all smallness and pettiness.
May I live in the consciousness of the Infinitude of God
And look to Him for all protection and inspiration.

Salient Thought for the Day.

Try to do everything humbly and with the utmost simplicity.

Lines to Memorize.

O Thou Infinite Life, dost Thou count even a lowly grain of dust as Thine own?
For this revelation my heart is speechless!

Lesson.

In the spiritual life there cannot be anything studied. In the realm of religion we thrive better when we cultivate the quality of simplicity, of guilelessness. We must be like little children. When real humility dawns in our heart, through the realization of the Infinitude of God, we realize our relation with that Infinitude and our finite nature fades into insignificance. Our dependence on meterial things, our egotism, our self-importance dwindle into nothingness and we taste true happiness.

Prayer.

O Thou Infinite Being, I lay myself humbly at Thy Blessed Feet.
Without Thee I can do nothing,
But with Thee all things are possible.
Do Thou direct my life and thought;
Do Thou lead me by Thy gentle Hand.
Fix my mind and heart on Thee;
And may I find all my happiness and peace in Thee alone.

MAY NINTH

Salient Thought for the Day.

Unless we are born again as little children, our burdens will not roll off.

Lines to Memorize.

I shall always remain ignorant, that Thou, All-wise One, may ever guide me:
I shall always remain a helpless child, that Thou, mighty Spirit of the universe, may ever protect me.
I thank my fate that keeps me ignorant of many things, so I may know naught else but One.
I bless my fate that keeps me ungrown, so I may cling to Thee alone.

Lesson.

The child has not the wisdom and calculation that a grown-up person has and he is always protected. The world is powerless to resist the charm, the appeal of a child. When a child is born, it seems to bring fragrance from an unknown region. Let us learn the art of being like little children. We are so grown-up, we have such a sense of independence and self-importance, that we cling to our burdens. When we gain a trusting spirit and give them up in complete surrender and simplicity of heart, our burdens drop from us of themselves.

Prayer.

O Lord, make my heart pure and clean and humble.
Help me to approach Thee with guileless spirit.
Make me childlike and simple,
That I may be able to lay all my burdens at Thy blessed Feet,
And trust wholly in Thy tender care.

Salient Thought for the Day.

Simplicity is a Divine gift.

Lines to Memorize.

Is it for my lack of knowledge that Thou art come to me in this garb of simplicity?
Is it to help the helpless that Thou hast made Thyself known to this lowly heart?

Lesson.

The spiritual life is never arduous; but when we take a wrong point of view, it seems to be arduous. There is nothing so simple as to open our heart humbly before that One from whom we have descended. But if any element of pride, calculation or doubt enters into us, it becomes unnatural. Sometimes out of fear childern try to hide something, but they find themselves entangled and their mind becomes blemished. If we want to gain anything in the spiritual realm, the direct, simple method is always best.

Prayer.

May the All-abiding, All-loving Spirit of the Universe,
Who is the embodiment of all blessedness,
May He purify my mind and cleanse it from all alien thoughts.
May I find my highest relaxation and joy in His Blessed Presence.
May He make me simple and free from all complexity.

MAY ELEVENTH

Salient Thought for the Day.

With lowliness of heart and with all the fervor of our being we must try to reach out towards the Goal of our life.

Lines to Memorize.

In the soft light of sanctity,
As I behold Thy transparent form of Divine loveliness,
My lowly heart is filled with unspeakable gladness.

Lesson.

Again and again the mind may fly away and follow its old habits, trying to forget that which has given it a glimpse of Reality; but we must try to bring it back. We must learn to purify our heart and simplify our life. When we have done this, the spiritual life becomes so natural that we do not even breathe without the consciousness of the First Great Cause. Then our struggle is over and we find peace.

Prayer.

O Thou Supreme Being, Thou art the Eternal among fleeting things,
Thou art the stable among all shifting things,
Kindle in my heart a more fervent love and devotion for Thee.
Make my yearning for Thee more ardent.
May I always follow thy path
Until I reach Thee, who art the Goal of my existence.

Salient Thought for the Day.

God is real to one who is spiritually awakened and humble.

Lines to Memorize.

Thou art the Maker of this life, the Giver of my sight.
Once I was ignorant of all this and sought happiness apart from Thee;
But now Thou knowest my only desire.

Lesson.

To have perpetual sense of dedication to God, we must carry Him in our thought and in our action, and realization will come as a result of this. When it comes, nothing can separate us from the allness, the all-abidingness of Deity. Then in the midst of all changing things we rest in That which is stable. It is through our understanding and a sense of consecration that we attain this state. Mere intellectual reasoning will not give it. A man must have a finer intelligence; he must be full of finer feelings and free from self-assertion.

Prayer.

O Thou Infinite Spirit!
Thou art my protecting Father,
Thou art my loving Mother,
Thou art the nearest of all beings.
Make me more conscious of that nearness
And help me to trust more wholly to Thy loving care.

Salient Thought for the Day.

When you have humility, no one can thwart you, no circumstances can overcome you.

Lines to Memorize.

Why art Thou fearful and trembling?
He is not a God of revenge.
Cast off thy false belief and let Him fill thee anew.

Lesson.

When our heart grows humble and guileless, we come close to the spiritual realm and gain spiritual vision. Then it does not matter what happens in the world. We remain indifferent to success and failure, victory and defeat. The ordinary man rises and falls with the change of circumstance. His life is fashioned according to the thinking of others. In order to find a place where we can rest and have a sense of security, we must sever ourselves from the outside material world and retire within our own soul.

Prayer.

I lift my prayer unto Thee, O Lord, who alone canst fulfil the desires of my heart.
Without Thee I can do nothing.
Help me to make Thee my safety
And turn to Thee in all distress and difficulty.
Help me to look to Thee always for protection
And rest my trust in Thee alone.

Salient Thought for the Day.

Too often through aggressiveness we step in our own light.

Lines to Memorize.

"The light is behind thee;
"When thou dost turn thy face it will shine before thee.
"This light,—the ever-burning candle of life,—was always with thee;
"But the phantoms of illusion blinded thine eyes."....
My soul, be thou vigilant!
Keep constant watch o'er this ever-burning candle of life.

Lesson.

When we cease to be in conscious touch with Divinity and turn our gaze towards the world, we forfeit the light. Then trouble, sorrow and disappointment overtake us. This goes on until we learn the great blessing of humility—that humility which is born of wisdom. The little man, the selfish man fades away, and another takes his place, one that is bigger, nobler, more efficient.

Prayer.

O Lord, kindle within me Thy Divine light;
That I may behold Thy Presence,
And see all things as they are in reality.
Free my mind from all darkness.
Cleanse my heart from all selfishness and unwisdom.
Make me humble and free from all that takes me away from Thee.

MAY FIFTEENTH

Salient Thought for the Day.

We must forget our littleness in bigness of vision, in a larger Ideal, in love of Truth and love of humanity.

Lines to Memorize.

Dark night of the soul is an illusion of mind.
Doubt of your Divine birthright will melt before the sun of Truth that will dawn in your heart.
In hour of meditation your thoughts will shine like the bright stars,
Illumining the firmament of the spiritual world.

Lesson.

There are two kinds of ego. One is unripe leading us into unending trouble. The other is the ripe ego which connects us with God. The only safe attitude a man can take is that he is an instrument in God's hands. This comes from an exalted state of mind and always leads to a bigger Ideal. It is reached through simplicity and spiritual devotion.

Prayer.

May that Infinite One who knows my innermost thoughts and feelings,
May He free me from all egotism, pride and unlovingness.
May He lead me to greater closeness with Him.
May He fill my mind and heart with His Divine Essence
And make me ever conscious of His Blessed Presence.

Salient Thought for the Day.

Be vibrant with love, faith and humility.

Lines to Memorize.

Faith, thou dost lift my humble heart.
Faith, thou dost show me His glory.
Faith, thou dost give me the nectar of love to drink,
To revive and refresh my spirit.
How oft thou dost bear me up
From the world of doubt and weight of self!

Lesson.

We can make and unmake our outer conditions by our thoughts and feelings. If we are humble, sincere and full of faith and devotion, we can change the whole order of things in our outer life. If our miseries are the result of a wrong point of view, we can remove them by discrimination, right feeling and nobility of purpose. Many times we may have to fail and stumble, but if our efforts are blessed with the Grace of the Supreme, they will always be fruitful.

Prayer.

O Thou Supreme Deity, I lift my heart to Thee.
Help me to assimilate the spiritual blessings which Thou dost bestow upon me so abundantly.
May Thy Presence kindle within me a more fervent fire of faith and devotion.
Thou art the Source of my life and strength.
Unfold my understanding, that I may feel myself at one with Thee in spirit.

MAY SEVENTEENTH

Salient Thought for the Day.

Spiritual qualities are infectious; also evil qualities are infectious.

Lines to Memorize.

In this great symphony of life
Where all is melody and music, save the voice of ego,
Sing, my soul, in harmony!

Lesson.

Those who have pure thoughts and noble ideals and loving characters exert a strong influence on others. Whenever we want to have a lasting effect on any character we must not expect to do it too quickly or too easily. If it is done too quickly, it will not last. It is like hay-fire. You set hay on fire and it makes a tremendous blaze, but in a moment it is over; while a log fire is slow to catch, but it lasts a long time. The real spiritual life is manifested when there is no element of fear, no ulterior motive, no bargaining. When we pray, we must not ask God to give us something in return. Our prayer must spring from a spontaneous desire to commune with what is beautiful.

Prayer.

May I feel the protection of the all-abiding Spirit within me.
May He so inspire my heart that I shall consecrate all my thoughts and efforts to His service.
May my love for Him be so sincere and spontaneous that others will feel it and gain new strength and inspiration from it.

Salient Thought for the Day.

If we live constantly close to spiritual forces, we become charged with them.

Lines to Memorize.

Thy immortal soul of sweet perfume
Hath risen to the throne of thy Lord;
Thou art no more separate from Him.
Thy humble heart hath taught me a holy secret,—
Yea, thou hast given thine all!

Lesson.

When we do our work through higher inspiration, which comes from contact with our Source, it has a special freshness. This inspiration comes with purity of heart. No one has a monopoly of it. The true heart is the same everywhere. The pure soul in its attitude and aspiration is always the same. There is no difference in the great saints anywhere. Spiritual wisdom is always the same and it never fails to fill the one who possesses it with higher power.

Prayer.

O Thou who art my Resting-place and Shelter,
I take refuge in Thy Sacred Being.
Rouse in me a new ardor of devotion.
I offer Thee my whole heart in humble worship;
Cleanse it and fill it with Thyself.

Salient Thought for the Day.

Simplicity, humility, whole-heartedness, can be cultivated by right direction of our thought.

Lines to Memorize.

Many times I have thought, as I scattered Thy unending gift,
That this vessel was emptied;
But it ever remains full of freshness.
I know neither to fill it nor empty it.
I only know that Thou hast placed this inexhaustible cup in my hand.
I carry it where'er I go.
'Tis Thou who givest and keepest,
I only know that I am Thy servant.
Thy humble cup-bearer.

Lesson.

There are people who find it difficult to be simple, humble and direct; but these qualities are essential in the spiritual life and we must develop them. They may not be natural to our life as it is, but we can change our life. We can make it whatever we want to make it.

Prayer.

Let me lift my heart in guileless simplicity.
May the Supreme Spirit of the Universe, who is Mother and Father and Divine Protector.
May He surround me and ever guide my steps.
May He ever make my heart glad
And graciously bestow upon me His peace.

MAY TWENTIETH

Salient Thought for the Day.

One cannot pretend simplicity and humility.

Lines to Memorize.

I lose all power of speech
Whenever I am before Thee;
My heart sings lyrical songs
Yet my tongue gives no sound
Whene'er I am before Thee.

Lesson.

All the great characters we have known have exhibited marvellous simplicity and directness. When one's mind is crooked, and travels by diverse ways, or when it is full of calculation, it cannot appear simple. There can be no pretending in simplicity. It is a natural, spontaneous, unconscious gift. We must unfold it in such a measure that we are not conscious of it. The moment calculation enters in, it is destroyed.

Prayer.

May the Inexhaustible Source of my life make me sincere and earnest in my search after Truth.

May I be simple and genuine in my spiritual life.

May I always look within and not without for help and guidance,

And may my devotion to the Highest be unfaltering.

MAY TWENTY-FIRST

Salient Thought for the Day.

We must be wakeful, sincere and devout. Let there be no pretense or arrogance in our life.

Lines to Memorize.

Wouldst thou pluck a flower in the budding?
Wouldst thou trample a newly planted seed?
Patient waiting and care bring them to ripening.
Our life's unfinished work and unexpressed thoughts
All have their season of harvesting.

Lesson.

There is not one so humble or so placed in life that he cannot carry out his spiritual convictions through his life. Every one of us can do it. All that it requires is simplicity, sincerity and devotion to our highest Ideal. Whether we believe in one thing or another makes very little difference. The whole theme of life lies in following a practical Principle.

Prayer.

Thou who art the Source of all my sustenance, I lift my prayer to Thee.
Thou art my Wealth and Wisdom;
Thou art my All-in-all.
Teach me how to offer up my whole being for Thy service.
And express Thy love through my life.

Salient Thought for the Day.

The aim of all spiritual teaching is to make us loving, pure, humble and unselfish.

Lines to Memorize.

Alter-flower, I have watched thee with deepest wonderment.
Thou fragrant beauty of delicate loveliness,
Thou hast given thine all!
Now thou art fading.
Art thou dead?
Nay, thou art risen to thy glory,—
Thou art ascended!

Lesson.

Religions do not differ fundamentally one from the other; they all point the way upward, Godward. They tell us never to be afraid to lift up our head to God. They strive to give us a greater vision, to make us forget our smallness and realize our Divine inheritance. They show us the way to attain fulfilment; they say we must cease to cling to the little notion of "I and mine" and cultivate humility and simplicity.

Prayer.

In this hour of worship, I gather up my thoughts
And lay them at the feet of That One who is my loving Mother.
May She lend me Her tender protection
And lead me in the path of humility and unselfishness.
May She protect me from all ignorance,
And enfold me with Her holy peace.

MAY TWENTY-THIRD

Salient Thought for the Day.

The one who is humblest, he is the greatest.

Lines to Memorize.

Tell me, O Thou wondrous Being, why dost
 Thou choose the lowly hearts?
Is it to make them bright with Thy footprints?
Is it to comfort the comfortless Thou comest
 down so low?

Lesson.

Some people are made more mellow, more humble, when they have success and glory; others lose their point of view. A common man always asserts his own attainments, while a superior man is only conscious that it is God manifesting through his bigger talents and lesser ones, through his success and failure, through his happiness and misery. In all his experiences he tries to realize one fact alone, —that God's Will is being fulfilled through his life, through his thought, through his activities.

Prayer.

O Thou Eternal and Infinite Being,
 find my delight in Thy vastness and majesty.
Teach me to be Thy true child, humble and pure
 of heart.
May the glamour of the world never blind me
 to Thy glory.
Thou art the One to be loved and worshipped.
Reveal to me Thy all-abiding Spirit
And keep me ever in Thy peace.

Salient Thought for the Day.

Ambition kills spirituality. Do everything humbly and without ostentation.

Lines to Memorize.

The dark walls of night stood before me as if in grim defiance, barring my vision.
I searched for light, but the face of the dark was ever before me.
"Light! Light! My soul cries for light!
"Help me to find the light!"

Lesson.

If sin or persecution leads us to humility, we should bless it: thus it is that saintly men bless their enemies. Even though we may feel the hurt, there comes a deep mellow feeling and we bless those who hurt us. Blows and wounds drive us to God. Life means struggle. God sends us hardship as a blessing, that we may unfold. When there comes real ripening, it makes one mellow, gentle and enduring.

Prayer.

O Thou Supreme One, open my heart to Thy blessing.
Plant in it the seed of spiritual fruition;
Take from it all pride and ambition,
And keep it simple and free from vanity.
Quicken in me higher desires.
May I feel the closeness of Thy Presence as I fulfil my daily tasks.

MAY TWENTY-FIFTH

Salient Thought for the Day.

Life is constantly radiating that which has either good or evil influence.

Lines to Memorize.

Sun, thou coveted light of the world,
The grey sky tried to hide thee;
That she might enjoy thee alone
In her blind, selfish greed.
But thou, universal Lover and Light-giver,
Tearing off her veil of mist,
Came forth to gladden our hearts.

Lesson.

When we have really found something deeper, spontaneously we try to live it. When Truth is lived in our life, it inevitably reaches other lives. Whoever comes near us, whatever life we touch, we give something spiritual. We give our atmosphere which we create through our attitude of mind and our physical habits. Whatever we have, that we share constantly. Our good and bad moods affect the whole of humanity. We are inseparable parts of one great Life and can possess or hold nothing apart from it.

Prayer.

O Thou All-pervading Presence,
Fill my life with Thy radiance,
That it may shine forth and brighten the lives of others.
Grant that I may never harm or wound any of Thy children,
Or turn them away from Thee.

MAY TWENTY-SIXTH

Salient Thought for the Day.

Practise humility. Never try to get ahead of anyone.

Lines to Memorize.

Thou Divine messenger,
Friend of the lowly,
Dwell Thou with me in my heart.
Be it in poverty or in wealth,
Be it in pomp or pain,
Be it in darkness or in light,
Do Thou dwell in my heart as my Friend and Guide.

Lesson.

The spiritual life can become very living. When our life moves along avenues of humility and simplicity, we are healthier and happier. That which represents simplicity, with order and tidiness, that is the best way and that is the spiritual way. Not by strain and struggle, not by aggressiveness and self-assertion, can we approach Truth. It comes to those who are humble and surrendered.

Prayer.

In prayer I lift my heart to the Infinite,
May He free it from all unkindness and unloveliness.
May He fill it with His love, leaving room for naught else.
May I serve all His children with humility and unselfishness
And shed forth His light at every step.

Salient Thought for the Day.

God picks up the humble life and makes it fruitful.

Lines to Memorize.

I found happiness nowhere till my self-will was lost in His Will.
Now I have no will of mine,
Nor do I want my will again.
His Will is my will
And my will is His.
In His Will is my delight;
His Presence is my peace.

Lesson.

The lowly ground, there the water rolls; there it fertilizes and enriches the soil. People who are great are never aggressive or domineering. There is no reason to be either arrogant or self-depreciative. When we depreciate ourselves, it is not humility. When we fall into despair and despondency, it means we have lost our higher instinct and forgotten our own true value. Our sense of values has become distorted.

Prayer.

O Thou All-blessed One, bestow upon me Thy grace,
That I may always yield my will up to Thine,
And seek Thy Will alone.
Free me from all sense of self-importance and arrogance.
Take from me all heaviness and sadness and make me worthy of Thy blessing.

Salient Thought for the Day.

If you keep your gaze on the right course, no one can turn you back.

Lines to Memorize.

My heart is full today, O Lord of my life, now
Thou art come.
I was lonely and desolate;
I dared not ask Thee to this lowly cottage;
But Thou, wondrous Lover, gavest me courage.

Lesson.

We have no existence separate from the Divine Existence. When, without any calculation, without any doubt or question, we learn in humble spirit to lose ourselves and be used as God pleases, there comes a greater dignity in our life. We refuse then to have our selfish will, because we know how limited it is. We have a peaceful feeling in knowing we are a part of the Great Will. As we mediate on this mighty fact, it becomes a reality for us and our heart is filled with humility.

Prayer.

O Thou who art my Guide and Friend,
Help me to come to Thee with humility and a
true sense of consecration.
May my gaze never be turned away from Thee;
May I never seek my joy apart from Thee;
May I approach Thee with faith and devotion,
And find all my strength and peace in Thee.

MAY TWENTY-NINTH

Salient Thought for the Day.

We can have no real sense of security until we become a conscious vital factor in the Divine life.

Lines to Memorize.

Alas, I follow Thee but with frail and faltering feet.
Wilt Thou not show me mercy
Thou friend of the lowly,
and halt Thy march a little moment?
Have pity on this poor pilgrim
And let him once worship Thy holy Feet.

Lesson.

One cannot define or calculate the loftier things of life. They are too big, too profound to describe. We must feel them with spontaneous soul-yearning and humble spirit. These feelings alone can destroy our pride, our doubt and despair. If our inner life is filled with humility and richness of spiritual understanding, nothing else matters. When we possess these, if good or ill fortune comes to us, we know how to meet it. We have found the Power which sustains us in all circumstances.

Prayer.

May the Supreme Being open my heart to His holy influence,
That it may be free from all doubt and darkness and ignorance.
May He enlarge my vision and increase my yearning for the Divine;
May He unite my life with His Divine Life
And keep me ever in His loving protection.

Salient Thought for the Day.

Spiritual feeling cannot be forced.

Lines to Memorize.

Language of the soul is spoken without tongue;
Its soundless symphony is heard not by keenness of ear,
But only by those who are deaf to the noise of the world.

Lesson.

Those who are truly awakened, those who have a real conception of spirituality, never try to force their ideas or views upon anyone, far from it, their sense of humility is so overpowering that they never raise their voice or try to interfere with others. If we have something in our life that is vital and real, we have little time to go about disturbing anyone. It is only when we have not reached the depths that we make much noise and we disturb our peace and the peace of others.

Prayer.

O Thou who knowest all my feelings and aspirations,
Make my yearning for Thee so earnest and sincere
That I shall seek Thee before naught else.
Sanctify my thought and dedicate it to the Highest.
Make me more firm and steadfast in my spiritual striving,
And grant me Thy peace.

Salient Thought for the Day.

God is within us, but we must awaken to the sense of His Presence.

Lines to Memorize.

In this flash-light of my soul,
As I read this unwritten book of Thine,
My life's unseen, intricate mysteries are unfolded
All veils are dropped.
I sit speechless, marvelling, in awe and wonder,
As I read and re-read this unwritten book of Thine.

Lesson.

We must try to develop pure spiritual consciousness. Whatever may be our ideal or faith, if we have sincerity of purpose and humility, if we have real yearning to know Truth, One who reads our hearts, our innermost feelings, will direct our thoughts and life to It. God is infinite, all-abiding. He is within us.

Prayer.

May the Infinite and Eternal One
Fill my mind and heart with the consciousness of His Being.
May He take from me all selfishness and egotistic feelings.
May I love and serve Him truly
And realize ever more and more His Presence within and without.

NOTES

Fear not, my heart,
Even the darkest night must end at dawn!
Clouds and mist may come and go,
But they cannot rob sun's radiant glow.
Look up, mine eyes, keep steady watch,
For never must ye lose your guiding star.
Hold fast! Hold fast!
Faith and courage are His tender blessings;
He will not hold these from thee when He sees
thy yearning, struggling soul.
Rest will come when thy toil is done.

June

FAITH AND COURAGE

O descendant of Bharata, the faith of each is according to his inherent nature. The man consists of his faith; he is verily what his faith is.

Fearlessness, vigor, forgiveness, fortitude, purity, absence of hatred and fear, these, O descendant of Bharata, belong to one born with Divine qualities.

Bhagavad-Gita

JUNE FIRST

Salient Thought for the Day.

Have faith ! It glorifies the life. It exalts it.

Lines to Memorize.

It is the flame of faith that sheds light upon our life's straight and narrow path.
Faith, how oft thou dost come to my rescue as I stand in the dark corners of life, puzzled and helpless.
O blessed Faith, thy transcendent glow hath filled my life !
Thy lustre hath brought me new sight.
I shall walk now with the light of thy holy sanctity.

Lesson.

What you need is a basis in life which will bring you upliftment, courage and resourcefulness. At no time do you need to feel lonely, destitute, devoid of help. All will come out right if you have faith. Faith always enriches the life and brings true understanding.

Prayer.

O Thou who are the Source of all goodness,
May I learn to work, worship and aspire with unfaltering faith and selfless spirit.
May I gain strength and vigor of mind, high inspiration and peace.
May Thy holy peace fill my heart and life.

JUNE SECOND

Salient Thought for the Day.

If we are faithful and fearless, we cannot exist without shedding the light of Truth.

Lines to Memorize.

When I reflect Thy light upon my heart
I become a part of Thy great effulgence.
All my doubts and despondent thoughts vanish
As doth the mist of night before the sun.
Do Thou teach me how I may keep this light ever shining in my soul like an altar flame.

Lesson.

Let us hope for big things, not only what is good for us, but what is good for the whole. Impossible hopes—let us even dare to hope for those. What if the world calls us dreamers! Let us dream those dreams which will lift us from doubt, fear, selfishness and self-seeking. Let us soar high with the wings of hope, and dream into the transcendental.

Prayer.

O Infinite, All-pervading Spirit, may I realize more and more my union with Thee.
May I learn to know that my little light is a part of Thy great effulgence,
That my little life is a part of Thy unbounded Life
And that in all things I partake of Thy vastness.

JUNE THIRD

Salient Thought for the Day.

Your faith must be fervent and living.

Lines to Memorize.

We pray that Thou dost open our eyes of understanding.
And place us in Thy kingdom of safety,
Where conflict of doubting life hath no entry.
We pray for this and this alone.

Lesson.

Your faith must be like an altar flame, burning every moment. Not only will it bring blessing to you, but it will bless others. There must be no doubt, no question, no hesitation. The worst enemy in our life, in all human life, is doubt. We can overcome it by the light of understanding.

Prayer.

O Lord, Thou art the unfailing Source of my sustenance.
Thou art the Source of all my power and strength.
Light in my heart a burning faith,
That all my doubts and questionings may be burned to ashes.
May I depend upon Thee at all times
And find my rest and peace in Thee alone.

JUNE FOURTH

Salient Thought for the Day.

Try to gain a sense of true manhood.

Lines to Memorize.

I live in this house of mine
Whose walls are not built by man.
None can invade my dwelling.
None can usurp my rights.

Lesson.

Although we are virtually constituted alike, we manifest different qualities. People are in different grades. Some are dense, gross; others are equipped with fineness of vision, fineness of feeling, fineness of thought. It is because some yield to their lower nature, others constantly strive to manifest their higher qualities. The choice rests with us. The individual becomes vital by his own effort. We must climb higher and radiate higher qualities in our life. To do this requires faith and courage.

Prayer.

O Thou Infinite, Indivisible Being,
Thou art the Eternal in this fleeting.
Thou art the abiding in the midst of the changing.
Teach me to cling to that which is stable and lasting.
May I draw all my inspiration and strength from Thee alone.
Unite my heart with Thine.
Fill my mind with noble exalted thoughts.
Guard me from all that is ignoble and weak,
And keep me ever in Thy peace.

JUNE FIFTH

Salient Thought for the Day.

That one is a master who is never crushed nor disheartened.

Lines to Memorize.

When my thoughts ascend to Thee, I dwell in peace.
My body is light,
My feet free,
My heart open to receive Thy blessing.

Lesson.

Courage, hope and cheer, let these three accompany you in your journey :—courage that is born of inner conviction and knows no fear, courage that is born of knowledge that we are heir to the Divine Power. That Infinite Majesty is ever free from the intoxication of material aggressiveness. Dauntlessness in all circumstances through selfless devotion to an Ideal is its attribute.

Prayer.

All-blissful One, flood my whole being with Thy pure Being.
Make me staunch and unshakable.
Grant that my faith may be undaunted.
That at all hours, in my work and play,
My spirit may be ever fixed in Thee.

Salient Thought for the Day.

When we have courage and give ourselves freely, our whole life is tranformed.

Lines to Memorize.

Withhold not Thy tender mercy from us.
The blessing of Thy Presence will lift our weight,
And our soul will sing again with new joy our thanksgiving.
Come, O come to us in this hour of need!

Lesson.

We all have setbacks, but this falling down does not mean defeat. Thousands of times we may fall down, yet we must rise up again. We need courage and poise to do this. He who is not afflicted by the dual conditions of life, he lives truly. Some people glorify their pain and adversity. If it is crusifixion, that crucifixion becomes a symbol of their religion and they bear it gloriously. This is not sentimentality, it is true courage.

Prayer.

O Lord, victory and defeat, elation and depression, good fortune and ill, all these things come and go;
But Thou art ever unchanging.
Help me never to rise and fall with these waves of circumstance,
But to find strength and steadfastness, by clinging with unshakable faith to Thee.

JUNE SEVENTH

Salient Thought for the Day.

We must be bold enough to love God and Truth above all other things.

Lines to Memorize.

Lingering perfume of Thy Presence is ever leading me on.
I as following its unseen track day and night
With longing in my soul.

Lesson.

At the present moment it is easy for us to have faith in physical phenomenal things—things we see and hear ; but, because spiritual things are not perceptible to the senses we are afraid to place our faith on them and depend on them. Yet God's Hand is ever working. The person who knows this has infinite blessing, one who does not know it, misses the security of that blessing. God's protection and love are unbounded and unceasing. They never fail us. Realizing this brings wonderful rest to our soul.

Prayer.

I lift my thoughts and prayers to Thee, Supreme Guardian of the Universe,
Who abidest in my heart and watchest over me at every moment.
May I never live apart from Thee.
May I find all my joy in Thee
And depend on Thee for all my needs.
May Thy blessing rest upon my life.

JUNE EIGHTH

Salient Thought for the Day.

When the Divine and the human become one through higher feeling, something mighty is born.

Lines to Memorize.

All this glory is Thine.
I am glorified in knowing this Thy infinite glory.
Thou dost take our frail and faltering hands
To do Thy work.
Our hands and hearts are strong
When they are in Thy keeping.

Lesson.

This machine of life does not run smoothly unless the right conditions exist. Meanness, pettiness, weakness, spring from lack of knowledge of our true heritage. We must be conscious of the Power which makes it run. We must have feeling. The outer alone cannot nourish the loftier impulses of the heart. It cannot satisfy the hunger of the soul. It cannot quench the thirst of the spirit.

Prayer.

O Thou Supreme, All-loving Spirit!
Through Thy Grace alone all things are possible unto me;
I pray that through that Grace I shall be able to surmount all weakness and imperfection.
Grant that my mind may be freed from all ignorance.
Lead me by Thy compassionate Hand
And fill my heart with love and understanding.

JUNE NINTH

Salient Thought for the Day.

When we forget our Source, we become isolated fragments without strength and efficiency.

Lines to Memorize.

When Thou art near, I feel strong
And my heart sings a happy song.
When I lose Thee, all my strength fails me
And darkness enshrouds my heart.

Lesson.

We are confronted by the problems of life and we seek consolation and help from some outside source; but wise men find these in the inner realm. They retire within themselves. This outer material life becomes much more beautiful, it acquires new grandeur, when it is connected with the inner spiritual life. The drudgery we too often feel arises because these two spheres of living are unrelated. We escape from this sense of drudgery by uniting the inner and outer. We do this through faith.

Prayer.

O All-loving Spirit, Source of my life,
May my heart rest close to Thy Divine Heart.
Fill it with Thy pure joy:
Grant unto me unswerving courage
And a trust that cannot be shaken or destroyed.
May I lean wholly upon Thy guidance and look
to Thee alone for protection.

Salient Thought for the Day.

The man of faith attains wisdom and illumination.

Lines to Memorize.

Flame of faith, let Thy radiant glow
Help me to find those who are in dark
And bring them to Thy light.
Thou dost put courage in my heart,
And quicken my body with new life,
And mind with undying vigor.
Thou blessed Flame!
Burn Thou without ceasing, in my heart
And let me walk on the path of life
Without fear, doubt, or thought of self.

Lesson.

By the power of faith one can remove mountains, bondage breaks, and sins are wiped out. Through faith the sick are healed and the lame walk. People who have not faith, nothing can be done for them. But it is not negative faith that can remove evil. It is not dogmatic faith that can heal or work miracles. It is a faith that takes form in action. This faith is fundamental and finds expression in wisdom and loving service. Be full of such faith.

Prayer.

O Thou Supreme Giver, rouse in me undaunted faith.
Kindle in my heart the fire of wisdom
That by its light I may see and feel Thee everywhere.
All my power comes from Thee.
May I use it wholly in Thy service.

Salient Thought for the Day.

As we live in the Great Light, we see more and more clearly the purpose of life and we learn to live more worthily.

Lines to Memorize.

It is flame without smoke;
It burns without fuel, save what is not visible to the eyes.
It burns in the mouth of the wise.
It dwells in heart of love.
It is the perpetual altar fire where saints pour their oblation of worship.
It is eternal life.

Lesson.

Everyone should carry the inner light of God, even when sorrow and misfortune come. There is no chance happening in this world. Great souls do not complain or rebel against adverse conditions, they convert them into benefits. They change evil into good. People who have any deep thought—how majestic and calm they are. Where does this calm spirit come from? From inner courage and bigness of vision.

Prayer.

I offer my heart's prayer to the Great one.
May I learn to carry His blessing without any obstruction.
May I be worthy of His gifts.
May His beneficent light shine through me
And bring understanding in my heart.

Salient Thought for the Day.

We must cultivate a sense of the immensity of God.

Lines to Memorize.

Art Thou in me or am I in Thee?
At times I feel that Thou art in me
As perfume in flower,—
Subtle, imperceptible, yet most real.
Again, in my inmost thought I see Thee
As vast, pervading like the infinite sky.
Then I know that my little life
Is like an ocean drop
Contained in Thy boundless Self.

Lesson.

When we are under the persuasion of ego and self-interest enters in, anxieties overtake us and our faith and courage grow weak. But when we come to realize how small our power is, how undependable is our intellect, how fleeting outer conditions are, we begin to draw more and more on that which is lasting. Then for the first time we have a real sense of rest and security, and new courage and hope awaken in our heart.

Prayer.

O Lord, through Thy Grace may I overcome all egotism, pride and self-will.
And realize that Thou art all in all.
I am only an instrument in Thy almighty Hand.
Do Thou use my hands and feet, my heart and mind to carry out Thy great plan;
And may I never forget Thy vastness and Thy glory.

JUNE THIRTEENTH

Salient Thought for the Day.

Those who revolve in the consciousness of the Divine are safe-guarded.

Lines to Memorize.

Didst thou not come naked from thy mother's womb?
Didst thou not have thy soul in safety even before thy body's birth?
Why art thou then fretful and anxious?
One who watched over thee then,
Watches over thee now;
One who loved thee then, loves thee now.
My mind remember this and be still.

Lesson.

Those who have noble aspiration in their heart not only seek light, they radiate light. The work we have to do is to remove the obstructions, as we clean our windows to let the light come into our house. The way to overcome fear and sorrow is by thinking on that One that is above all sorrow and fear. The way to conquer weakness is to think on that One who is infinite strength. The way to overcome littleness is to think on the great Immensity.

Prayer.

O Thou Compassionate Spirit, bestow upon me Thy abiding protection.
Grant that I may acquire strength of mind and fearlessness of heart.
Destroy in me all delusion and weakness
And make me worthy of Thy unfailing blessing.

Salient Thought for the Day.

We are eternally protected. Know this and be fearless.

Lines to Memorize.

Take my hand and lift me to that plane where abide harmony and unbroken union with Thee.
I was not ready when Thou didst give me Thy Hand of mercy;
Now I come ready to follow Thee.
Lift me and lead me!
I will follow Thee;
I will not look back nor fear.

Lesson.

When a man feels that in spite of shortcomings, in spite of faults, he has something abiding, something that is his very own, which no one can rob him of, he gains fresh hope and courage. If under pain and sorrow a man can stand up and say bravely, "Thy Hand guides me," it is a very beautiful thing; but only he can do it who is master of himself.

Prayer.

O Thou Divine Protector, make Thy protecting Presence real to me.
In my silent hours may I feel Thy Presence.
In all my actions, may I feel Thy guiding influence.
In my hours of waking and sleeping, may I ever carry Thy blessed Presence in my consciousness.
Grant me a new sense of peace and security in Thee.

JUNE FIFTEENTH

Salient Thought for the Day.

Fearlessness comes through the practice of unselfishness.

Lines to Memorize.

It is not ambition that lifts us to our goal;
Nay, not ambition, but our humble acts, void of self.
Give us wings for flight!

Lesson.

Souls who are full of self are always troubled and fearful. We cannot hope not to have moments of anxiety, but we can learn how to meet them with calmness and courage. Until we are able to give up clinging to the self, we can never enjoy the blessing of rest in God's protection. So long as we have the slightest feeling that we are able to live our life and do our work without a sense of consecration, the fever of struggle will never cease and our aim will never be reached.

Prayer.

Grant unto me, O Lord, greater closeness to Thy Holy Spirit.
Give me clearer vision, deeper understanding,
That I may realize how little I can depend on my own frail self,
And how great is my need of Thee.
I lay my life and love at Thy Blessed Feet in humble devotion,
And ask only for greater power to give myself wholly to Thy service.

JUNE SIXTEENTH

Salient Thought for the Day.

When the selfish side of our life dies away, the nobler, bigger, braver God-side will manifest itself.

Lines to Memorize.

Pay no heed to voice of ego;
It is false, yea, and always out of tune.
Sing thou after the Beloved's voice!
It is Divine harmony;
It is sweet melody,
And it is perpetual peace.

Lesson.

The more we can release ourselves from the bonds of slavery to fear and selfishness, the freer we shall be to enjoy the blessings of the Infinitude of God. All selfishness and weakness must be washed clean by the water of a new spiritual understanding. We do this through prayer, when it is earnest and sincere. By constant longing and yearning and a prayerful attitude, we create a great power within us.

Prayer.

All-loving, All-beneficent Spirit!
Make my life free from all inharmony and discord,
That I may grow more conscious of Thy Presence.
Purge my heart of egotism and vanity.
In this hour of prayer and at all times may I draw my strength and inspiration wholly from Thy Being.

JUNE SEVENTEENTH

Salient Thought for the Day.

Our life must ring true. In the realm of religion we cannot pretend.

Lines to Memorize.

When thy mind is filled with noble thoughts,
There is no room for small, petty, and selfish whims.
Keep thy heart then well-filled with feelings that are noble and true.
Then work with thy hand;
For no act can enslave us when our heart and mind are true.

Lesson.

There is a finer type of spiritual manhood. If you can manifest that, you will always glorify whatever you do. But to do this, you must be genuine and you must look beyond yourself. You cannot live this life worthily unless you relate it with what lies behind this life. If you would enter into a more exalted realm of being, you must have patience, faith, perseverance and courage. Without these you cannot partake of the Spirit of Godhood.

Prayer.

I lift my heart to that One who knows all my struggles and my shortcomings.
Grant that I may direct my whole life to that One, never to the fleeting objects of this material world.
May my prayers be so sincere and earnest that they will always reach Him.

JUNE EIGHTEENTH

Salient Thought for the Day.

Make your religious faith fundamental.

Lines to Memorize.

Waiting for Thee, my Love, my Life, Soul of my life!
Many hours of day and night have passed me by,
Yet faith kindles my hope and in the light of hope I see Thy approach even in dense dark of night.
I shall wait for Thee now
And let me wait for Thee always!

Lesson.

What we have in abundance in our heart, in our mind, in our habitual consciousness, that will come uppermost in every circumstance. People who are loving and forgiving, when they are oppressed, will show their loving, forgiving nature. The outer life always intensifies what we have within. Therefore we must try to keep our spiritual point of view clear and unwavering. Faith must not be a quality of mind which varies with the varying conditions of life.

Prayer.

Thou Eternal, All-pervading Presence!
Thou art the Source of my existence.
Thou art my Resting-place.
Make me ever conscious of Thy abiding Spirit,
That my heart may be purified and freed from doubt.
Strengthen my faith and awaken even greater and greater devotion within my soul.

Salient Thought for the Day.

When the heart and soul yearn with living faith for the Unseen, it purifies the life and brings a deeper vision.

Lines to Memorize.

Thou art the sweetness of my life;
Thou art the soul of my body;
Thou art the vigor of my limbs;
My clear sight and power of action.
Why dost Thou ever leave me?
When Thou dost abandon me, I find darkness in light and sadness in gayety.
Who art Thou? What art Thou?
These mysteries of Thy Being I cannot fathom.

Lesson.

A house should never be kept in the dark. It becomes desolate and loses all its charm and atmosphere. The same way with human life. We may have all the ornaments and gifts, but if the spiritual light does not glow and glorify everything, that life is dead and in darkness. When the light of faith and hope illumines it, it is safe; otherwise it is in danger, because it is not sanctified and protected.

Prayer.

Grant, O Compassionate One, that I may feel Thy all-abiding Presence within my soul,
And that I may rejoice in that Presence.
Dispel all darkness and depression from my heart
And fill it with Thy radiance,
That I may shed forth Thy light in every act of my life.

Salient Thought for the Day.

Never do anything that will destroy another's faith. Even the simplest faith leads Godward.

Lines to Memorize.

Wouldst Thou receive this unworthy gift of mine?
Then let me lay it prostrate at Thy blessed Feet.
I came with an eager heart,
Though courage had I none to approach Thee.
But Thou, All-seeing, didst know my
Heart's yearning and didst call me to Thy side.
I am wonder-struck at this, Thy mercy!

Lesson.

When we learn the art of connecting ourselves with the Source of life, this little distracted fragment of life will become glorified and we shall find peace. Our little life will be blessed and we shall not again weep and mourn. We shall learn to practise the beautiful attributes of life—calmness, peace, steadfastness, faith. These are the adornments of life which beautify a man's character.

Prayer.

Kindle in my heart the light of understanding, O Lord,
That I may learn to be a true instrument in Thy Hand.
May I never do aught to hurt or hinder my brother in his search for Thee.
May I always serve truly and faithfully all Thy children.
Accept my offering of prayer and bestow on me Thy holy blessing.

Salient Thought for the Day.

Even a thin thread of faith is better than all worldly splendor without faith.

Lines to Memorize.

Thou hast placed me on this other shore
Where virtue and vice, sin and merit,
Praise and sensure, all are one;
Where light and dark, life and death
Are commingled in eternal unity.
I stand on this strange shore and look upon the swift-flowing current of life
With amazed wonderment.

Lesson.

It is only when there is lack of light that we see things in wrong way. How like a little cloud is worldly grandeur blown away. Man can never be self-sufficing. But when he learns a higher dependence there is no more anguish of mind, no more rebellion. To be able to see our connection with every condition of life is to see with a new eye—the spiritual eye. Patience, endurance, courage—these come when that eye opens. Then we can turn all our forces Godward. For one who sees with the spiritual eye there are no evil forces; it is we who create evil by the misdirection of our energies.

prayer.

All-encompassing Spirit, Thou art the Giver of all life.
Thou art all that is manifested and all that is unmanifested.
Thou are all that is within and all that is without.
Do Thou uplift my mind and heart and give me a new sense of Thy Reality.

Salient Thought for the Day.

The one who lacks faith misses his point of contact with Divinity.

Lines to Memorize.

Virtue and vice, good and ill,
Ever play surging havoc in the dual conflict of life,
I abandon them forever and sit with Thee.

Lesson.

Divine Mother's glory is infinite, and whoever learns to float in the Ocean of Her love knows neither fear nor care. Simple trustfulness is all She wants of us. Be therefore of good cheer and unwavering faith. All will be right through Her Divine Grace. Do not bother about what you have not. She knows. She will not deny any blessing when the time comes.

Prayer.

I pray with yearning spirit that I may be true to that One, from whom has come my life.
May I never forget or be separated from that holy Source of my being.
May that One fill heart with understanding, faith and compassion.
May true devotion for that all-abiding One grow ever stronger and stronger within me.

JUNE TWENTY-THIRD

Salient Thought for the Day.

There is a Higher Power that guides our steps.

Lines to Memorize.

Thou canst make my frail vessel to cross o'er these rough waters of life.
Thy Will is my hope of safety.
I know no other art nor skill
Save to trust in Thy Will.
Thy Will is my safety,
My source of all peace and joy.

Lesson.

This mind served from its Source is weak and faltering. Too often we have fear in our heart, we dare not go forward. What can we fear? What should we fear? We possess something within us that is living and vibrant, but if we are closed to that Divine influence it cannot make any impression on us. As we grow conscious of this Higher Power, we throw away our littleness. We feel exalted and uplifted.

Prayer.

O Thou Infinite and All-powerful Sustainer of the Universe!
Thou art the Consciousness abiding in the heart of every conscious being.
Thou art the Giver of all blessing.
Thou fulfillest the desires and needs of every living thing.
Do Thou reveal Thy Divine Self unto me,
That I may learn to live in Thy consciousness
And find my safety in Thy never-failing protection.

Salient Thought for the Day.

Faith is the one sure antidote for doubt and fear.

Lines to Memorize.

Flame of Faith, burn Thou in my heart day and night without ceasing.
In Thy glow I shall read this book of life,
And walk my path of destiny without fear.
Flame of Faith, burn Thou without ceasing!
For I have no other guide to show my course.

Lesson.

Do you think you can ever weigh or measure spiritual things? And yet people cannot cease doing it until they find something bigger. If you dispute and argue you lose your vision and faith. Through faith one attains God. Through argument and discussion God goes further and further away. When we come in contact with something higher, we are lifted above the noisy, lower self and we grow silent.

Prayer.

O Thou Infinite Being, free my mind from the bondage of the finite.
Make me free from the delusion of egotism, anger, self-assertion
And all that severs me from Thee.
May I learn to partake of the blessed qualities of the Supreme,
That doubt, imperfection and weakness may vanish from my heart.

Salient Thought for the Day.

Faith and courage are always constructive.

Lines to Memorize.

O Thou, who givest Thy bounty
With ceaseless love and tender blessing,
Alas, how oft we come to Thee,
Our hands and hearts already filled
With fear, doubt and all this world's endless possessions.
Thou who givest Thy bounty,
We pray that Thou givest us power of sanctity
To receive Thy blessing.

Lesson.

Fear is never constructive. People who are dauntless, through faith, through courage, through higher inspiration, they attain fulfillment; because their being is quickened, all their powers are aroused. A person who is exhibiting courage and faith in every circumstance is a model character.

Prayer.

Thou who art my protecting Father and loving Mother,
Fill my whole mind and consciousness with Thy blessings
That I may learn to depend wholly upon Thee.
Make me fearless and strong, full of child-like faith and holy inspiration,
So that all I think and do may be productive of good.

Salient Thought for the Day.

Be not disheartened. Never lose courage.

Lines to memorize.

This, my little vessel, is tossed and tossed by the angry waves of life.
If Thou dost not hold the rudder and guide its course.
It will break and sink.
At Thy Will, tempest will cease;
At Thy command, the sun will light the dark;
In Thy Presence, my fear-stricken heart will embrace peace.

Lesson.

Fear and depression have no place in the realm of Spirit. We all have to pass through the slough of despondency sometime or other. You must not let your spirit go down under any circumstances. Do your duty bravely and faithfully. Never feel that your life is a failure. Try not to brood over such ideas.

Prayer.

Help me, O Lord, to make my heart pulsate in harmony with Thy holy Being.
Thou art my one sure Refuge.
Thou art my one safe Protection.
May I never yield to heaviness or anxiety,
But may I rest all my life in Thee and be at peace.

JUNE TWENTY-SEVENTH

Salient Thought for the Day.

A hindrance ceases to be a hindrance when we face it with courage.

Lines to Memorize.

Thou dost change all earth's harsh notes into heaven's unspeakable sweetness.
At Thy touch a broken reed sounds Divine harmony,
And mortal voice sings immortal song.

Lesson.

In all entanglements, in the midst of turbulence and adversity, we can walk safely if we have spiritual courage and unfaltering faith. Those who are calculating and dependent on their own strength stumble many times; while those who are fearless and trusting and unspoiled by the vanities of the world, they go through the hardest experiences with undaunted spirit. They triumph over every obstacle.

Prayer.

Almighty One, help me to turn my whole thought and aspiration to Thee.
Thou knowest my innermost struggles and difficulties.
Thou alone canst remove them.
Open my heart to Thy beneficent influence.
Grant unto me an undaunted spirit.
May I live this day bravely, looking to Thee for strength and wisdom to meet each step.

JUNE TWENTY-EIGHTH

Salient Thought for the Day.

Man is born to conquer nature, not to be afflicted by nature or the world.

Lines to Memorize.

Be not a puppet in ambition's hand, beaten and buffetted!
Wouldst thou be enticed and enslaved by a ruthless tyrant?
Should a child of Eternity stoop so low?
Nay, be not trapped or befooled by the seeming.
Verily thou art ever free, an heir to eternal and omniscient Life.

Lesson.

One who is attached to the things of the world, the world claims that one. One who is wholly given to God, the world cannot hold or harm him. No matter how much we have blundered, we all have a right to go to our home. We should never give way to discouragement or doubt.

Prayer.

O Thou Infinite and Eternal Being
Thou art the One to be known;
Thou art the One to be worshipped.
Free my mind from doubt and ignorance
That I may know Thee truly;
And find in Thee new courage, light, strength and fearlessness.

JUNE TWENTY-NINTH

Salient Thought for the Day.

Never lose faith in yourself.

Lines to Memorize.

Behold, the saving light dispelling darkness!
Let all mortals rise to-day and inherit their immortal state.
Let all mortals, forsaking sleep of doubt, ascend with the glory of dawn.

Lesson.

We must have faith in ourselves, and we cannot have faith in ourselves without having faith in others. We are all parts of that Infinite One, and we cannot have faith in one part more than another. True religion does not allow a man to lift his hand or his thought or his heart against aught that lives. Loving kindness is an attribute of genuine faith. One cannot have faith in God and in humanity without being loving and having eager desire to serve.

Prayer.

O Thou All-loving Mother of the Universe!
I am Thy child, my real nature is one with Thine.
My spirit is eternally united with Thy Spirit,
My life is bound in Thy life.
Grant that I may realize my union with Thee
And express it through my every thought, word and deed.

JUNE THIRTIETH

Salient Thought for the Day.

Do not let your faith waver or weaken.

Lines to Memorize.

O Faith, holy Redeemer,
My Divine Protector!
Put Thou Thine armor about me.
I am always safe with thee.
This conflict of life.
Hath no fear for me.
When thou art in me and with me.
Holy Redeemer, Divine Protector!
Put Thou Thine armor about me.

Lesson.

Faith is the greatest reformer. One becomes saintly through faith. Faith gives life, faith gives exaltation. Through genuine faith one can accomplish anything. Complete faith and surrender are essential factors in the spiritual life. When you have them, all your troubles cease—not that they have been eliminated, but you have risen above them. Unless a man has patience, faith, perseverance and courage, it is impossible for him to enter into the spirit of holiness.

Prayer.

May the Fire of Faith burn in my heart,
Consuming all my impurities and weakness.
May it sustain me and protect me from coldness
and indifference.
May it make me brave and enduring in the hour
of trial.
May the Fire of Faith never grow dim or die in
my heart.

Hold aloft the light and stand firm to thy post,
Till all wandering souls have reached their goal in
safety.
Service brings strength and renewed life,
Love cures all weariness,
And Faith, the shining jewel of life, performs all
miracles.

July

BLESSING OF SERVICE

The self-subjugated Truth-seers, whose impuritics are washed off, whose doubts are destroyed and who are engaged in doing good to all beings, attain supreme liberation.

Bhagavad-Gita

JULY FIRST

Salient Thought for the Day.

The proof of our love for the Ideal lies in service.

Lines to Memorize.

O awake, brother! Linger thou no more!
Come and see this newness and freshness of love, life and joy!

Lesson.

A truly happy life is one which radiates happiness, which gives happiness to others. Let us make ourselves open channels to receive and transmit joy. May we not only receive it, but let us make ourselves able to retain it, that we may give it to others. Let us pour out ourselves in love and service. What comes of it, let us leave that to The Lord. Every time we think of our own self, it brings us sorrow in one form or another. We may attribute our unhappiness to other things, but its cause lies in self-seeking. We can create a boundary between ourselves and such selfish thoughts through selfless devotion and consecrated service. That boundary of selflessness nothing can penetrate.

Prayer.

O, All-loving Spirit, remove all selfishness and egotism from my heart,
That I may be able to love and serve truly.
May I realize Thy Presence within and without,
And carry its radiance into the world.
May Thy blessing rest upon my life,
And may I share that blessing with others.

Salient Thought for the Day.

Pray to the Lord that you may be able to serve wisely.

Lines to Memorize.

I was sad at heart, most doubtful of my thankless task,
But I stood firm, obedient to Thy Will.
At last a few came and paused and asked me what manner of light was this that burned without oil or wick.
I told them it was Thy unfailing lamp that needs no aid of human hand;
I begged them to kindle their own, but they were afraid and hesitant.

Lesson.

The best thing we can do for others is to inspire them with new hope and courage : by doing this we also benefit ourselves. We can never hold lofty, noble thoughts without benefitting both ourselves and others. Man needs action, he needs prayer, he needs service, he needs love, he needs cheer. Do everything with selflessness and a true spirit of service and you cannot fail to bring blessing.

Prayer.

O Thou inexhaustible Source of life and wisdom,
Grant that I may feel Thy all-abiding Spirit within me.
Reveal Thy Divine wisdom unto me
That I may convey it to all Thy children.
May I bring to Thee a willing service
And may Thy love flow through my heart to all living things.

JULY THIRD

Salient Thought for the Day.

We cannot all be great, but we can all serve.

Lines to Memorize.

With Thy holy lamp in my hand, I stood at the corner of the street of life a long, long time.
At first I thought that no one would ever see my precious light;
My heart grew anxious and I called aloud.
They turned and looked, but saw no light nor understood my voice.

Lesson.

Those whose hearts are full of spiritual light, they long to impart that. Everyone may not be open to the highest Truth. It cannot be apprehended by mere intellectual cleverness, nor can it be imparted by a little oratory. But even the most unlettered can serve God and His children. If Truth is clarified by the life, and the one who serves proves his fervor and sincerity, then the sense of Divine Presence will be behind the service and it will be living. If it is living, it cannot fail to be productive of good.

Prayer.

O Lord, open my heart to Thy Divine influence,
That it may be from pride and arrogance,
I know that Thou art never far from me.
Grant unto me the power to serve Thee humbly
And to live with true selfless devotion and steadfastness of purpose.

Salient Thought for the Day.

Every task should be for the good of many.

Lines to Memorize.

I plead with them with all my might,
But they would not leave their accustomed ways of darkness and of shadow, the enemies of life.
O unhappy fate that leads the weary travellers from light to dark!

Lesson.

There is not a moment in your life when you cannot render service and set an example. Every one of us can bring something to this world every day. We can sound a note that will resound rhythm and harmony. When we cultivate our inner sense of values, we cease to be fretful, we cease to complain and we always have something to give. If we give with wholeness of heart, we shall be able to remove mountains of obstacles and difficulties and all our struggles, which arise from our imperfections and which make our life so full of suffering, will vanish as light before the day. This is the higher ideal of life,—oneness in faith, oneness in hope and oneness in cheer.

Prayer.

May the Infinite Being protect me from selfishness and narrowness of vision.
May He enlarge my heart and expand my love until it embraces all His children.
May I never be impatient or weary in His service,
But may I feel at peace in my own heart
And bring peace to other hearts.

Salient Thought for the Day.

No man can perform any service bigger or better than his thoughts inspire him to do.

Lines to Memorize.

Let him speak whose spirit flows like the river
in flood-time, full and strong;
Let others keep silent—
The tongue that speaketh soulless words
But scattereth pebbles before hungry mouths.

Lesson.

There is a selfish type of humanity which does not sense what is happening to others, but a man who has evolved his soul nature and found access to the higher realm, that one is full of concern for his neighbour. We cannot afford to sever ourselves from our fellowman. We do not realize this so long as we have not established an inward relationship with him. Until we know God as our Father, we shall not feel that he is really our brother and our service will always have an element of selfishness in it.

Prayer.

All-loving Father and Mother of this universe,
I lift my prayer to Thee in humble supplication.
Free me from all pettiness and smallness
Help me to consecrate all my efforts and
thoughts to Thy service;
Fill my heart with fresh inspiration and
strength.
May all my words and thoughts and actions be
worthy of Thy loving blessing.

Salient Thought for the Day.

Those who can turn more within, they will get more joy out of service.

Lines to Memorize.

I know that Thou art in my soul.
I know this in my dreaming;
I know this in my sleeping;
I know this in my waking,—
That Thou art my very life
Today, tomorrow, aeons hence and forevermore!

Lesson.

Love, forgiveness, tolerance are qualities that come from within. They are the result of an expansion of the soul. There is but one standard in life,—to love and serve and not pay heed to the world. The great thing in any kind of work is to keep ourselves quiet and serene, never fretful or morose. We cannot render true service until we have made our body and our mind fitting channels. When are we happiest? When we have a sense of spiritual relationship with mankind, then the veil of selfishness is lifted from our inner vision and we realize the oneness of our soul with the Great Soul and with all humanity.

Prayer.

O Compassionate Being, do Thou fasten my life to Thee with steadfast devotion and faith.
Remove all self-limitation from my heart,
And make me untiring in loving service.
May I feel blessed as I serve
And may I express love through every act of my life.
May I never forget Thee or Thy children.

JULY SEVENTH

Salient Thought for the Day.

We owe a certain obligation to our own spiritual being. We serve others by cultivating it.

Lines to Memorize.

Dost Thou know, who knowest all,
That I need Thee at all hours of day and night,
Both in joy and sorrow, dark and light?

Lesson.

When we do not seek to unfold our higher nature, we weaken our spiritual fibre and it suffers. It cannot die because it is immortal, but it can suffer through our carelessness. When it suffers, everything suffers within us. Others also suffer through us. When we live our life carelessly, we defeat its purpose; we shatter our faith and we lose our power to serve wisely. An illumined soul always understands the needs of others and perceives the best way to meet them. He has a sense of kinship with all living things and sympathy, forbearance and loving-kindness are natural to him. He expresses these qualities spontaneously through every act and word.

Prayer.

May the Infinite Being help me to gather up my thoughts and feelings and offer them unto Him;
May He make my life, my thoughts and actions more worthy;
May He remove from me all imperfections and grant me His loving blessing.

Salient Thought for the Day.

Purify and strengthen yourself and make yourself ready to do your part in the world.

Lines to Memorize.

Dream, my soul, where love dwells in harmony
And beauty in its virgin loveliness.
Dream of Divine ecstasy
Whose eternal melody is sung by all created things.

Lesson.

We are responsible for all discord in the world, we are also responsible for all the peace and happiness of the world. The best way we can do our part is to release ourselves from self-interest, self-pity and self-importance. They rob us of our opportunities to serve our fellowmen. As long as there is any sadness or sickness in the world, we cannot be wholly happy. The individual consciousness must expand. We must learn to live in the world sharing our blessing with the world; but we must never forget from where these blessings come. If we do, we fall short in doing our duty and cannot have real happiness; nor can we bring happiness to anyone else.

Prayer.

O Thou Eternal Spirit, I ask Thee Thy holy blessing
And Thy protection from all weak and selfish thoughts.
Grant unto me this desire;
That I may never fail in Thy service
Or prove unworthy of Thy love.

JULY NINTH

Salient Thought for the Day.

We can only receive in exact proportion as we give. If we give wholly, we receive the whole.

Lines to Memorize.

I told them of Thy song, but they heard it not for their own voices were loud; they laughed and mocked me.
I sat alone with streaming eyes, yet these drops were not from sadness;
They were through fullness that Thou, merciful One, hadst given me hearing for Thy precious song.

Lesson.

Life and lack of life, light and lack of light—these are the two phases of life. There are people who are so glowing that they radiate light and life everywhere. Then again we find a person in whom the light is almost extinct. Our task is to rescue all those who are in darkness by increasing the power of their waning flame and making it strong and steady. How can we be harsh, how can we turn a deaf ear, when Truth stands out everywhere so clearly and shows us that we are in no way separate from any living being!

Prayer.

O Thou who art the Spirit of all,
Grant unto me the power to spread Thy blessing among all the children of men.
Make me a channel of ever higher and higher service.
Help me to give freely and without stint,
Knowing Thou art an inexhaustible store-house of love and power.

Salient Thought for the Day.

We cannot help anyone until we have found help ourselves.

Lines to Memorize.

When thy feet are tired rest them.
If mind is weary, refresh it.
Pause awhile in the still peace of thy inmost cave;
Then rise again with renewed spirit of faith, hope and courage.

Prayer.

We can feel secure only when we have found our connection with a Higher Power. Without this life is a sham. To be genuine it must be founded on truth. This inward connection with something which is absolutely dependable, we must seek. If wc cannot seek it every hour, let us seek it sometimes at least. It we do seek and find even a little access to it, our service and all our actions will be enriched.

Prayer.

O Thou Giver of all blessedness, who abidest within me and without me,
Grant unto me a sense of Thy Reality,
That I may never fail to turn to Thee in hours of darkness and distress.
Help me to seek all my inspiration from Thee;
And grant me the power to carry that inspiration
To all with whom I come in contact.
Purify my thought and sanctify my life
And grant me Thy holy peace.

JULY ELEVENTH

Salient Thought for the Day.

When our heart is full of love, we always find ways of expressing it.

Lesson.

Glory to Thy all-conquering love!
Yea, Thy love is my armour,
My impenetrable shield,
My unfailing safe-guard.
I bathe in Thy love and am refreshed;
I feed on Thy love and my soul-hunger is appeased.

Lesson.

One who possesses love in abundance, he does not remain content with mere theory; he becomes practical in his spiritual living. Carrying the Ideal with us in our every-day life is the real aim of spirituality. What we have in our heart, that we are bound to manifest in our life. If it is love, then we shall not fail to speak the kind word, or do the kind act, or give silent expression to love by our sympathetic attitude of mind.

Prayer.

All-compassionate Being, help me to open my heart
That it may become one with all that lives.
Make me pure and spotless,
That I may be free from all bondage of selfishness and fear.
Lead me from the darkness of ignorance to the light of wisdom
That I may shed that light in service to all Thy children.

JULY TWELFTH

Salient Thought for the Day.

When we find our sense of peace, we contribute something towards the good of the whole.

Lines to Memorize.

Amid chaos Thou dost create Divine Beauty;
Amid dire disorder Thou dost plant the seed of harmony that beareth the sweet blossom of peace.

Lesson.

When we have wisdom and the willingness to cast aside our own lower nature and ally ourselves with our whole heart to the Higher Power, we find a sense of peace. This creates an atmosphere which influences every one who comes in contact with us. A person who has a peaceful heart, who is quiet and self-controlled, cannot fail to radiate a quietness and power which every one feels. We cannot be in contact with something that radiates blessing without conveying it to others. It never fails us. A high point of contact will redeem us and bless others.

Prayer.

Thou who art One without a second,
I offer Thee my whole being,
That I may be made fit to serve Thee and do Thy work.
I am but an instrument in Thy Hands.
Fill my heart with Thy peace,
And pour out upon me and on all Thy children
Thy loving blessing.

JULY THIRTEENTH

Salient Thought for the Day.

Life is a constant struggle, but struggle is good, It makes us strong.

Lines to Memorize.

What avails wailing if thou art bound to the stake of self ?
Thou art not born a bondman.
Why then dost thou make thyself a slave of thyself ?

Lesson.

It never helps another to worry with him. Instead of worrying and complaining of injustice to ourselves or others, we must try to strengthen the life and get a right sense of values. We cannot help anyone more when he is in trouble than by giving him a proper sense of proportion. When he comes to see things in their right light, he will be able to meet his own problems. Being misunderstood or criticised is sometimes good. It gives us a sense of helplessness and makes us turn to the Higher Power.

Prayer.

May the All-merciful Deity grant me light and awakening.
May He make my vision true and bestow on me His wisdom.
That I may do His work wisely and in right spirit.
May I always bring to all His children true joy and peace.

JULY FOURTEENTH

Salient Thought for the Day.

Only as you live in the Soul-Principle yourself, can you convince another.

Lines to Memorize.

Thy sweet perfume hath spoken to my soul its language of love.
Spirit of rose, teach me more of thy subtle and wondrous ways of love;
I am thine ignorant brother, stranger to this new world of thine.

Lesson.

You cannot help anyone, unless you have faith and fervor in your own heart. If you have any doubts about anything, your words will not carry conviction because you have not convinced yourself. If you talk of the power of love, you convince through loving. But if you have any hatred in your heart, or are a slave to anger and jealousy, what you say will have little effect. We impart moral principles through our action and by the way we serve.

Prayer.

O Thou Supreme Goal of the Universe,
Thou art the abiding and the sustaining Life-Principle within my soul.
May I never be unmindful of Thy Presence.
At every step may Thy guiding Hand lead me.
May I think only as Thou makest me to think.
May I speak only as Thou makest me to speak.
May I act only as Thou makest me to act.

Salient Thought for the Day.

The best language is the language of the heart.

Lines to Memorize.

What I feel now I cannot say;
The words are not yet made for its utterance,
Speech is powerless to speak of That which hath given it power to speak.
Thus it is, friend, so oft I keep silent when thou wouldst have me speak.

Lesson.

We may theorize and sermonize about many things, but this does not satisfy us. The practical part of spirituality and religion lies in loving, silent service. Service opens a new chapter in our life. It is a fundamental thing, not something indefinite. Service is the living expression of our thought and feeling. If they are right, we shall never desire to enjoy any blessing apart from our fellow-men.

Prayer.

O Eternal Spirit, open my heart to Thy all-embracing love,
That it may flow through me and bless all Thy children.
Make me a worthy mouthpiece that Thou mayest speak through me.
Keep me humble and simple and free from harshness.
May my life radiate Thy peace and bring joy to all weary souls.

Salient Thought for the Day.

We cannot sink without dragging others down.

Lines to Memorize.

[Ego!]
Henceforth stay thou out of this land, for it is guarded by His sentinels.
When thou didst first enter my home as a friend I trusted thee, also thy companions;
But thou art no friend of mine.
Thou hast brought me vanities of self-love, pride and possession.

Lesson.

It is a diseased state of mind when we look at another or speak to another harshly. It implies a low grade of humanity. When we strike at another, we deal a blow at ourselves. We cannot harm another without having a harmful reaction in our own life. When big forces stir in small vessels, it rouses the worst in them. When anger and hatred sweeps over a little nature, it acts like a fever or delirium; it causes havoc and disaster.

Prayer.

O Thou Infinite One, awaken in my soul a sense of Thy Reality,
That I may never do anything unworthy of Thy Presence.
Thou knowest my innermost thoughts.
Cleanse them of all impurity and imperfection,
And uplift my mind and heart
That they may never fail to seek Thee.

JULY SEVENTEENTH

Salient Thought for the Day.

When we learn to go through the difficult places holding our Ideal ever before us, we elevate ourselves and help others.

Lines to Memorize.

Compassionate Spirit, guide our steps!
Do not let us blunder or be led by self-will.
We know not how to follow nor what to follow amid these, our life's endless ways.

Lesson.

When we lift our mind to that which coincides with our higher aspirations, we create happiness and peace in our own life and we carry them into other lives; because what we have in abundance ourselves, we are able to share with others. We do share with others constantly. Not only when we talk about higher things, but at all times we share, consciously and unconsciously. We cannot receive blessing without giving it.

Lesson.

May the Supreme Being who abides within me,
May He grant me evenness of mind and a peaceful heart.
May He make me staunch and steadfast in my daily life.
May He help me to remain calm and serene in all circumstances,
And may I never forget to turn to Him at every hour.

JULY EIGHTEENTH

Salient Thought for the Day.

The best way we can influence another is to be consecrated to a lofty Ideal.

Lines to Memorize.

Motionless tree, speaking its welcome with a living tongue to the tired birds at nightfall, offering them shelter,
How silent is its language of love!
How, by the gentle fanning of the leaves, it soothes its weary guests to their sleep!
How staunch it stands, watchful and firm
In its vow of selfless service!

Lesson.

Only way we can serve truly is to realize we are all inter-related. We realize this by realizing our connection with our Source. In the world of life souls seem to differ, but there is a blending harmony running through all. We perceive this only by realization of spiritual relationship. Serve like a mighty tree. If you cut its branch it still continues to give shade and shelter.

Prayer.

O Thou All-abiding Spirit, may my prayer ascend unto Thee;
Make it so genuine that it may reach Thee.
May I draw all my strength from Thee, in sorrow and hardship or in joy and ease.
Bestow upon me Thy peace and grant me Thy tender blessing.

15

JULY NINETEENTH

Salient Thought for the Day.

When God blesses us, everything that we do, every life that we touch, is touched with His blessing.

Lines to Memorize.

Since Thy holy touch, I have lost all craving for sense-pleasure;
Things of this great world please me no more.
Life's momentum may carry me on through passages old, new and unknown;
But amidst it all, my heart yearns for Thee alone.

Lesson.

If we have God's blessing, we carry it everywhere; we have it all the time. Even in our blunders, when we fall down and make mistakes, even then we cannot be crushed, we cannot be lost; because we have found something which upholds and sustains us. We gain this through faith. That is why such tremendous importance is laid on faith. It is a very precious thing and we can acquire it through the sincere and earnest outpouring of the soul.

Prayer.

O Thou Giver of all blessings, embodiment of all love and wisdom,
Help me to carry Thy love and blessing to all mankind.
May I never cease to serve Thee through my words and actions.
Grant that I may draw all my inspiration from Thee,
And rest my life in Thee alone.

Salient Thought for the Day.

Spiritual fragrance is not limited by any boundary line. It reaches all hearts that are yearning for the Highest.

Lines to Memorize.

[Love, hope and joy]
These three flowers of fruitful life
Scatter their precious perfume with wings of angels.
Their unseen power transforms world's ugliness to beatific vision,
Storms of anger to gentle peace,
And brute passion to Divine affection.

Lesson.

The only way we surmount the evils and limitations of the world is through the realization of love. When we know we are all children of one Divine Being, we naturally become united. This is something we do not realize through theory. We find the centre of this realization in our own heart. When we have found it there, we realize it in the universe. But if we do not realize it in our heart through humility and devotion, we may seek it everywhere in the world but we shall find it nowhere.

Prayer.

May the Infinite Being in this hour of prayer,
Direct my whole thought and feeling to Him.
May I never cease to be conscious of the sweetness of His Divine Presence,
And may I convey that sweetness to others.

Salient Thought for the Day.

He whose prayers are always for others is truly happy.

Lines to Memorize.

Love is a miracle!
Behold its working in life!
It is life. It is soul.
It is beauty. It is joy.
It is peace.
It is all! It is all!

Lesson.

The awakened man seeks not revenge, nor tries to injure those who injure him. He does not complain or condemn, but strives to benefit those who maltreat him. He feels that he would rather be defeated and cheated again and again than grow distrustful of his fellowmen. A person who is ignorant does not recognize the oneness of all mankind. It is easy for him to bring pain and suffering to others. But he who is awakened, he sees all men as his brothers and he shrinks from hurting any living thing.

Prayer.

O Thou All-abiding One, abide in my soul
And fill it with Thy holy love.
May I pour out that love freely upon all Thy children.
Make me so unselfish that I shall never ask anything for myself,
But may I be ready always to share all my blessings with my fellow-men.

Salient Thought for the Day.

We are such cowards at times, we are afraid to give.

Lines to Memorize.

Can we with all our might, offer Thee aught worthy in Thy blessed sight?
Can we ever make our heart so free of earthly stain that Thy light of love may shine and glow unceasingly?

Lesson.

Our life can be like a lamp-post; travellers pass and find their path revealed. Let us become like such a lamp-post, that we may throw a glow not only on our own path but on the paths of all God's children. We cannot help giving; we are constantly giving something. Whoever touches our life, whomever we touch, we give something to that person unconsciously. The influence we exert depends upon our inner life and our power of vision. If our Ideal is uppermost in our life, we shall always exert a noble influence. If our own higher consciousness is dormant, we shall be unable to appeal to the highest in others.

Prayer.

O Thou Effulgent One, may I never enjoy anything apart from The Divine light.
May that light shine through my every thought and action.
May Thy love flow through me
And unite me with all Thy children.
May I share gladly what Thou givest unto me.

JULY TWENTY-THIRD

Salient Thought for the Day.

You serve most by the example you set.

Lines to Memorize.

But I read on thy face
That thou art destined for thy goal.
Thy faith is not broken;
Thy courage not gone.
Call them forth and hold awhile
Till thy journey is done.

Lesson.

We cannot check or impede our own progress without impairing the happiness of others. We cannot fail ourselves without weakening others. Failure will never overtake us as long as we keep our contact with the Ideal. Evil cannot touch us when we realize our oneness with the Divine. But we cannot be united with our Divine Self until we have been disunited from our lower self. When we have union with our higher Self, we have an asset that is permanent. Then poverty, sickness, misfortune, may come but we are untouched by them.

Prayer.

May Thy touch quicken my heart with new life.
Do Thou fill every corner of my being with fresh strength and determination.
May I never falter or turn back in following Thy path.
May I glorify Thee and make myself worthy of Thy loving protection.

Salient Thought for the Day.

You may be an unconscious instrument through which power may flow to another.

Lines to Memorize.

Let the stream of love flow on and on.
It will bring life and loveliness;
It will bring calm and happiness.
Let the stream of love flow on and on,
Unhindered and unblocked by fear or inner storm.

Lesson.

If you serve with pure and whole-hearted devotion, it must all go well with you and you will feel more blessed every day. The strength of all service is in harmony and tolerance. To bring even a shadow of anything else would be to weaken it. The spirit of self-surrender and prayer will enable us to accomplish this. There are certain qualities we require to love and serve,—introspection, deeper vision, fervor of spirit. To love truly is the greatest triumph of life.

Prayer.

O Thou Inexhaustible Source of my being!
My heart and soul yearn for Thee.
Purify my vision, that I may perceive Thy bounty and the fullness of Thy blessing.
Help me to realize that when I have Thee I have all things.
Thou art the Source of all my wealth and wisdom.
Fill me with Thy blessed Presence,
And may I find all my joy and strength in Thee.

JULY TWENTY-FIFTH

Salient Thought for the Day.

Try to have living spiritual intuition and feel the pulse of others.

Lines to Memorize.

Let the stream of love flow in thy soul, unbarred.
Hinder it not through fear,
Nor let petty thoughts block its course.
Let the stream of love flow on.
It will wash and clean;
It will revive and redeem.

Lesson.

Unless you can do everything through intuitive observation, you will have to be told always what to do and your service will be lacking. There are three types of people,—one serves by intuition, by direct inspiration; another must be told or corrected once only and never forgets; a third type must be told again and again and never remembers. Try to belong to the first type.

Lesson.

May the All-loving Deity grant unto me a greater understanding,
That I may serve His children with true wisdom.
May He fill me with spiritual yearning
And may I manifest His Divine Spirit in my life and action.
May His love infill my heart and make me a worthy instrument in His Hand.

Salient Thought for the Day.

To raise the standard of the world we must raise our own standard.

Lines to Memorize.

Thou hast vanquished my formidable foe by
Thy coming;
He fled before Thee as night before the day.
I feel safe now that Thou art come—
Stay Thou always near me,
For I have no strength apart from Thee.

Lesson.

A little association with worldly life is good, when it shows the difference between that and the spiritual life. Through it we gain knowledge to help others and understand our position better. Everything depends on our attitude and motive. When they are right and unselfish, we are perfectly safe. The basis of true service lies in realizing oneness with our Source. Each individual gives what is uppermost in him. He cannot give more or less. He can give only what he has.

Prayer.

O Thou who art the Resting-place of all souls,
Kindle in me a new light.
May I never live in the darkness of selfishness
and ignorance.
May I strive always to manifest Thee in all I say
and do.
Grant that I may see Thee in all living beings
and learn to transform evil into good, hatred
into love!

JULY TWENTY-SEVENTH

Salient Thought for the Day.

Education is unfoldment.

Lines to Memorize.

My adoration to Thee, great One!
It was Thy mighty hand that broke the chain which held me bound upon the shifting sands of life.

Lesson.

The greatest service we can render anyone is to unfold his higher faculties. Education does not mean tearing down everything we have learned already. We do not tear down the body to find the immortal soul. We look within for that which gives life. When we open the mind to the radiant light of the soul, we accomplish the true end and aim of all education.

Prayer.

To that One who alone can guide me to light and wisdom,
I offer up my body, mind and heart.
He alone can save me from the darkness of ignorance
And bestow upon me the light of understanding.
May He lead me and direct me in all things.
May I depend upon Him alone.

JULY TWENTY-EIGHTH

Salient Thought for the Day.

Service wipes out all egotism, all blemish, and silences all harsh discordant notes.

Lines to Memorize.

Do Thou fill my heart in full measure with
Thine inexhaustible love
That I may scatter it abroad;
For Thy love is all-saving life-giving.

Lesson.

If mind and heart are full, the overflow finds expression through service. Whenever you have a great Ideal or a lofty feeling, it finds its practical application through service. When you serve selflessly, you do not lose anything, you come into your own. You have a new majesty and grandeur of spirit. Service always opens up new avenues for the soul's expression.

Prayer.

Thou who art my loving Mother and protecting
Father,
Imbue me with the spirit of consecration,
That I may lose myself wholly in Thy Divine
Being.
Help me to forget my own pains and struggles,
And think only of the needs of all Thy children.
Fill my heart with new love of service,
And help me to bring Thy peace and blessing to
all that lives.

JULY TWENTY-NINTH

Salient Thought for the Day.

Service brings strength and renewal.

Lines to Memorize.

My life's wounds are healed at Thy touch,
O Thou, my soul's Physician!
Never had I hope for such benediction;
But Thou, Divine Healer, knowing my heart's prayer didst come of Thine own compassion.

Lesson.

If your heart has only love, no evil can bind you. The love element heals; it heals diseases of mind and body. It restores and redeems. People who heal thus through love are not aware of it. Such healing is a very beautiful thing. It is done just as the flower gives its fragrance. To accomplish such healing, you must have faith as well as love—a living faith. If we have even a little grain of true faith, our service will soothe and heal and restore.

Prayer.

May that One who is the Giver of all blessedness,
Bestow upon me ever greater strength to live the life and serve His children.
May I find a greater and greater joy in that service.
May I lose all selfishness and calculation
And give freely with gladness of heart.
May His blessing flow through me to all mankind.

Salient Thought for the Day.

Service makes us bigger, more enduring, more full of compassion; and these are the qualities which makes for spiritual understanding.

Lines to Memorize.

All our resolutions are but brittle deceptions
Save when Thou givest us Thy tender Hand of safety.
Knowing this in my heart of hearts,
I shall banish all unrest of mind,
And wait here at Thy door in peace and gladness.

Lesson.

Spiritual qualities manifest spontaneously through our life. When we are imbued in even a small degree with these qualities, we find the nearness of God far more quickly than when we merely cling to dogmas or beliefs, however, lofty they may be from an intellectual point of view. We come nearer to our Ideal through our feelings, through our devotion and through selfless service.

Prayer.

O Lord, enlarge my heart, that I may bring truer service to Thy children.
May a new and strong love dawn in my soul.
May my vision grow clear, that I may serve more wisely.
Make my life more fruitful and full of helpfulness.
May it never fail to bring Thy peace to all weary hearts and suffering souls.

Salient Thought for the Day.

Try to serve truly. All power comes through true service.

Lines to Memorize.

Love is a miracle.
Behold its working!
It bringeth life to the dead;
It bringeth joy to the sad;
It bringeth light to the dark and despondent soul;
It waketh the spirit that slumbereth in doubt.

Lesson.

My earnest prayer is that God may give you strength and wisdom to follow ably what is best for your wealfare, and for those who look to you for help. This world cannot prove dangerous when our heart is steadfastly fixed in God; but without love of God and His mercy, life is altogether unsafe and full of peril. Pray to Him earnestly for light; try to do your duties with non-attachment; practise purity and self-control in all your thoughts, words and actions; this will give you peace.

Prayer.

Supreme Spirit, awaken in me an ever greater consciousness of Thee.
That I may never fail to follow Thy guidance.
Bestow on me wisdom to serve the needy, gladness of heart to cheer the sorrowing, and loving-kindness to comfort the distressed.
Grant unto me the power to help all who are in need of help.

NOTES

Sing when joy fills thy mind!
Sing when sadness crowds thy heart!
Sing when thy life-stream runs its fullest!
Sing when death brings its darkest gloom!
Sing that song which will never change with time or tide of life!
Light and shadow, joy and pain,
Fame, infamy, loss and gain—
These are all set hours for our life's eternal song.

August

TRANQUILLITY AND CHEERFULNESS

The wise, who knows That One hidden in the cave of the heart as God, is liberated from the fetters of joy and sorrow.

A mortal having realized through discrimination the subtle Self (Immortal Spirit) rejoices, because he has obtained that which is the Source of all joy.

Katha-Upanishad

AUGUST FIRST

Salient Thought for the Day.

Never let your heart become ruffled by pain or pleasure, joy or despondency.

Lines to Memorize.

Our life hath both its summer and its winter, with their heat and cold.
The great Creator knoweth our need
And giveth unto us season of cold and the summer of heat.

Lesson.

A person does not begin to do his best until body is focused and unified. But body cannot be focused without the mind being focused. It is not by thinking on the body you control your body, it is rather by thinking on higher things and relating them to body. Body and mind are both unified by this means and you gain poise. When shall you practise poise? Always. When you are in the crowd and when alone. You must maintain a sense of sanctity and serenity at all times.

Prayer.

O Thou Infinite Spirit, quiet the turbulence of my outer and inner life.
Grant me quietude of heart and mind.
Help me to silence the voice of the world
And to maintain calmness and tranquillity in all the varying conditions of the day.
May Thy peace fill my being
And make me open to Thy blessing.

AUGUST SECOND

Salient Thought for the Day.

Poise does not come accidentally. It springs from intuition and self-conquest.

Lines to Memorize.

For this madness of mine I can find no cure;
There is no help save when Thou art near....
Now at last Thou art come, I am well,—yea, my spirit is still!
My body, mind and sense all sing in perfect unison the joy of Thy coming.

Lesson.

When mind becomes established in quietude, then all sorrows cease. All our forces should be so in tune that there is no room for things to happen by accident. In reality there is no such thing as accident. Whatever happens is the result of a previous state of mind. Mind is not meant to rest in outer influences. In order to get out of gloom or disturbance it must have a point of contact that is different. The mind must be interested in a higher point, where everything is living and vibrant.

Prayer.

May the Supreme Being grant me power to keep an even tenor in all the happenings of my daily life.
May I live in unbroken contact with His Divine storehouse,
And draw all my strength and inspiration from Him alone.

AUGUST THIRD

Salient Thought for the Day.

We must learn to establish ourselves on a foundation which does not waver. That alone will give us quietness of mind.

Lines to Memorize.

Not knowing the ways of this strange world,
As I journeyed alone, self-dependent,
My heart was wounded and my body was torn.
But Thy tender touch of brooding love hath revived me.
Thou hast made my wounded heart Thy throne;
Thou hast transformed my pain into sweet solace.

Lesson.

So long as we dwell on the sense plane, it is impossible for us to maintain calmness of mind. We may plan that, no matter how the world may treat us, we shall remain calm and serene; yet in spite of our calculations we are overwhelmed. We forget our determination, because the material condition which confronts us becomes a reality for us. There is only one way that we can establish a calm attitude of mind,—by fixing our consciousness in that which does not change and which will not fail us.

Prayer.

O Lord, Thou art my resting-place and only protection.
May I never lose my vision of Thee.
May I never give way to sorrow or despondency.
May I remain undaunted and unfaltering in my spiritual life
And serve Thee with steadfast heart.

AUGUST FOURTH

Salient Thought for the Day.

We attain tranquillity by finding it in our own soul.

Lines to Memorize.

I am stillness of the night.
Perfume of the flowers am I.
Majesty of the mountains am I.
The quiet solitude of thy soul is my home.
The peace of thy heart is my rest.

Lesson.

Tranquillity never means dullness or passivity. Dullness and lethargy are great obstacles in the spiritual path; but when our heart is filled with high inspiration we are never heavy or dull. We do not attain tranquillity through calculation or by any material means. We attain it by finding tranquillity in our soul. Stillness of heart is a great blessing. When our outer life is still, it opens up new avenues for spiritual unfoldment. That is why the practice of silence is so helpful and beneficial.

Prayer.

O Thou All-loving Spirit, do Thou glorify Thyself through my life.
Fill me with Thy Divine Grace,
And keep me ever in peace and tranquillity of mind.
Take from me all anxiety and heaviness.
May I always act and think with lightness of heart.

AUGUST FIFTH

Salient Thought for the Day.

Only when the turbulences of self cease, do we have the peace and tranquillity which are absolutely needful for spiritual vision.

Lines to Memorize.

The touch of Thy holy Hand is my sole adornment.
A glance from Thy smiling eyes hath poured upon me a shower of countless blossoms.
Now I gather these scattered flowers day and night with ecstatic joy,
For they bear the blessing of Thy Divine fragrance.

Lesson.

If we have the courage to give ourselves wholly to Truth, what will happen? This question will not rise. There will be no more questioning or calculation. We shall possess the most inspiring, most sustaining vision; and Divinty will become a reality to us. A new vision is born from within. Our whole life is filled with it. Suppose we lose our vision. Instead of giving way to dejection, let us close our eyes and fix our gaze on something within. That will lift our blindness and restore our spiritual sight.

Prayer.

O Merciful One, bless me that I may never bar the stream of Thy love and wisdom in my heart.
May it flow freely and wash away all petty selfish thoughts.
And may I never fail to keep my gaze fixed on Thee.

AUGUST SIXTH

Salient Thought for the Day.

Keep your mind and heart tranquil and your life peaceful.

Lines to Memorize.

Driven by the storm of life I have come to Thee, Thou eternal Tree of shelter!
As I sit under Thy protecting boughs
My storm-pressed heart sighs with relief.
Thou hast given me long-lost peace.

Lesson.

The practical province of life is to make our connection with our Source, and one of the best ways to make this connection is by the establishment of tranquillity. One who lacks tranquillity has a hard road to travel. Tranquillity is the real test of character. We need tranquillity in all the varying conditions of life. Unless we can maintain calmness of mind, we lose all our blessing.

Prayer.

May the All-abiding Presence keep me quiet and peaceful.
May It infill my life, my thought and action.
May I manifest that Presence through love and harmony.
May the Divine blessing rest upon me and upon all living creatures.

AUGUST SEVENTH

Salient Thought for the Day.

A peaceful heart alone gives us the vision of the closeness of the Divine Spirit.

Lines to Memorize.

Mystic heart, rejoice!
This day thou art blessed.
He for whom thou hast cried and sung,
Yearned and waited for these many days, is come.

Lesson.

The principal work is to live the life. This we must ever bear in mind. We must do everything with peaceful and serene attitude. In talking and walking, in dealing with people, at every hour we must carry balance in our mind. We cannot have a peaceful mind unless it is fixed at a high point. We must give it something loftier and greater to think about than the concerns of this ordinary outer life. A man may apper meek and gentle, but if his mind is tranquil and controlled, he is tremendously powerful. Even those in high places fear him, because he has a background of something invulnerable.

Prayer.

May the Eternal One, who is the resting-place of all troubled souls,
May He free me from all disturbance of mind and distress of body.
May He grant me power to carry His peace in my heart
That it may inspire all my thoughts, words and actions.

Salient Thought for the Day.

We must learn to be quiet and cheerful. It not only helps us, it helps others.

Lines to Memorize.

Thou hast chastised me by Thy sad countenance;
I lose all courage when Thy benign face is turned away from me.
Thy displeasure is my long night of living death,
The blessing of Thy smile is my perpetual day of unbroken life and bliss.

Lesson.

Suppose a man loses his balance; if you come with peaceful, quiet mind, you exert a quieting influence on that person and help him regain his equilibrium. You can always set a standard. The way you do everything can become an example. When you do things casually, it means that you have acted thoughtlessly and lack ardor of spirit. The true art of performing action means doing things with poise and calmness. Our thought can make us careful or careless and dull. When our heart is full of lofty aspiration, we move swiftly, lightly and thoughtfully; we are never agitated or careless.

Prayer.

O Lord, still all turbulence in my heart.
May I be so surrendered to Thy Will
That I shall gain quietness of spirit.
May I always trust in Thy loving care and protection
And find my peace in Thee.

AUGUST NINTH

Salient Thought for the Day.

He attains who always remains the witness and never loses his tranquillity.

Lines to Memorize.

It, [my *vina*] is renewed and refreshed ;
It is revived by the touch of Thy Hand,
The touch of Thy Hand is ever fresh life.
Heart of my *vina,* its voice and music art Thou ;
Verily Thou art the Soul of my song.

Lesson.

When you lose yourself, you gain poise, tranquillity and steadiness. When outer happiness comes, you must not be too elated. You must stand as a witness on guard that you do not forget and let yourself be carried away by the temptations and distractions of the material world. There is a higher state of calmness and security that no amount of calculation and planning can give. It comes through connection with the Source of all peace.

Prayer.

O Thou Infinite Being, may my vision never become one-sided or distorted through self-limitation.
Make me steady and unfaltering in my spiritual path.
May I always look with serene heart upon all the happenings of life, depending wholly upon Thy protection.

AUGUST TENTH

Salient Thought for the Day.

We should be thankful for every ordeal every misfortune. They lay the foundation for serenity and cheerfulness of mind.

Lines to Memorize.

Seeking for my soul's freedom I have wandered far.
Oft in my haste I have embraced far greater fetters than those I have sought to break.
In search of happiness oft have I plunged into the unenduring glamour of life,
Like the foolish moth in the flame.
In vain have I struggled;
In vain have I sought my liberation apart from Thee.

Lesson.

Serenity is a very desirable quality. It is like a tonic to body and heart.. It brings great strength. We all need it. When we lose our serenity, we do what is disturbing to ourselves and to others. Now we depend too much upon our own thought and calculation. When we learn to depend upon God, then we shall grow quiet and know true serenity.

Prayer.

O Supreme One, help me to follow Thy way of wisdom,
And learn to maintain evenness in all the uneven circumstances of my daily life.
May I be undaunted in my search for Thee;
And may I trust wholly to Thy guiding Hand at every step.

AUGUST ELEVENTH

Salient Thought for the Day.

When the world distracts us and makes us forget God, that is the greatest misfortune.

Lines to Memorize.

Season of blossoming is the time of love.
Heart of the bud bursts with the fullness of its love.
The flower speaketh its inmost heart by giving us its fragrance.
Let thy heart, like the flower, blossom with love
And give to the world peace perpetual and abiding joy.

Lesson.

When we forget our complex nature and relate ourselves wholly to the Supreme, a sense of peace and rest falls upon us. Outside darkness and distress cannot count for us if we have inward light; and the inward light comes through our knowledge of the Supreme. This knowledge can be gained only when the heart is humble, receptive and turned towards God.

Prayer.

O Infinite Spirit of the Universe,
Thou art my one safe Shelter.
Thou art my one sure Refuge from the distractions of this world.
Help me never to forget that Thou art the root of my life;
My strength and joy depend wholly on Thy Grace;
Bestow that Grace upon me out of Thine infinite mercy.

Salient Thought for the Day.

Your start determines your day.

Lines to Memorize.

Torch of faith He will give thee, and a staff of Endurance.
When thou art thus equipped and set on this mystic road,
The hidden will be disclosed before the torch of Faith;
All darkness and dangers will cease to be.

Lesson.

One type of person begins the day reluctantly; another type rises up with vitality, with a song in his heart, joyful that a new dawn has come. We must approach the day thoughtfully, since what we do in the early morning fixes the temperature for the hours which follow. We must not waste our time in idle talking and laughing. Exuberance is good, but too much of it disturbs the balance. We can be joyous without losing our equilibrium. The whole day will be in rhythm when we begin it with peaceful, tranquil mind.

Prayer.

May the Giver of all peace and blessing make this day peaceful and wholly consecrated to Him.
May His Presence sustain me at every hour.
At the time of loneliness and discouragement,
May I turn to Him with trusting heart,
And look to Him for all my needs and inspiration.

AUGUST THIRTEENTH

Salient Thought for the Day.

We gain cheerfulness when we live close to the heart of Truth.

Lines to Memorize.

Now I sing only one song,
The song that Thou hast taught me.
It never grows old to my ear.

Lesson.

Never destroy your own happiness through impatience and thoughtlessness. The same thing can produce both happiness and unhappiness. We can make ourselves so uncontrolled, so unworthy of the blessings that surround us that we are not able to take good opportunities when they come. Truth is a light, a glowing spiritual light. When that light shines, there can be no darkness. Heaven is not a vague, visionary thing. It is something we create within ourselves. We make it out of the exuberance and radiance of our cwn soul.

Prayer.

O Thou All-abiding Spirit, make Thy care and guidance a reality to me.
May the consciousness of Thy Presence become so vivid
That I may find all my rest and strength in Thee alone.
May I walk by Thy light only and never turn away to follow darkness.

AUGUST FOURTEENTH

Salient Thought for the Day.

The weight of the world falls on those who throw their weight on the world.

Lines to Memorize.

Thou hast shielded me by Thy protecting love.
Now I depend on Thee, nay, I cannot live without Thee.
I crave no other blessing than Thy benign Presence.

Lesson.

Our happiness depends on the happiness of others. We should expand our little nature. There is no such thing as selfish happiness in political life; there is no such thing as selfish happiness in social life; there is no such thing as selfish happiness in spiritual life. Unhappiness means that we close our hearts to the higher avenues of true joy. True happiness is contained in the Infinite and Eternal.

Prayer.

May the Divine Spirit protect me from selfishness and pettiness.
May I never yield to dejection or discontent.
May He grant me brightness of spirit and cheerfulness.
May I find all my happiness in Him, not in the things of this world.
May He bestow His peace and blessing upon my life.

Salient Thought for the Day.

God will do everything for us, if we bring Him one flash of soul-joy.

Lines to Memorize.

Verily, Thou art the Master of miracle!
Thy approach filleth our soul with light of gladness.
Where Thou dwellest the gloom of darkness can never be.
Thou art the perpetual sun that feedeth my soul with ever fresh life.

Lesson.

Complaining never accomplishes anything. God is eternally blissful. If we approach Him wtih a sick soul, our sickness is cured. Whenever we connect ourselves with Him, all our ills are healed. God never wants us to live with sad heart. He is always ready to carry our burdens.

Prayer.

In this hour of prayer I lift my heart to Thee, O Thou all-protection Deity.
Free me from all fretfulness and complaining.
Make me strong and contented.
May I take cheerfully whatever Thou sendest, and bear my burdens bravely.

AUGUST SIXTEENTH

Salient Thought for the Day.

God has given us life that we may express joyousness of heart.

Lines to Memorize.

My soul is happy with an inexpressible joy
Since I saw His smiling face turned towards me.

I can never forget that radiant smile;
Where'er I go it haunts me by day and it haunts me by night.
When in grim despair of life, it brightens my path with hope and love.

Lesson.

No man can attain his goal without practising the higher principles of life. No man can be truly happy who is selfish. What possible use is outer light if there is darkness inside? Happiness is a quality of the soul. It enters the soul which has tasted God-consciousness. God is ever cheerful. Life is given to us to work out our freedom and lasting happiness.

Prayer.

O Thou Giver of all joy, may I not be unworthy of Thy gifts,
But may I radiate happiness and cheer in every hour of my daily life.
Help me to realize that when I am sad, it is because I am separated from Thee.
All my sadness and sorrow will vanish when I seek Thee with open heart.

AUGUST SEVENTEENTH

Salient Thought for the Day.

We need joy for the expansion of our soul.

Lines to Memorize.

Thou art the root of this life-plant.
Not knowing the secret of its being,
It lifted its head to the light,
Spreading its limbs in space
As if eager for flight.
But earth held it firm to its root
While sun, rain and air,
By their unfailing care,
Brought it to ripening.

Lesson.

We must make our life deep-rooted in God. When it is thus rooted, we can walk through life with smiling heart. The whole world is full of the Spirit of God. Sometimes we close our doors and nothing can penetrate. Our heart becomes barren and dry. Self-consciousness dries it up and attaches it to the finite. Everything becomes parched within us. Only as we open the door to the Divine, can we taste the sweetness of Divine joy.

Prayer.

All-effulgent Spirit, may I make myself open to Thy holy blessing.
Help me all through this day to walk in Thy light with joyous heart.
May I seek my joy and my support in Thee alone.
Do Thou enfold me with Thy loving and abiding protection.

AUGUST EIGHTEENTH

Salient Thought for the Day.

When we are resourceful and have found our contact with something higher, we are never sad.

Lines to Memorize.

He is come,
Behold Him standing at thy gate,
Art thou blind with joy?
Art thou mad in ecstasy?
He is come.
Keep Him not standing at thy gate.
Mystic heart, thou art blessed,
Yea, thou art blessed this day.

Lesson.

Joyousness characterizes all great souls. Man is constantly looking up. He is never reaching out for something higher. He is full of unrest. He feels intuitively that nothing but the higher can make him happy. Happiness requires a great deal more than material things. We all find this out sooner or later. We must come in contact with the highest and holiest, and we must have willingness to receive. Our inner being must be made fertile soil, then our life becomes fruitful and joyous.

Prayer.

O Thou Compassionate One, help me to express the spirit of joy in all my thoughts, words and actions.
May I never yield to sadness or gloom.
Grant that my contact with Thy Divine Being may grow ever closer and closer,
And may my happiness rest wholly in Thee, who art the Source of all joy and peace.

AUGUST NINETEENTH

Salient Thought for the Day.

Joy is in the Unbounded.

Lines to Memorize.

The blessing of Thy love, like a heavy shower, fell upon me unaware.
It washed me of all dross clean and free.
In this freshness of bareness my soul is happy,
For it hath found the Hidden,
And hath attained the Unattainable!

Lesson.

Man cannot come in contact with God without feeling happiness. When the soul is truly awakened, it expands and expresses itself in blissfulness. Such a one refuses to recognize anything but the voice of God. He refuses to see anything other than God's Will working through all. He sees the whole world as the manifestation of Divine joy. When there is Divine joy and peace in your soul, the Supreme will always protect you, cheer you, give you strength and fill your heart with bliss.

Prayer.

May the Divine Mother of the universe flood my heart with pure love and holy joy,
That I may at all times be worthy to live close to Her Divine Heart.
Through the day may I seek refreshment at Her holy Feet,
And depend always on Her tender care and protection.

AUGUST TWENTIETH

Salient Thought for the Day.

Carry the torch of joy with you everywhere.

Lines to Memorize.

O Thou heavenly smile of strength and cheer.
Thou art my soul's sunshine!
Thou art my heart's ecstasy!
Thou art the consummation of my life.

Lesson.

The religion must awaken in us a sense of joy. It teaches us to carry a light with us everywhere. How wonderful it would be if every one would carry his own light! How beautiful life would be if each one would shed the light of joy into the world! In vain we seek this joy without; it is only to be found within. A person who has this light sheds blessing everywhere. He sees all things in the pure light of Truth and people come to him eagerly for help.

Prayer.

May the Supreme Spirit of the universe guide me in all that I do,
And help me to express joy and fervent devotion through each task of the day.
May I bear aloft the light of Truth in my every thought and action;
And bring brightness into other lives.

AUGUST TWENTY-FIRST

Salient Thought for the Day.

We cannot be happy without casting that radiance into the world.

Lines to Memorize.

The blessing of Thy smile hath filled my soul with radiant joy.
When I am in Thy Presence my heart is always light and my feet do not touch the ground.
Verily, Thou hast transported me to a sorrowless land!

Lesson.

It is good to have at least one person in every household who radiates joy. Often a light is kept burning before the shrine; so in the soul must we keep burning the light of understanding. Then no evil can touch us. Vision does not come to one whose heart is soiled by the world and heated by the fever of life. A person cannot convey constructive thought who is not in tune with the universe; but when his heart is in perfect tune, he benefits and comforts the whole world. His life is like a radiant light shedding brightness.

Prayer.

O Lord, make my life a blessing to all Thy children.
May I never bring darkness or heaviness to any heart;
But may I shed the radiance of true joy on all who cross my path.
Grant that I feel the bliss of Thy Presence within my soul.
And may Thy Presence protect me from all gloom and sadness.

Salient Thought for the Day.

Happiness means that our life is rhythmic and harmonious.

Lines to Memorize.

It is rhythm of life I sing at dawn,
Calling thee to rise with new life.
My mandate is to bring thee blessing from the Ever-blessed,
And to fill thy heart with joy.
Dear dreamer, live in the rhythm of life in waking and in sleeping,
Then thou shalt know the spirit of my song.

Lesson.

It gives new courage when we meet a joyous person. We need joy for our own upliftment and for the upliftment of others. But how can we bring cheer to the world if we have not cheer in our own hearts ? We have a living soul, but we know that it is living only when we establish our contact with the Soul of the universe. When we touch the Eternal, we gain our access to what is everlasting. Then we cannot feel gloom.

Prayer.

May the great Eternal One expand my thoughts through lofty aspiration.
And bestow on me gladness of heart.
May my life move in rhythm with the universal Life.
May my mind think in harmony with the great Mind of the universe.
May he grant me a peace that can never be broken or destroyed.

AUGUST TWENTY-THIRD

Salient Thought for the Day.

We must make our life so rhythmic that it will be invulnerable to attack.

Lines to Memorize.

I sing the song of life,
With the smile of the sun and the dance of the twilight.
I float in the sky in rhythm,
With free spirit and joyous heart.

Lesson.

Rhythm means balance. We protect ourselves by balance and poise. If a person comes with evil tongue or intent and you are quiet and dignified, the person becomes ashamed very soon. He is silenced and powerless to hurt. Without saying anything you put a check on him. As we gain in calmness and serenity, we become charged with higher power. We must always maintain balance and spiritual sanctity.

Prayer.

O Thou almighty Deity, help me to keep my body and mind harmonious and tranquil.
Grant unto me a courage that never yields to weakness,
A joyousness that never gives way to sadness.
Make my heart invincible to the attacks of the World,
And may I turn to Thee at all times for help and guidance.

AUGUST TWENTY-FOURTH

Salient Thought for the Day.

We must find the way of access to happiness.

Lines to Memorize.

When Thou art near me, time puts on wings and flies speedily;
Space melts into nothingness and my life's cares are forgot.
Yea, Thou hast thrown a magic aura around me—
I forget myself so wholly when I am near Thee.
Oh, how my soul delights in this total self-oblivion!

Lesson.

We hold the key to happiness in our own hand. Whenever we desire, we can open the door and enter into the storehouse of joy, inspiration and strength. Our thought can make us unhappy or it can expand our whole life and fill it with radiant joy. The one who brings a real picture of joy and exuberance is a true benefactor. It shows that he has found access to the realm of happiness. When we cease to run after passing things and seek within, we never fail to find joy. Then whatever we touch, it blossoms.

Prayer.

O Compassionate Spirit, Thou who abidest within me as peace and bliss,
I pray unto Thee to make Thy radiance manifest in my heart and life:
Bestow upon me a sense of prayerfulness and gladness,
That in the dark hours I may still remain grateful for Thy unfailing blessing.

AUGUST TWENTY-FIFTH

Salient Thought for the Day.

We can always control our inner life. Joyousness comes from within.

Lines to Memorize.

My Lord, my Love!
Thus I pray unto Thee with holy joy and ecstasy,
Knowing that Thou enterest my soul as pure prayer.

Lesson.

Great souls are invaribly buoyant and joyous. Whatever comes to them, they are imbued with joy. One cannot imagine a highly illumined soul without seeing light shining through and through him. Spirit is never sombre. Wheeping with the afflicted does not help. It may create a point of contact, but it does not bring a remedy. Joy is the antidote for sorrow. What we need is a basis of unfailing joy for our daily life. This alone will bring us courage and resourcefulness. When we are exuberant and happy, no trial can overwhelm us. This higher spiritual joy fills our heart only when our gaze is fixed steadily on our Source.

Prayer.

Grant that the Infinite Being may hold my life in His Hand
And shape it according to His Will.
May He help me to realize that I need never feel lonely or desolate;
That in the hour of gloom, if I but turn within, I shall never fail to find His blissful Presence to console and cheer me.

Salient Thought for the Day.

We can block the channel to joy and nothing blocks it so much as morbid self-pity.

Lines to Memorize.

I dream now in waking,
I see with closed eyes,
I walk without feet
And grasp without hands.
Since Thou hast brought me
To this unearthly and ethereal land.

Lesson.

Dire distress, misfortune, sorrow, calamity—nothing can overwhelm the man who has tasted the joy which comes from transcending all sorrow by spiritual consciousness. It is indeed a cloudy dark day for the soul when man loses sight of God and forgets through doubt and self-pity that he is of God; that his life is absolutely in God's Hands. No calculation or thought can bring this higher happiness. It rises only in the heart that is full of faith and selflessness.

Prayer.

O Divine Mother, make my life so pure and humble and free,
That the light of Thy Truth may shine in it and through it.
Hold my heart close to Thy great eternal Heart,
And fill my mind with Thy great eternal Thoughts.
Grant that I may live and act in harmony with Thy Divine Will,
And be a clear channel through which Thou dost speak and act.

AUGUST TWENTY-SEVENTH

Salient Thought for the Day.

When our soul is awakened we are habitually cheerful; it becomes natural to us.

Lines to Memorize.

Thou, Friend of the poor, didst come to me when my heart was heavy with helplessness.
Now I am drowning in a river of joy!
Tell me, O Thou Merciful One, ere I am swept by this current of bliss:
What can I do to repay such love?

Lesson.

If we are truly sanctified we can never be unhappy. How can anyone who lives close to the Lord be anything but cheerful? We are all struggling for a point where we shall no longer have gloomy, morbid feelings. The world gives us a sense of incompleteness and we do not know where to look for something that is complete. Thus we struggle and strive. But struggle does not always bring peace, although it can pave the way to it. Where there is exuberance of spirit and radiance of soul, we find peace and we share it with others. We cannot help it.

Prayer.

Divine Spirit, Giver of all happiness,
Fill my soul with higher spiritual joy.
In the presence of Eternal Good no evil can gain access,
In the presence of Eternal Joy no gloom can enter;
Grant that I may live always in Thy blissful Presence and find lasting joy in Thy blessing.

AUGUST TWENTY-EIGHTH

Salient Thought for the Day.

We must make our contact with the Bilssful One.

Lines to Memorize.

Our life, our strength, our joy and peace—all are in Thy Hand.
Give us what Thou wilt.
Keep from us what Thou wilt not give.
But this we pray:
Do Thou never turn Thy face of grace away from us.

Lesson.

No man can come within the radius of the Divine and not feel the burdens of life drop away. A simple person, full of faith, full of devotion, full of openness of heart, may know a great deal more about God than a philosopher of brilliant intellect. Sometimes it becomes a great advantage to know less. We have not so much to unlearn. We gain contact with God, not through intellectual keenness, but through a sense of consecration, through the feeling that He is the Guiding Spirit abiding within us and working through us.

Prayer.

O Thou Beneficent One, surround me with Thy tender protection.
That I may be shielded from all that may cloud my mind or heart.
Lead me from the realm of affliction and sorrow
To Thy Divine realm of joy and peace,
Help me at every moment to feel Thy nearness,
And may I draw my joy and strength from communion with Thee.

Salient Thought for the Day.

The All-Blissful Mother of the Universe never wants to see Her children sad.

Lines to Memorize.

O Thou unasked, unceasing Giver,
Thou hast given me Thy endless blessing,
Thou hast drawn me close to Thy Heart.
Thy bounty runs through my life to overflowing.
Yea, tender Lord, by Thy magic charm Thou hast driven away all my past wretchedness.

Lesson.

Melancholy thoughts are a great detriment to our health and to our happiness. All our successes and failures, our pleasures and pains, come and go. They are not lasting. Why should we take them so seriously and make ourselves miserable ? The sun is a great symbol and what is it a symbol of ? A symbol of light and joy. It teaches us that we must find avenues through which the light of the soul may flood our whole being and fill it with radiance. We can kindle this light only when we establish our contact with a Higher Power that will shield us and radiate through us.

Prayer.

May the Divine Presence within me quicken my soul with new understanding
May It kindle in my heart a new fervor of joy
And may the light of that joy drive away all darkness and gloom.
May my life bring happiness to others
And prove more and more worthy of God's love and blessing.

AUGUST THIRTIETH

Salient Thought for the Day.

There is a song for every hour. Life is a constant song to those whose ears are open.

Lines to Memorize.

At times I catch the echo of Thy voice in my song.
Then my madness grows with joy
And I sing again and again
Not to hear my own voice
But to catch the echo of Thy voice in my song.

Lesson.

It is not a strenuous effort to sing this song of life. It comes easily in the heart that is directed towards God. It is because we are not trusting that we do not sing that song. A man cannot have happiness until he has earned the right to happiness. When our heart is in tune with the Infinite Heart, a joyous song of life arises spontaneously in our soul. That song is never boisterous or noisy. It sings itself in silent communion with the inward Presence.

Prayer.

O Thou All-radiant Deity, help me to live this day with radiant spirit.
May I do each task joyously and with contented heart.
May Thy voice sing in my soul, Thy flame of love burn in my heart.
May my own voice be silent, my own will lost in Thy Will.

AUGUST THIRTY-FIRST

Salient Thought for the Day.

You cannot be cheerful with gladdened heart without dispelling some of the gloom of the world.

Lines to Memorize.

Once in the dark I stood alone aimless but expectant,
But an unlighted lamp appeared; whence, I knew not,
Its unkindled flame led me on, forward, ever onward; up or down,
I knew not, for space was no more
O Thou mysterious light, He who sent thee to guide me, I am His forevermore.

Lesson.

Our thoughts are magnified, our action is made beneficial through the light of cheerfulness. When a man is gloomy, you do not help him by weeping and wailing with him. Bring in the light and that will lift the gloom. Cheerfulness heals and unifies. It stirs new hope in the despondent and discouraged. It is a constructive force. It stimulates to new thought and action.

Prayer.

Blessed Lord, help me to carry light of Thy Divine Spirit into the World
That I may never cast gloom over any heart.
May Thy holy radiance shine in my face
And find expression through my words and actions.
Grant unto me the power to cheer the sad, comfort the distressed and bring Thy blessing to all lives that touch my life.

NOTES

Love ! Great immensity !
Unfathomed mystery !
Sacred current of life !
Vibrant resplendent flame that burneth eternally,
Consuming all our imperfections,
Healing all our wounds,
And bestowing peace upon our turbulent heart !
Hail to Thee, Thou holy Spirit !
Hail to Thee again and evermore,
Thou Giver of pure sight !
Let me lie in Thy protecting arms
And sleep in the warmth of Thy bosom,
And in waking behold Thy beneficent face
That never changeth its tender mercy.
To Thee I turn my face.
And on Thee I fix my eager gaze
Now and let it be through eternity.

September

SELFLESS LOVE AND DEVOTION

Fill thy mind with Me, be thou My devotee, worship Me and bow down to Me, thus steadfastly uniting thy heart with Me alone and regarding Me as thy Supreme Goal, thou shalt come unto me.

Bhagavad-Gita

SEPTEMBER FIRST

Salient Thought for the Day.

Think not of self. There are so many great things to think about.

Lines to Memorize.

Time will pass,
Nay, time exists not in love.
Love will melt time and all but One,
Then the anguish of thy heart
Will cease in serene contemplation.

Lesson.

Selfishness places a terrible weight on the life. When we are tied by selfishness, the soul suffers. We feel weighted down with life because we have no higher avenues of expression. Self-limitation always defeats a man, but if we can turn our mind and heart to the Divine, it will make our faith stronger and stronger, and give us joy, selflessness and true devotion.

Prayer.

May the All-loving Spirit of the Universe
Quicken my soul with new life and a deeper understanding.
May He surround me with His protecting love,
That I may be safeguarded against selfishness and all that leads me away from Him.
May He inspire me with more and more love.
May He increase my devotion and strengthen my faith.

Salient Thought for the Day.

There is no calculation, no bargaining in true love.

Lines to Memorize.

Lo, they came to rescue me with their frail boats.
My heart shivered with apprehension and I cried aloud :
Current of love ! Current of love !
Carry me swiftly where Thou wilt.
I want no rescue !

Lesson.

We look at beautiful scenery, we love it, but we ask nothing from it in return. We love it because it is beautiful. We should love God in the same way, because He is the most lovable Being in the universe. Such understanding love is the greatest gift in life. We get more than we ask for when we reach that point.

Prayer.

All-beneficent Deity, enlarge my heart that I may love Thee with wholeness of being.
Do Thou rouse in my soul an ever greater and greater power of love.
May I learn to give myself without reserve or calculation.
Grant that I may never again fall under the bondage of self,
But look to Thee always for guidance and protection.

SEPTEMBER THIRD

Salient Thought for the Day.

A sincere devotee gives up all he has and by giving up he acquires immensity of life.

Lines to Memorize.

To Thee whose holy Hand kindled my heart with this fire of love,
I consecrate my soul's outpouring.
I lay at Thy tender Feet, whose sacred touch fills my whole being with ecstasy, this, my inmost secrecy.

Lesson.

All the power that manifests through you comes from one Source. You open the channel for it through constant loving service, humility and devotion. Let it always flow steadily and the current will grow mightier and mightier every day, so that whoever comes in contact with you will be blessed. It is when your heart is humble that the light of love sheds its radiance through you. That light reaches every one whose life you touch.

Prayer.

May the Supreme Being grant me this blessing,
That I may always walk in High light,
And shed forth His love.
May I realize that I am always in danger when I sever myself from His protecting care.
May my life move in union with His life,
And may my heart be filled with a new sense of His peace.

SEPTEMBER FOURTH

Salient Thought for the Day.

God pleads tenderly with us like a mother to give up self.

Lines to Memorize.

God is thy Father.
Gentle King is He.
He rules with sceptre of love
And He wears the crown of compassion.
Be thou then like unto Him in love.
If thou wouldst inherit His heavenly realm.

Lesson.

Always hold your position with dignity and selflessness. Know that you are a channel through which the Ideal is manifesting. Keep yourself pure and one-pointed in your devotion, then there will be no difficulty. If you have given yourself entirely to Him, your body, mind and heart, with all their powers and possibilities, then nothing can distract you or overwhelm you.

Prayer.

O Thou All-loving Ruler of the Universe,
Make me worthy of Thy tender care and blessing.
May I never fail to hear Thy voice;
May I never fail to obey its call.
Thou dost never forsake me.
May I never forsake Thee.
Make me Thy true child,
And keep my heart fixed on Thee through every hour of the day.

SEPTEMBER FIFTH

Salient Thought for the Day.

He who has attained conquest over self, no one can overwhelm him.

Lines to Memorize.

I was sad to think of all lost opportunities;
But Thou, Divine Forgiver, hast called me again to sing before Thee.
My heart is full of gladness!
Strange that my mind knew not it was Thy voice that sang in me, and Thy music gave its rhythmic chord.

Lesson.

All our miseries spring from self-interest. Self-interest makes us unsteady and calculating. A man who can go over the rough places and still maintain his ardour, that one is blessed. He is a great asset to himself and to others. Unless we learn the art of living, we cannot maintain steadiness. No one need think that some special place or condition will give it. They help, but unless we ourselves cultivate it, too often we throw away our opportunities to exhibit it.

Prayer.

O Thou Infinite Deity, in this silent hour
May I feel Thy love and protection.
May I rest in that love and lose all fear and weakness.
In both my sleeping and waking may I have the consciousness of Thy Presence,
And may that consciousness destroy in me all self-interest and self-importance.

Salient Thought for the Day.

We do our best when we are least conscious of ourselves.

Lines to Memorize.

Ah, the quiet, blessed hour,—
The hour of union and fulfilment,
The hour of joy complete!

Lines to Memorize.

Every time you forget yourself, you are renewed and rested. It is done sometimes through higher understanding or it may be done through devotion to an Ideal. What will become of a man when he gives up self? Renunciation of self—what does it mean? Renunciation in every form is very sacred. It is the motive that determines its value. When you limit yourself to selfish vision, everything becomes distorted and your balance is destroyed. You must give your whole life freely, if you would have true, undistracted power of action.

Prayer.

O Thou Eternal Light of the Universe,
Thou art the Source of my life; my inspiration and my joy.
May my gaze ever remain fixed on Thee;
May it never turn back upon myself.
Help me to keep my spiritual fire burning;
May I never let it grow dim or be extinguished.
May I devote my whole heart to Thy service,
And find my strength ever in Thee.

SEPTEMBER SEVENTH

Salient Thought for the Day.

By love and aspiration, you open yourself to the Divine blessing.

Lines to Memorize.

When our thoughts rise with the perfume of purity,
We can offer them to Him who accepteth our oblation.

Lesson.

Whenever you try to serve Him with spontaneous feeling, without thought of self, then nothing can resist you. Know this, and nothing will ever be able to thwart you. When you start with generous devoted spirit, all your efforts must meet with success. Spirituality is a revelation. It is revealed not only to the prophet or the teacher, but also to the devotee who is humble, enduring and selfless. Unless you have spiritual vision, when difficulties arise you will not be able to meet them. You must safeguard yourself by acquiring wisdom. Wisdom is abiding and always sustains.

Prayer.

O Lord, grant that in my ordinary tasks of the day
I may be ever mindful of Thy guidance.
Help me to do each duty with loving helpful spirit
May all that I do be pleasing to Thee.
In my work, worship and aspiration, may I seek ever to glorify Thee.
Increase my endurance and grant me wisdom,
That I may manifest Thy spiritual grace in all my words and actions.

Salient Thought for the Day.

Selfless devotion to an Ideal plays a vital part in the spiritual life.

Lines to Memorize.

Freely am I bound to Thee,
Freely do I remain bound,
For Thou hast poured upon me Thy unbounded love unasked—
Unasked will I make my offering unto Thee.

Lesson.

Try to cultivate the true spirit of discipleship. The world is so full of teachers—everyone wants to be a master; but the spirit of discipleship is indeed very rare. But going through the form of discipleship, however, is not everything. You must stir yourself up. You must never go to sleep. It is too hard to awaken oneself.

Prayer.

O Thou All-wise One, bestow on my heart the blessing of humility,
That I may learn joyfully the lessons that come to me through this day.
Keep me fearless and steadfast in my devotion to the Ideal.
May I never fail in my loyalty to it.
May I fasten my life to Thy infinite Life,
And forget myself wholly in my service to Thee.

SEPTEMBER NINTH

Salient Thought for the Day.

Real love and devotion always bring strength.

Lines to Memorize.

Once this heart of mine was barren like yon desert.
Lacking in grace and lacking in life;
Till the stream of love made it fertile,
It was full of waste and unlovely land.
The stream of love hath transformed my barren grounds.
To a flower garden and a fruit orchard.

Lesson.

Pray to the Divine Mother to make you unflinching in your devotional life. Pray to Her to rouse greater love for Her in your heart and free you from all pride, ambition and vanity. Honour, praise and recognition can be great drawbacks for the soul; they awaken the subtle ego and prevent spiritual progress. Pray to the Divine Mother always to protect you from such dangers. Always try to glorify Her by your life.

Prayer.

May the Infinite Mother accept my offering of prayer and devotion.
May I gain light and a larger love through my daily worship.
May I grow strong in thinking on Her infinite Strength.
May I grow tender and loving in thinking on Her infinite Love.
May all unrest and discontent vanish from my heart,
And may I find peace and joy in Her Presence.

Salient Thought for the Day.

Can God accept the worship of one who has not loving-kindness in his heart?

Lines to Memorize.

Beauty in the rose draws my heart;
Beauty of dawn exalts my soul;
Stillness of the night fills me with wonder;
Beauty of face and beauty of sight
Awaken in my soul love and ever greater love.

Lesson.

When you find others harsh and irritating, it is because you have those feelings in yourself. When there is only love and gentleness in your heart, the harshness of others does not touch you. Unselfishness is a very real thing, but it is something that cannot be defined. You lift yourself to a higher point and become unselfish when you serve God and His children with true consecration and devotion. When the light of love shines in your heart, it charges you with power to do the right act and speak the right word. Your work and your worship become acceptable to God.

Prayer.

O Lord, take from me all harshness and unkindness,
And release me from all that binds me to my little self.
Help me to love and serve truly all Thy children.
May I always extend a helping hand to all those in need,
And never turn away from any living creature.

SEPTEMBER ELEVENTH

Salient Thought for the Day.

The true disciple hears in silence. If he is corrected he does not rise in self-defense.

Lines to Memorize.

Lover, sit still and wait;
Whom thou desirest will come.
Being alone is not lonely.
And how wilt thou receive Him if thou art not alone?
Waiting is for preparing;
Watching with longing is sweet;
And when He comes all this will end
And thou thyself will be lost in love.

Lesson.

It is necessary to open the deeper side of one's nature by patience, humility and obedience before one can take spiritual teaching. That is why the great sages of India were so insistent in their discipline. Those who cannot bear reprimand, it shows they are shallow and empty. Discipleship is a very sacred thing and it cannot be given to one who is not fully prepared for it.

Prayer.

I lift my heart to the All-pervading One, who is the giver of all strength and blessing.
May He free it from pride, rebellion and all unworthy thoughts and feelings,
That I may realize that He is the Source of my existence;
That from Him comes all my joy and sorrow.
May I take humbly whatever He sends, whether it be pain or pleasure,
And place my unfaltering trust in Him.

Salient Thought for the Day.

Steadfastness, love, unselfish devotion and unfaltering loyalty to the Ideal,—these are the blessed qualities essential to spiritual attainment.

Lines to Memorize.

Thou alone canst save us from the tyranny of self
And restore unto us selfless love,
Whose fragrance bringeth life and healing.

Lesson.

The small concerns of the little self are áll detrimental to a man. Try to cultivate selfless love, steadfastness and loyalty and a new world will open before you. These qualities cannot flourish in the soil of selfishness. They do not come to one who is a slave of himself. They are to be found only in one who has learned to turn within and listen to the inner voice of the soul.

Prayer.

O Thou infinite Being, make Thy Presence felt in my soul,
That I may know Thee as the Embodiment of all blessedness.
Inspire me with love and holiness.
Cleanse my nature of all vanity and self-interest.
Vnfold my spiritual insight that I may realize, Thee both wihtin and without.
Free my heart from all inharmony and keep me ever in Thy peace.

SEPTEMBER THIRTEENTH

Salient Thought for the Day.

The stream of love purifies and redeems,

Lines to Memorize.

It was a flood unlike all other floods,
For it made no devastation.
It was love's flood.
Its vehemence came upon me when I was lying still.
This full flood-tide carried me to the midstream;
There I lay content—drifting far, far away from all that was once so near.

Lesson.

We must never criticize or find fault with anyone or see evil in any person. If we do, the love in our hearts will grow weak. If we can keep our gaze fixed on the good side and can rejoice in another's victory or good fortune, the blessing of an ever greater love will come to us. There is something in us which is the greatest teacher, that is devotion. When people do anything with pure devotion, they succeed. The stream of love always purifies the vision and we see everything more clearly. When truly consecrated souls come together in ardor of selfless devotion they can perform miracles.

Prayer.

May the Supreme Spirit strengthen my devotional life,
That I may gain a more vivid sense of the nearness of Divinity.
May that Spirit throw light upon my path and give me a greater understanding,
That I may love more wisely and serve more worthily.

SEPTEMBER FOURTEENTH

Salient Thought for the Day.

The selfless heart is always in rhythm.

Lines to Memorize.

The vioce of love hath melted my life into sweet harmony ;
Thy holy compassion hath filled my heart with endless song.
My soul breathes now in peace and music.

Lesson.

Steady devotion and unfailing selflessness always bring joy and satisfaction to the heart. May these holy qualities grow daily stronger in you. May the world learn through you what true devotion means. You have all the strength you need. What we require is great ardor of devotion to direct it. If you have an earnest spirit and a prayerful attitude, you can break down any obstacle. We do not gain devotion by chance. It comes through unselfishness and practice of inner harmony.

Prayer.

O Thou Mother of the Universe, make me a worthy child.
May I never fail in trust or surrender.
Help me to follow Thy Will with unwavering devotion,
That I may never be out of rhythm in my thoughts or actions ;
May my life ever be turned in perfect unison with Thy Divine Life.

SEPTEMBER FIFTEENTH

Salient Thought for the Day.

We have great need of forgetting ourselves, otherwise the world-consciousness will grind into us.

Lines to Memorize.

Great Liberator, deliver us from the bondage of self;
Cure us from its mad intoxication.
Thou alone canst draw our hearts away from its hypnotic spell.

Lesson.

When you find yourself brooding over self, turn your thought elsewhere. How much we need the Divine blessing! How much we need to think on the Ideal! We need to safeguard ourselves. Life never runs with perfect smoothness, so we need to place ourselves under higher protection. The whole spiritual life is based on unselfishness, in being and becoming something other than the little self. Living devotion to an Ideal alone will make us selfless. Contact with a spiritual Ideal always fortifies us and brings us a saving sense of consecration.

Prayer.

May I transcend all self-limitation, pride and egotism;
May I be so humble and pure-hearted that the light of Truth will shine steadily
And shed its radiance through my whole being.
May my mind be so fixed on God that I shall forget myself utterly.

Salient Thought for the Day.

Unless a man is bereft of self, he cannot find God.

Lines to Memorize.

Love will give you light,
Love will give you faith and hope,
Love will bring you bliss;
Love will lead you,
Love will shield you—
Let love dwell in your soul.

Lesson.

Do you suppose you can lose your self-will through analysis? The only way it is wiped out is through excess of love. If unconsciously you become a larger center of self-expression, a greater Power will take your hands and mind and heart and express greater things through them. But this cannot come through calculation. What a wonderful treasure house the soul has through selfless love. You wipe out all, yet you have everything.

Prayer.

May the All-loving Spirit pour through my life a flood of Divine love.
May that love wash my heart clean of all selfishness.
May He grant unto me a new sight that I may see Him in all.
May I look to Him alone for all my joy and sustenance.
May I never grow weary in seeking Him;
And may my vision of Him always remain clear and unwavering.

SEPTEMBER SEVENTEENTH

Salient Thought for the Day.

Give and ask nothing in return.

Lines to Memorize.

Live and Love!
Love and live!
Where love reigns death can never be.
Love is mother of both joy and peace;
From that heart where love always lives peace and joy will never part.

Lesson.

We must have a focusing point. Light is everywhere, but we must focus it to use it. Similarly we must focus our spiritual thought, and we do this by serving our Ideal. A sense of worship and reverence is a very wonderful thing in this world. People who are cold, hard and aggressive miss a great deal.

Prayer.

All-merciful Lord, may I learn to serve Thee with my whole heart,
May every act of my life be an act of worship.
May my mind be fixed on the inward vision of Thy nearness,
And find peace and quietude in Thy Presence.
Bestow upon me humility of spirit, loyalty and unswerving devotion,
That I may live wholly for the Ideal
And seek to manifest it in every task of this day.

SEPTEMBER EIGHTEENTH

Salient Thought for the Day.

You cannot be devoted—heart and soul devoted—and not lose yourself.

Lines to Memorize.

Bereft of self,
Bereft of thought,
Save that Thou art all,
That I am wholly Thine
And all in Thee contained.
I am lost, and lost is all but Thee.

Lesson.

We cannot think of two opposite things at the same time. A man cannot think of God and at the same time keep his mind on his little self. Being devoted and whole-hearted in service to the Ideal, we realize the essence of all ideals. As we gain more understanding, the unfoldment of our higher nature takes place of itself. Then trust and surrender will come naturally to us and there will arise in us a sense of peace and quietude.

Prayer.

May the all-abiding Spirit dwelling within me
Make me a ready instrument in His Hand.
May He free me from all egotistic sense
And teach me to be wholly dependent on His Will.
May I forget all selfishness and limitation
And partake of His Divinity.

SEPTEMBER NINETEENTH

Salient Thought for the Day.

True devotees are those who never forget their Source.

Lines to Memorize.

When thou hast naught, thou hast all.
When thou art naught, thou art all.

Lesson.

Be an ideal devotee, an ideal disciple. Never forget that your indebtedness to God is incalculable. You can never do enough for Him and His children. To please Him by your life is the greatest thing that you can do. To displease Him by thought, word or action is your greatest misfortune. Nothing is more vital than to have the habit of constant mindfulness of your Source. You cannot afford to lose consciousness of that for one moment. Let your heart rest unceasingly in the thought of God.

Prayer.

O Lord, fill my heart with such pure love and devotion that there will be room for naught else.
Grant that I may be a worthy part of Thy Infinitude,
And learn to love and serve all Thy children worthily.
Thou art the Guardian Spirit of my soul ;
I offer to Thee my whole life.
Take it and make of it what Thou wilt.
I desire to be nothing apart from Thee.

Salient Thought for the Day.

The first duty of a devotee is to love God.

Lines to Memorize.

Thou hast bound me with Thy subtle thread of love.
I bless this fetter that binds me to Thee.
Bind Thou me more: my hands, my feet, my hearing and sight, my mind and heart; yea, bind them all by Thy magic thread of love.
I seek freedom no more.
Henceforth I am Thy captive,
To Thee I surrender my all!

Lesson.

Devotees are those who go direct to God. They say: "I want to know Him, I want to feel Him, I want to commune with him, I want to become one with Him." To know God vividly is to plunge into Him in silence. There is no time especially suited for this. At all times we can pray. In every hour of our life we can have a sense of consecration.

Prayer.

O Thou Eternal Unchanging One, unveil Thyself to me,
That I may find my peace and rest at Thy blessed Feet.
Thou art the Giver of all good things.
Grant unto me the power to love Thee with my Whole heart;
And to express that love in all that I may say and do through this day.

SEPTEMBER TWENTY-FIRST

Salient Thought for the Day.

Devotion is a thing that we feel inwardly. It is also a great power.

Lines to Memorize.

Thy flame of love touched my garment.
I was startled and affrighted lest all my possessions and cherished hopes be burned to nothingness.
I fled for fear of life, but Thy unquenchable fire ever followed me.
With troubled heart and misgiving I opened my eyes only to find
That Thy bright and blazing flame was not of destruction.
It burned, yet destroyed it naught.

Lesson.

There is nothing more potent than the heart of a pure, simple aspiring devotee. His prayers are potent because he does not pray for himself. They are answered because there is no selfishness or impurity in them. He can forget himself because he has something better to think of than himself. All doubt, scepticism and struggle give way before the light of the Spirit.

Prayer.

O Thou who art the Protector of all, protect me from my lower self,
Purify my heart and increase my devotion.
Take from me all discordant, selfish feelings;
And make me worthy to retain the blessings Thou dost pour upon me.

SEPTEMBER TWENTY-SECOND

Salient Thought for the Day.

Devotion unites us with the Cosmic Universe.

Lines to Memorize.

Thy love's lightning struck me;
I was dazed and motionless.
The fear of death, like a dark shadow, hung over me;
But Thy lightning danced and glowed and in its flash I found life again.
For this new gift I am more wholly Thine than I am mine.

Lesson.

When man really yearns for higher perception, when he feels that he must have his doubts removed, his darkness dispelled, then he opens his heart and gains Truth through the force of devotion. By faithful striving he earns access to his higher Being and becomes illumined. The Cosmic is always in our inner life, but we must call it out. We do this through steadfast faith, meditation and prayer.

Prayer.

O Thou All-pervading Deity, I offer Thee my thought and prayers in humble worship.
I approach Thee with wholeness of heart.
Help me to give all that I am, that I may be worthy to receive Thee.
May I never forget that only as I give all,
Can I be united with Thy infinite Being.
Accept my offering and grant me Thy peace.

SEPTEMBER TWENTY-THIRD

Salient Thought for the Day.

Through love one gains higher inspiration and light.

Lines to Memorize.

O Thou effulgent Spark, I fear Thee no more.
I love Thy Presence ; my soul delights in Thy Presence ;
Thy Presence is my supreme joy !

Lesson.

We are all waiting for the moment when we shall blend our feelings with the great feelings, our life with the great Life, Human beings can never be satisfied until they find ultimate vision. Now we are intoxicated with the sense of "I" and "mine". This "I" and "mine", this idea of separation from the Source, both are born of ignorance. When we partake of the universal, we lose all sense of limitation and separation.

Prayer.

All-blessed One, Thou art the shining radiance of the Universe
Through Thy light all things are revealed ;
Through Thy light we have the power of intelligence.
Fill my life with Thy Divine light that all my ignorance may vanish.
May I feel Thy Presence within my soul.
May I manifest Thy Presence in my life.

SEPTEMBER TWENTY-FOURTH

Salient Thought for the Day.

The practice of devotion gives us tangible power by which we experience things which at present seem unattainable.

Lines to Memorize.

Thy countenance of compassion has transfixed me.
All my wants are forgot ; I am lost yet fixed in Thee.
Lost am I in this wonder of wonders !

Lesson.

Spiritual attainment seems at times so distant that we even doubt our ability to acquire it, but all these doubts vanish when we approach the Light. When we turn our back to the Light, we do not see it. But when we turn our back to ourselves and our face towards the Light, we see it shining there steady and unfailing. Then if we follow it with undaunted spirit and fervent devotion, we reach the Highest.

Prayer.

May the Giver of all blessing bestow upon me the gift of a truer devotion.
May He teach me to depend upon Him for all power and strength.
May He help me to realize that He is behind my every thought and act,
That I am but His humble child, at all times led by His all-wise Hand.
May I walk in His light and follow His path at every step.

Salient Thought for the Day.

Whatever we do with whole-heartedness brings abundant results.

Lines to Memorize.

Love is a Divine essence.
Its inbreathing is life.
What is opposed to love is enemy of life.
Those who love truly, they live;
For love abounds in unending life.

Lesson.

There cannot be any devotion without whole-heartedness. There cannot be any devotion with calculation. As long as there is any element of calculation, there cannot be any real spiritual devotion. In the crude form of religion man may pray out of fear. He is afraid of a powerful revengeful Deity, so he bends his knee to be forgiven of his sins. But the man who is truly devoted bends his knee out of pure love and humble worship.

Prayer.

In this hour of prayer I lift my heart to the Divine Being;
May it receive the Divine touch and be inspired with new fervor.
May all the wounds of my heart be healed by that touch.
I bring all that I have and all that I am to that One
Who alone can give me fullness of life.

Salient Thought for the Day.

If we have true love in our hearts we can never be unhappy.

Lines to Memorize.

When Thou art near me I am filled with irrepressible joy.
Oft am I held speechless as I gaze on Thy unformed beauty.
Thou art ever silent, yet Thy voice resounds the sweet music of the universe.

Lesson.

How can anyone who has lived close to the Lord be anything but happy? Unless we can maintain unshaken devotion to the Ideal, we shall lose all our blessing. We must never doubt or question. When we learn to love and trust without reserve or questioning, there comes upon us a great peace and that peace has wonderful healing influence. It soothes and cheers. It makes us over and sets us free.

Prayer.

All-tender Lord, Thou art the embodiment of love.
Shed its purifying influence upon my mind and heart.
Quicken with new ardor my life of devotion, my aspiration and my prayers
Rouse in me greater spiritual yearning.
May my love for Thee be so great, my delight in Thee so unbounded
That I shall never yield to discouragement or discontent,
But shall ever live with Thee in peace.

SEPTEMBER TWENTY-SEVENTH

Salient Thought for the Day.

Selfless devotion unlocks the hidden door of the innermost Shrine.

Lines to Memorize.

Prepare for His coming;
Weave a garland for the Beloved,
Gathering all the sweet flowers from thy inner garden.
Hast thou not raised these cherished blossoms to please Him?
They are fragrant with thy love!
Lover, in excess of longing forget not the garland.

Lesson.

There is an outpouring of the soul, and in that outpouring there is a language strange to outer ears, but there are moments when this strange note brings great solace. We may utter beautiful prayers, but unless we are tuned in the same rhythm, they will have no power. Our heart will remain cold and unmoved. There is great strength in prayerful devotion. When the yearning soul prays with yearning voice from the depths of the heart, it cannot fail to reach the Lord and bring rich blessing.

Prayer.

O Thou Holy One, make me so pure and untouched by the world,
That I shall be worthy to enter Thy Divine sanctuary and lay my love and devotion at Thy blessed Feet.
May my life be as a fragrant flower, offering its sweetness unceasingly to Thee.

SEPTEMBER TWENTY-EIGHTH

Salient Thought for the Day.

A true lover always loves.

Lines to Memorize.

Think of love and speak of love;
Dream of love and sing of love—
Let love reign in your life.

Lesson.

Love cannot be a compulsion; but if you have not this rare gift, both human and Divine, what have you? You are deprived of everything. Why do we love? Because we have made ourselves avenues through which love flows. Love is a lubricant. Life is a machine which needs frequent oiling and love does this. We must never forget that hatred is conquered by love, harshness by gentleness. Do not brood over harm. Any ordinary man can brood over an injury, only the noble man forgives.

Prayer.

O Thou All-loving Deity, make me a clear channel through which Thy love may flow out to the world.
May I never harbor hatred or resentment in my heart.
May I be so pure and selfless that I shall be worthy to enter Thy Holy of holies,
And taste the sweetness of Thy Divine love.
Grant that I may never fail to share that love with all who suffer and are oppressed.

Salient Thought for the Day.

It is not that anyone lacks love, but the love is often misdirected.

Lines to Memorize.

It is beauty I love.
Though like the foolish moth
Oft I burn my limbs in the flame,
Yet evermore my soul craves its attainment,..
In love and with love
I seek the Maker of the Beautiful.

Lesson.

What bars the stream of love? Fear, petty thoughts, anxiety. If you would have it flow freely, you must free yourself from the habit of complaint and discontent. Never any complaining spirit enters into true discipleship. Love and selfless devotion to something higher alone give access. If we keep our mind fixed on the main end of our life, we shall attain it.

Prayer.

I lift my thought to the Supreme, who knows all my struggles and failures.
May He awaken in my heart a new sense of His abiding love,
And may that love flow back to Him in unceasing worship and devotion;
May it never turn to the objects of this world.
May He give me the power to consecrate myself to Him more fully,
And live in ever closer and closer contact with His holy Presence.

Salient Thought for the Day.

If you have enough love in your heart, you can overcome everything.

Lines to Memorize.

Love will conquer all your ills;
Love will heal your wounds;
Love will cleanse your stains;
Love will bring you peace.

Lesson.

We do our best work when we have least concern for our good fortune or ill fortune. All pain and hardship come from selfishness and lack of love. We create the web of self that binds us. We cannot love without bringing greater love and joy into our own life. Love is always a miracle. It breaks down all barriers. It is not by harshness that we can subdue harshness. It is by manifesting that which will make others feel the gentle, tender Power abiding in our heart.

Prayer.

O Lord, Thy gifts and blessings are distributed to all equally;
Unlock the door of my heart that I may receive them in fullest measure.
Flood my whole being with selfless love
That I may give myself freely in willing service;
And meet all trials and difficulties with undaunted spirit, because I find my strength in Thee.
May I love all men for Thy sake,
And serve them in Thy name.

Walk in the rhythm of life;
Your limbs will not tire.
Sing with the rhythm of life;
Your voice will gain sweetness.
Dance in the rhythm of life;
Your feet will not touch the ground.
Breathe in rhythm.
Think in rhythm.
Talk in rhythm.
Walk in rhythm.
Sing in rhythm.
Dance in rhythm.
Let rhythmic be your life.

(NOTE: The lines to be memorized throughout the month of October are taken from the Swami's translations of the Bhagavad-Gita and the Upanishads.)

October

RIGHT THOUGHT AND RIGHT ACTION

That man attains peace who, abandoning all desires, moves about without attachment and longing, without the sense of "I" and "mine." This is the state of dwelling in God; having attained this, no one is ever deluded. Being established in this knowledge even at the end of life, one attains oneness with the Supreme.

Bhagavad-Gita

OCTOBER FIRST

Salient Thought for the Day.

Keep your life in rhythm.

Lines to Memorize.

Surrendering mentally all actions to Me, regarding Me as the highest goal, resorting to Self-knowledge, do thou ever fix thy heart on Me. Fixing thy heart on Me, thou shalt, by My Grace, overcome all obstacles; but if, through egoism, thou wilt not hear Me, thou shalt perish.

Bhagavad-Gita

Lesson.

People who are in rhythm are full of mellowness; their voice is sweet. People who are unrhythmic, their voice is harsh and their life discordant. When you establish your life in rhythm, you do the right thing spontaneously. It is the way of wisdom to tune ourselves and bring ourselves into rhythm—our whole body, our mind, our heart, that they may all beat in unison. Nothing is impossible to us if we hold the right attitude of mind.

Prayer.

I lift my thoughts and prayers to the Supreme Being of the Universe;
May He make my heart free from all unworthy and alien thoughts,
That I may feel His great Infinitude
And dwell ever in the consciousness of His Presence.
May He free my heart from all discord and disharmony.

Salient Thought for the Day.

Rhythm is essential in every department of our life.

Lines to Memorize.

A wise man should control speech by mind, mind by intellect, intellect by the great Self, and that by the Peaceful One (the Supreme Self).

Katha-Upanishad

Lesson.

When a man is out of rhythm, whatever he undertakes cannot be in harmony with the universe. We can make ourselves rhythmic by going deeper and finding a point of contact with the inner Source of life. If we do everything with harmonious, sympathetic spirit, then we shall never fail to be in rhythm. It is a blessed privilege to be connected with the Lord's great human family and to serve it faithfully. We all possess the power of higher service. When we serve in true spirit, the seed of spiritual fruition is sown and we are bound to reap a rich harvest. The truest service is inward and consists in keeping ourselves in harmony with God's plan for our life.

Prayer.

May the All-abiding Spirit, Father and Mother of all living beings,
Grant me His loving, unfailing protection;
May I think only thoughts that are holy and uplifting to my soul.
May my heart be filled only with that which is pure, spiritual and sublime.
May all my words and actions be in unison with His great Heart and Mind.

OCTOBER THIRD

Salient Thought for the Day.

Your action must be vibrant. Your words must be sweet.

Lines to Memorize.

He who neither rejoices, nor hates, nor sorrows, nor desires, and who has renounced good and evil, he who is thus full of devotion is dear to Me. He who is the same to friend and foe and also in honor and dishonor, the same in heat and cold, pleasure and pain, free from all attachment, (he is dear to Me).

Bhagavad-Gita

Lesson.

Learn gentleness of speech, of step—gentleness in all your motions. Those who are in a higher state of evolution have great lightness in their touch and in their movements, in all they do. The tendency to be destructive, to overturn and to break indicates a wrong state of mind. When we move in perfect rhythm, we never destroy or hurt anything. Gentle manner and a sweet voice disarm all hatred and harshness. When we resist and assert ourselves, our action has no power other than to awaken a like spirit of resistance. Gentleness alone will overcome condemnation and anger.

Prayer.

O Lord, fill me with the spirit of love.
May I never wound or injure any living thing.
May self-interest never dominate my actions.
Make me gentle and kindly in all my dealings with my fellow-men.

Salient Thought for the Day.

Life is a ladder up which we go step by step.

Lines to Memorize.

The good and the pleasant approach man. The wise examines both and discriminates between them; the wise prefers the good to the pleasant, but the foolish man chooses the pleasant through love of bodily pleasure.

Katha-Upanishad

Lesson.

Balance is necessary. You cannot climb a ladder without balance. What does poise imply? That we are in a balanced, normal state. We should definitely cultivate this. There are certain fundamental principles which underlie everything, and life is not complete until we have our grasp on these. Poise and higher aspiration are among them. When life is full of non-essentials, we have no time for the essentials. We cannot lay emphasis on what is superficial without affecting the course of our destiny.

Prayer.

O Thou Eternal One, grant me wisdom,
That I may learn to fasten my little life to Thy great Eternal Life.
Merge my love in Thy unending Love.
Give me higher aspiration, more fervent devotion;
And help me more and more to realize that naught exists apart from Thy Supreme Existence.

OCTOBER FIFTH

Salient Thought for the Day.

If our real interest is in the Higher, the whole life will manifest it.

Lines to Memorize.

> The good is one thing and the pleasant another. These two, having different ends, bind a man. It is well with him who chooses the good. He who chooses the pleasant misses the true end.
>
> *Katha-Upanishad*

Lesson.

When we enter into true relationship with our fellow-men and with Divinity, we find our own true worth. We would all like to feel that fortified state of mind which comes from conscious connection with the Whole; but the ego brings a harsh, discordant note into our life and makes it barren and unhappy. It also creates unhappiness for other lives. It is through the ego that we say something unkind to another or that we hurt another; but we hurt ourselves more, because we cannot harm another without harming ourselves. Only one who is master of himself can help others to be happy.

Prayer.

O Thou Abiding Presence, do Thou manifest Thyself in my life.
May I never think of myself as a mortal perishable and frail;
But help me to realize that I am born of Spirit.
May I express spiritual grandeur in all I do and say and think,
And glorify Thee at every step.

OCTOBER SIXTH

Salient Thought for the Day.

Manifest Divine wisdom in your daily life.

Lines to Memorize.

Dangerous are the senses, they even carry away forcibly the mind of a discriminative man who is striving for perfection. The man of steady wisdom, having subdued them all (sense), becomes fixed in Me, the Supreme. His wisdom is well-established whose senses are under control.

Bhagavad-Gita

Lesson.

Chaos rises when all the lower instincts of man become uppermost. The bite of a rattlesnake is not half so dangerous as the sting of anger, envy, jealousy and hatred. They distort the mind and poise the whole system. The ways of the mind are countless. Every thought and deed causes a ripple or a wave in the mind-stuff. The most harmful ones we recognize are anger, hatred and jealousy. They are counteracted by waves of love, generosity, patience and unselfishness.

Prayer.

May the Supreme make me so strong and resolute in the spiritual path
That I may never follow my lower instincts
Or yield to the promptings of the senses.
May I show forth His love in all my service.
May I never give way to anger or hatred.
May my mind dwell in holy thought,
And my heart rest in His Infinite Heart.

OCTOBER SEVENTH

Salient Thought for the Day.

We must carry such balance with us that anyone looking into our face will feel new strength.

Lines to Memorize.

He who has not turned away from evil conduct, whose senses are uncontrolled, who is not tranquil, whose mind is not at rest, he can never attain this Great Self even by knowledge.

Katha-Upanishad

Lesson.

We must find time to balance our forces and faculties. Our spiritual power can be tremendously increased. It depends upon our balance and the common sense we use. Our character must be sound, our life must be rhythmic, then order and harmony will become natural to us. A mind that has a sense ot order puts everything where it belongs.

Prayer.

O Thou Infinite One, bestow upon me the gift of discrimination,
That I may cross over all difficulties and rough places trusting to Thy protection and guidance.
Kindle in me a new faith, a new surrender.
May I never seek to follow my own will
Or shape my life according to my own plan.
Help me never to retard my spiritual growth
By acting contrary to Thy Divine plan.
May I seek my peace in Thee alone.

OCTOBER EIGHTH

Salient Thought for the Day.

Bring fullness of spirit into every task.

Lines to Memorize.

If thou art unable to practise devotion, then be thou intent on working for Me. Even by performing actions for My sake, thou shalt attain perfection.

Bhagavad-Gita

Lesson.

If you have the right feeling, you do not need any other training. You cannot better yourself or equip yourself for your daily duties without getting a hold on the higher principles of life. It is only when we have the higher view that our lower instincts drop away. You must keep your mind clean and polished. It grows dull through neglect and collects alien substances. The secret of right action is to learn to do the greatest amount with the least output of energy. We do this by keeping in constant touch with the Source of supply.

Prayer.

May I never fail to serve the Ideal in all that I say and do.
May there be quickened in me a new and greater loyalty to It.
May my devotion for It grow ever more fervent.
May I be more earnest and ardent in my love,
And may my whole life become consecrated to the Highest.

OCTOBER NINTH

Salient Thought for the Day.

Every good action inspires one for another.

Lines to Memorize.

He who, with devotion offereth to Me a leaf, a flower, a fruit and water, that love-offering I accept, made by the pure-hearted,
Even if the most wicked worships me with undivided devotion, he should be regarded as good, for he is rightly resolved.

Bhagavad-Gita

Lesson.

You must do your work with a sense of sanctity and not feel that it is work. Do it in silence and without noise. We must not talk of it and make much of it. We must never bring a critical attitude towards it. Better not to work at all than to work with wrong spirit. Nothing is more purifying than unselfish work.

Prayer.

Compassionate One, I pray unto Thee to purify and spiritualize my whole life.
I have no power to do aught of myself,
But Thou art an inexhaustible Storehouse of power.
Inspire me to noble thought and action;
Lift my aspiration and make me steadfast in seeking and manifesting only that which is lofty and up-building.
May I never fail to serve Thee with unfaltering faith and devotion.

OCTOBER TENTH

Salient Thought for the Day.

A noble soul is always noble in all circumstances.

Lines to Memorize.

When a man is satisfied in the (higher) Self by Self alone and has completely cast out all desires from the mind, then he is said to be of steady wisdom. When he completely withdraws his senses from sense-objects as the tortoise withdraws its limbs, then his wisdom becomes well-established.

Bhagavad-Gita

Lesson.

Thoughts are as fragrant as flowers. They sweeten our life. He who is protected by pure spiritual thought is always safe. Whatever we put in the soil of life, we must expect a like fruition. The seed of discord is planted in the human heart and the spirit of inharmony is born there. Also the spirit of harmony and peace and nobility come out from that same heart.

Prayer.

O Thou All-pervading Deity, help me never to forget that I am a child of Divinity.

May I speak only what is worthy of a child of God.

May I think only what is worthy of a child of God.

May I do only what is worthy of a child of God.

May my life be wholly one with Thy universal Life.

OCTOBER ELEVENTH

Salient Thought for the Day.

Freedom is a condition of greatness; it is self-caused. We bind and free ourselves.

Lines to Memorize.

Those who constantly practise this teaching of Mine with true faith and devotion and unflinching heart, they too are freed from the fetters of action. But those who find fault with My teaching and do not follow it, such self-deluded ones, devoid of all knowledge and discrimination, know them to be ruined.

Bhagavad-Gita

Lesson.

As long as our mind is confined and narrow and self-centered, we can never bring anything fruitful into our actions. We must live in the material world without becoming material. We must gain knowledge without the arrogance that learning sometimes brings. From our thought comes our inspiration for action. When our mind is peaceful and focused, we gain a tremendous power for usefulness.

Prayer.

O Thou All-beneficent Spirit, who alone knowest my innermost feelings, who alone canst answer my prayers,
I open my heart to Thee with childlike and guileless simplicity.
Do Thou free me from all that is unworthy, —from pride, ambition, vanity and egotism;
From all that binds me to my lower selfish nature.

OCTOBER TWELFTH

Salient Thought for the Day.

We are made strong by our thought. We are weakened by our thought.

Lines to Memorize.

Those whose ignorance is destroyed by Self-knowledge, their knowledge of the Self, like the sun, illumines the Supreme. Those whose heart and soul are absorbed in That Supreme, who are steadily devoted to That and regard That as their highest goal, they go never to return, their sins (impurities) being washed off by wisdom.

Bhagavad-Gita

Lesson.

How necessary it is that we guard our thoughts and do not make evil contacts. If we do not guard our thoughts, we shall be the losers. We contact the high points and the low points of the universe by our thought. It we keep our mind on a high point with steadfastness and continue to hold it there, the result will be a great awakening. If it is not held there, it will drop to a low point. It rests with each individual to determine where the mind will make its contact.

Prayer.

I offer up my thoughts and my prayers to the Supreme Being.
May He make my heart in tune with the great Infinite Existence.
May He shake off from my mind all petty, ignoble thoughts,
And fill both my mind and heart with loving, harmonious and pure feelings
That through these feelings, I may gain contact with His Divine Being.

OCTOBER THIRTEENTH

Salient Thought for the Day.

We can magnify our problems and we can minimize them.

Lines to Memorize.

> If, actuated by egoism thou thinkest: "I will not fight," in vain is this thy resolve. Thine own nature will impel thee. . . . Take refuge in Him with all thy heart; through His grace thou shalt attain Supreme Peace and the Eternal Abode.
>
> *Bhagavad-Gita*

Lesson.

No one can solve our spiritual problems for us. No one can hinder their solution. We ourselves hinder our own life and spiritual possibilities. We must find some higher way of working out our problems and the practical way is the higher way. When a man becomes conscious of his spiritual value, he will no longer be tempted to do anything petty or ignoble. If we do not order our life, if we do not fortify ourselves, how can we hope to flourish?

Prayer.

May that One from whom nothing is hidden,
May He surround me with His blessings
And guide me by His wise and unfailing Hand.
May He give me strength and wisdom to follow His path.
Through His Grace, may I learn to be God-abiding in all my thoughts, words and actions.

OCTOBER FOURTEENTH

Salient Thought for the Day.

We must fortify ourselves with practical wisdom.

Lines to Memorize.

He whose mind is not agitated in calamities and who has no longing for pleasure, free from attachment, fear and anger, he indeed is said to be a saint of steady wisdom. He who is free from all attachment and neither rejoices on receiving good nor is vexed on receiving evil, his wisdom is well-established.

Bhagavad-Gita

Lesson.

It is not everything to find out the cause of our misery, we must find some means to eliminate it; and nothing does this so well as practical wisdom. There is no need of failing down, if we fortify our house against attack. We fortify our houses against flies and insects; all the more should we fortify our spiritual house against jealousy, hatred, anger and petty thoughts. If mind is not regulated, we shall not accomplish even the outer results we desire.

Prayer.

May all the pulsations of my body, mind and heart be in rhythm and harmony,
That I may feel the Presence of the great Infinite within me and all about me.
May the Supreme Spirit of the Universe bestow on me the light of true understanding.
May He help me to do each task of this day wisely and with ardor of devotion.

OCTOBER FIFTEENTH

Salient Thought for the Day.

You outrage yourself and your spiritual Ideal when you harbor any evil thought.

Lines to Memorize.

> Those who are full of desires for self-gratification, ... whose discrimination is stolen away by the love of power and pleasure and who are thus deeply attached therein, (for such people) it is impossible to obtain either firm conviction in purpose or God-consciousness.
>
> *Bhagavad-Gita*

Lesson.

Our state of mind opens or closes certain avenues for us. In one state of mind, we get answers to our problems ; we are contended and happy. In certain other states of mind our thought is distracted and we accomplish nothing. If we know how to operate and organize and govern the forces of our life, we derive great benefit from them. We also gain balance, poise and efficiency.

Prayer.

O Thou Bestower of Peace !
Do Thou awaken my spirit
And fill my heart with unbroken love.
Make me conscious of Thy Divine Presence,
That I may rise above all the afflictions of the world of matter,
And live ever in joyful communion with Thee.
May I serve Thee with wholeness and earnestness of heart.

Salient Thought for the Day.

Motive is the greatest factor in all action.

Lines to Memorize.

One whose attachment is gone, who is liberated, whose mind is well-established in wisdom, who works for sacrifice alone, his whole Karma (bondage) melts away ...... Thus by performing actions with the consciousness of the Supreme, he reaches the Supreme alone.

Bhagavad-Gita

Lesson.

It is the natural thing that when there is any vacancy, Mother Nature fills it. It is filled with that for which we open the channel. If we form the habit of holding wholesome, beneficial, upbuilding thought, it will act like magic in our life. There is great harm done by discordant thought; but there is no harm we cannot remedy, nothing we cannot mend. Thought when it becomes inward has such power that it can transform our life and other lives.

Prayer.

Thou who art the Giver of all,
Give unto me the spirit of understanding,
That I may learn to rely on Thy Grace
And find my sustenance in and through Thee.
Abiding Spirit, surround me with Thy protecting love.
Grant me greater earnestness and wisdom,
And fill my life with Thy holy Peace.

OCTOBER SEVENTEENTH

Salient Thought for the Day.

Do not let us play false with ourselves.

Lines to Memorize.

> He who, restraining the organs of action, sits holding thoughts of sense-objects in his mind, that self-deluded one is called a hypocrite. But he who, controlling the senses by the mind, follows without attachment the path of action with his organs of action, he is esteemed.
>
> *Bhagavad-Gita*

Lesson.

You must order your life in such a way that you need not explain yourself. Your action will be sufficing, your word will be sufficing. Whatever thought we send out to the world, we receive similar thoughts in response from the cosmic universe. A thought is like a note in music, it produces a volume of sound which has a broader scope than we imagine. We may think that our thoughts are only for ourselves, but they cover a large area and have a wide influence. That man is noble who thinks and does his best when he is unseen and unheard.

Prayer.

O Thou Embodiment of all blessing,
I lift unto Thee my prayer with guileless heart.
Free it from all discordant feelings
That I may sense Thy Presence within me,
And breathe the atmosphere of pure holiness
radiating from that Presence.
May It purify and strengthen me
And make me more worthy.

Salient Thought for the Day.

Man is born erect.

Lines to Memorize.

He by whom the world is not afflicted and who is not afflicted by the world, who is free from elation, envy, fear and anxiety, he is dear to Me. He who is free from all external dependence, pure, efficient, unattached, undisturbed, and has given up all selfish undertakings, he who is thus devoted to Me is dear to Me.

Bhagavad-Gita

Lesson.

The first stepping-stone to manhood is manhood itself. A man must be a man. He must exemplify manhood. What is a gentleman? He is gentle, big, noble; he is independent of opinion. He does not think evil. Evil thoughts are as creative as good thoughts. A man cannot have happiness until he has obtained certain qualities of mind. When he has obtained these qualities, nothing can overthrow him.

Prayer.

May my thoughts turn to Him from whom comes all my blessing.
May I bring unto Him with childlike simplicity my actions and all that is produced through my actions.
May He sanctify my life and every part of my life.
May nothing be hidden from Him;
May nothing remain without His sanction.

OCTOBER NINETEENTH

Salient Thought for the Day.

You should think and act in direct line. There must be no crookedness in your thought or action.

Lines to Memorize.

He who is without discrimination and whose mind is always uncontrolled, his senses are unmanageable, like the vicious horses of a driver. But he who is full of discrimination and whose mind is always controlled, his senses are manageable, like the good horses of a driver.

Katha-Upanishad

Lesson.

Mind embraces that which is disturbing and undesirable; but it is not a natural state, not a natural state because every individual suffers when his mind is out of balance. Man cannot take a destructive attitude without destroying himself. He cannot indulge in hatred, anger, jealousy, without working his own ruin. You must try to cultivate lofty thoughts and feelings. Then it will be impossible for you to do anything ignoble.

Prayer.

O Thou Revealer of all things!
It is Thy light that reveals all the hidden-most parts of my being.
Safe-guard me against all ignorance and darkness.
Fill my mind and heart with Thy radiance,
That I may walk on the path of life as Thou dost reveal it to me.

Salient Thought for the Day.

Every thought you think has its special weight and import.

Lines to Memorize.

> He who is moderate in eating and recreation, moderate in his efforts in work, moderate in sleep and wakefulness, his spiritual practice becomes the destroyer of all misery.
>
> *Bhagavad-Gita*

Lesson.

When mind is afflicted, bodily health shows it very quickly. A well-ordered mind and body bring health and happiness. There is an order in the system ; and when we work in harmony with that order, health and happiness result. We do not need to be disturbed by outside things. It rests with us how we shall be affected by them. If we eat normally, drink normally, think normally, our power is bound to increase. That which we acquire normally, that is abiding. When all our actions and thoughts are balanced and normal, life does not weary us. It is not work or activity which tires. Work never wears us out. It is the state of mind which wears or renews.

Prayer.

In this hour of silent prayer, I give myself wholly to That One,
Who alone can grant the desires of my heart.
He alone can fill all emptiness.
He is the life-giving Breath of all beings.
He is the Divine principle of all existence.
May my mind and heart rest in Him.

OCTOBER TWENTY-FIRST

Salient Thought for the Day.

Your whole nature is built of the thoughts you hold in your mind.

Lines to Memorize.

> Therefore, at all times, think of Me and fight (perform actions). Having offered thy mind and intellect to Me thou shalt without doubt come unto Me.
>
> *Bhagavad-Gita*

Lesson.

If you think of holy things you become holy. If your heart is always filled with love, no hatred can penetrate; nothing can mar your peace and tranquillity. But the law works the other way also. If you are careless and let alien thoughts persist, they will change your nature. Whenever you criticize anyone, or find fault with anyone, or think evil of anyone, that evil comes to you. By dwelling on a saintly character we become saintly. That picture of saintliness will inspire us, throw light on our path and transform our nature.

Prayer.

I open my heart, my mind, all the avenues of my soul,
That I may feel the Presence of the blessed Infinite One.
May my life be in tune with that great abiding Spirit;
May my heart sing supplications unto Him.
May my spirit surrender unto Him with understanding and devotion.

Salient Thought for the Day.

We lift our thought by constant devotion to our Ideal.

Lines to Memorize.

> By the steadfast practice of meditation with unwavering mind (not moving elsewhere) and constant thought of the Supreme Divine Being, one goes to Him.
>
> *Bhagavad-Gita*

Lesson.

We have to meditate on something. Our mind must dwell on some object. According to what he thinks upon, a man can create an atmosphere of radiance, exuberance, buoyancy; and this brings joy. Or he can carry gloom with him. It is a matter of habit of thought. If a man's thought, aspiration and action are one, that man is free. He does not blunder. We must build up our own life by our thought. There are many ways by which we can do this. Art, music, even manual work, all can bring ripening to the soul.

Prayer.

Grant, O Lord, that through this day nothing may disturb the peace of my thought.
May I radiate love and joyousness.
May I keep my eyes fixed upon Thee
And meet each problem with courage and surrender.
Help me to keep my heart pure and full of devotion,
And at all times may it rest close to Thy Divine Heart.

OCTOBER TWENTY-THIRD

Salient Thought for the Day.

Every man must have a lofty Ideal.

Lines to Memorize.

He who thus understands truly My Divine birth and action is not born again on leaving his body, but he attains unto Me. Freed from attachment, fear and anger, being absorbed in Me and taking refuge in Me, purified by the fire of wisdom, many have attained My Being.

Bhagavad-Gita

Lesson.

Our spiritual experience is not shut away from our human experience. Our daily life is closely inter-related with our spiritual life. We mingle the two by prayer and devotion to an Ideal. But it is not enough to ask for material things; our prayer must be that our eye of understanding may be opened. It is very necessary for us to cleanse and polish the mind. A clean mind is one of the most beneficial thing we can acquire. It can become like a polished mirror, giving a perfect reflection.

Prayer.

O Thou All-wise One, teach me in each task to act wisely and with understanding spirit.
Grant that I may rest wholly in Thy Being,
And draw my inspiration only from Thee.
May I seek Thy aid in the moments of perplexity,
And turn to Thee alone for help and guidance.

Salient Thought for the Day.

It is not by thinking of ourselves we save ourselves.

Lines to Memorize.

> Those who, surrendering all actions to Me and regarding Me as the Supreme Goal, worship Me with single-hearted devotion, for them whose hearts are thus fixed on Me, I become ere long the Saviour from the ocean of this mortal world of birth and death.
>
> *Bhagavad-Gita*

Lesson.

Great souls are never caught in the net of the personal. They are not conscious of small, petty things. When people lack higher idealism, they give way easily to brooding and despondency and they depress others. We cannot conceive of God as other than all-loving. Fear is not the seed of religion. More we are actuated by love, more inspiration we shall have, more imbued we shall be with higher feeling.

Prayer.

All-pervading Deity, quicken in me a new sense of Thy Divine Being,
That my little self may be lost in Thy great Self.
Make my heart humble and free from all selfish concerns.
Grant that I may always extend a helping hand to others,
And lose myself utterly in service to all Thy children.
May I trust at all times to Thy saving Grace.

OCTOBER TWENTY-FIFTH

Salient Thought for the Day.

We must keep our mind pure, watchful and open to the higher realm of thought.

Lines to Memorize.

> Forsaking egoism, power, pride, lust, anger and possession freed from the notion of "mine" and tranquil; one is thus fit to become one with the Supreme. Becoming one with the Supreme, serene-minded, he neither grieves nor desires; alike to all beings, he attains supreme devotion unto Me.
>
> *Bhagavad-Gita*

Lesson.

The reaction of one who keeps on brooding is gloominess, like a thick cloud. We can never afford to take a discontented or careless attitude. When we understand the law of life, it is seldom we take a frowning attitude, towards ourselves, towards others, or towards God. No aloofness from our fellow-men can insure us connection with the Heart of God. When we perceive that a thing is detrimental, what can we do? Counteract it. In the presence of light, darkness vanishes. In the presence of God, evil falls down.

Prayer.

May the All-loving Spirit of the Universe free me from all self-interest and self-assertion;
May I shed abroad love and love alone.
May love be to me an armor and my only weapon.
May His life-giving power infill me
And cleanse me from all arrogance.

OCTOBER TWENTY-SIXTH

Salient Thought for the Day.

We do not lift our burden by ceasing our work but by learning how to do it.

Lines to Memorize.

> Therefore, being unattached, perform thy duties (the work that ought to be done) unceasingly; for through the performance of action, unattached, man attains the highest.
>
> *Bhagavad-Gita*

Lesson.

If we want to succeed in life it must be through unification of effort. All parts of our being must cooperate. It is not enough to have material prosperity, we must also have knowledge; otherwise we cannot truly prosper. We must not keep on doing those things which are detrimental to our soul's well-being. Under anger, fear, jealousy or vanity, the better part of us suffers. Vanity is one of the greatest drawbacks in human life. It springs from a shallow nature.

Prayer.

May I realize more and more that my life is what I make it by my silent thoughts and actions.

May I never yield to vanity, discouragement, or envy of others more fortunate than myself.

May all my habits of body and mind be wholesome and strength-giving.

May I be faithful in the performance of each task;

And never grow weary or prove unworthy of blessing.

OCTOBER TWENTY-SEVENTH

Salient Thought for the Day.

The great secret of life is to learn to maintain an even tenor in the midst of all things.

Lines to Memorize.

The steady-minded, by giving up all attachment for the fruits of action, obtains peace, born of steadfastness. The unsteady, being attached to fruits through desire, is ever bound by action.

Bhagavad-Gita

Lesson.

We must give up, not because we are dejected or battered. We must give up because there has come a certain ripening within. Life as a rule does not run evenly. It has many ups and downs. It has many changes. But those who have found the way of wisdom, have learned how to maintain evenness in spite of all the unevenness which circumstances offer. We do not accomplish this by calculation or by any material means. We accomplish it by going within and attaining inner tranquillity.

Prayer.

O Thou who art One and All-abiding,
I offer up my thoughts, words and actions unto Thee.
Grant that each act of the day may be an act of devotion.
Thou art the Source of my being;
I turn to Thee in whole-hearted love and trust.
In Thee alone do I find rest and satisfaction.
From Thee alone can I draw life and strength.

OCTOBER TWENTY-EIGHTH

Salient Thought for the Day.

One who wants nothing gets everything.

Lines to Memorize.

Those who worship Me and meditate on Me without any other thought, to these ever steadfast devotees I secure safety and supply all their needs (I carry their burden).

Bhagavad-Gita

Lesson.

One can have nothing, yet possess a sense of princely heritage. What is renunciation? It is giving up self-limitation; it means no longer yielding to a lower order of things. So many people want happiness with a fervent longing, but the fever of self keeps them from attaining it. As our outlook changes, we outgrow the limitations of greed, pride, envy and all the narrowness of the little self. An awakened soul is never touched by earthly things. When we have very high fever we are delirious and everything is distorted. So with the fever of the world—it makes us lose our sense of proportion.

Prayer.

May the All-abiding Deity liberate me from the bondage of desire;
Through His Grace may I never forget that He alone is my Wealth and the Source of my life.
May I seek no possession apart from Him.
May He help me to realize that the objects of this world are fleeting and perishable,
That He alone is eternal, unchanging and indestructible.

OCTOBER TWENTY-NINTH

Salient Thought for the Day.

When a sense of our oneness with the Infinite comes, all the petty details of life cease to bind us.

Lines to Memorize.

He who works for Me, has Me for his highest goal, is devoted to Me, is free from attachment and bears enmity toward no creature, he enters into Me.

Bhagavad-Gita

Lesson.

The small mind cannot partake of the big. Now we have formed the habit of living in a certain consciousness and we are afraid to change, although we know that what we have is not the best. If, however, we consent to change, a new world will open before us—the world of Spirit. We breathe freely in that higher sphere of consciousness and we become imbued more and more with the Spirit of God.

Prayer.

O Thou Infinite Being, so infill me with Thy Presence
That I shall never bind myself by self-created fetters.
Expand my heart and mind,
That I may gain bigness of vision and largeness of feeling.
May I no longer be content with what is small and non-essential,
But may I live wholly in Thee who art the essence of all things.

Salient Thought for the Day.

Forsake harsh speech.

Lines to Memorize.

From anger arises delusion; from delusion, loss of memory is caused. From loss of memory, the discriminative faculty is ruined and from the ruin of discrimination man perishes. But the self-subjugated attains peace and moves among objects with the senses under control, free from any longing or aversion.

Bhagavad-Gita

Lesson.

Let there be nothing harsh, nothing discordant in your heart. How can anyone dare to be unkind? If you were not thwarted, how would you practise forbearance and fortitude? Humility, gentleness and forbearance will save you. Great souls, when they are humbled or condemned or crushed, rise up stronger than ever. Arm yourself with gentleness and non-resistance and you will always be safe. A lasting impression is made only by a subtle gentleness. Aggressive methods never create anything enduring.

Prayer.

Thou who art the Embodiment of all blessedness,
Grant me the blessing of kindness, forbearance and gentleness.
May I never hurt or wound any one of Thy children.
I open my heart to Thee—cleanse it of all selfishness and harshness;
And fill it with Thy Divine love.

OCTOBER THIRTY-FIRST

Salient Thought for the Day.

Remember : Humility, Love and Tolerance every hour of the day.

Lines to Memorize.

He who is alike in praise and blame, is silent, content with everything, homeless, steady-minded, such a devoted soul is dear to Me. Those who follow this immortal teaching as declared by Me and who are possessed with faith, regarding Me as the Supreme Goal, such devotees are exceedingly dear to Me.

Bhagavad-Gita

Lesson.

When our heart is humble, then we never quarrel or criticize; we only love, and love ever breeds tolerance. Without humility, love and tolerance we cannot be in harmony. Try to cultivate these three with tireless spirit. When we succeed in keeping our mind in tune, in intuitive rhythm, then, whatever difficulties may overtake us, nothing can thwart us.

Prayer.

All-tender Mother of the Universe, I bring Thee yearning heart;
Make it lowly, forgiving and gentle.
May I feel sympathy with all living things.
May my whole life be imbued with Thy Divine tenderness,
And may each hour of this day be filled with loving acts and loving words.

NOTES

Beloved Guide, my soul's Safe-keeper,
Thy firm but gentle hand of wisdom hath saved me from falling over the precipice of life many, many times.
In my childish whims how oft have I disregarded Thy pleadings and warnings,
Yet Thy tender love and unchanging patience have ever shielded me.
Oft my own hope and courage abandon me,
But Thou dost never forsake me.
Thou hast given me all; yea, more than this small vessel of mine can hold.
Naught have I to offer Thee save this unworthy life,
Which is already Thine.

November

UNFALTERING TRUST AND SURRENDER

Take refuge in Him with all thy heart; through His grace thou shall attain Supreme Peace and the Eternal Abode.

Bhagavad-Gita

NOVEMBER FIRST

Salient Thought for the Day.

We are led and guided by a Divine Hand and that Hand is never absent.

Lines to Memorize.

It is Thy Hand that tightens my heart-strings through pain.
Again Thy gentle Hand slackens the cords.
Master Musician, Thou playest on this frail instrument.
I sing or sigh at Thy touch.

Lesson.

God is watching over us all, those who are gone beyond the border line and those who are in the flesh. He is taking care of us now and always will do so. Let your heart rest in peace. Our safety and protection are in His keeping and He never fails us. He may chide or He may bless us in tender indulgence, but both rebuke and blessing come from Him and must be fruitful of good.

Prayer.

O Thou All-protecting One,
Not one moment can I live apart from Thee.
Thy Hand guides me,
Thy love shields me,
Thy wisdom leads me—
Help me to realize this
And yield myself up wholly to Thy guidance and protection.

NOVEMBER SECOND

Salient Thought for the Day.

Our life flourishes when it is connected with its Source.

Lines to Memorize.

In this hour of meditation I lift my whole heart to Thee.
Fill it, my Lord, else I dwell in emptiness!
Charge me with yearning thought.
Let my heart be filled with Thy all-absorbing love;
Let there be no vacant space in me where Thy love hath not entered.

Lesson.

We can only receive in exact proportion as we give. We must give fully, if we would receive fully. The Divine Mother knows Her own and when She attracts, no power can resist. Blessed are those who are attracted to be blessed. The Divine Mother will take all possible care of us and give us Her Divine protection, if we will only put our trust in Her and pray to Her unceasingly.

Prayer.

May the Divine Mother who is the Source of my life and strength,
May She surround me with Her wise protection.
May I look to Her for all things,
And never lose hold on Her Divine Hand.
May the veil of selfishness never blind my eyes to Her glory;
May my heart never be closed to Her all-filling love.

NOVEMBER THIRD

Salient Thought for the Day.

The all-beneficent Power never fails us. It is always ready to shield us and guide us and help us.

Lines to Memorize.

Great Mother Heart, how tender art Thou!
Thy love, transcending all mine iniquities,
Pours upon my life its benign sweetness.
How oft my imperfect nature lies mortified and by Thy unfathomed tenderness;
Who art Thou that givest this endless bounty to me, meritless and ignorant?

Lesson.

Surrender yourself entirely unto the Divine Mother, then there will be no danger. Take good care of your spiritual life in every way and never neglect anything. Then Mother's blessings will ever surround you and keep you safe. She will guide and protect you. Be always careful about everything. Remember She has a tender mother heart and always holds you close!

Prayer.

All-protecting Mother, help me to open my heart to Thee with sincere and spontaneous devotion.
I am Thy little child, ever in need of Thy watchful care.
Make Thy mother-love felt in my heart.
May I yield myself up wholly to Thy love.
And never fail to lean upon Thee in willing submission to Thy Will.

NOVEMBER FOURTH

Salient Thought for the Day.

No man is strong enough to stand alone.

Lines to Memorize.

How long wilt Thou play this game of hide and seek ?
May we not play another that keeps us always together ?

Lesson.

Those who have their eyes open, instead of lifting their own hand in defense, they look wholly to God for protection. Whenever, we lift up our petty little self, we strike a discordant note and we deal a blow at our higher Self. When we have perfect trust in God, we cease to be petty and small in our thought and action. It is always the ego that betrays us and makes us unworthy. If we see only God everywhere and trust entirely to Him, what will happen to us ? It will purify us ; it will sanctify us ; it will free us from all pain and selfishness.

Prayer.

May the All-campassionate One shield me from the onslaughts of pride and egotism.
May He fill my heart with undaunted trust
And make me holy, selfless and uplifted.
May I look to Him at every hour for guidance
And cease to live or act apart from His all-encompassing wisdom.

NOVEMBER FIFTH

Salient Thought for the Day.

We must have whole-hearted devotion, if we would establish our connection with the Highest.

Lines to Memorize.

Divine Mother Heart, proof of Thy
unceasing care I find in every turn of life.
With many arms dost Thou shield me;
With many hearts dost Thou love me;
With many minds dost Thou guide me to the road of safety.

Lesson.

It is indeed a great blessing when we realize the emptiness of the vanities of the world and our utter helplessness, and turn to God with our whole heart. Pray that a new awakening may come in your heart and make you steadfast and faithful to your Ideal. If you depend solely on the higher resources and put all your devotion into your task, you can accomplish anything. Intuition and feeling are our safeguards. We better ourselves only as we make our connection with the abiding Essence of our existence.

Prayer.

In this hour of communion I lift up my prayer unto Thee,
Make it living and vibrant.
Fill me with spiritual longing,
That I may gain access to the Unlimited and Eternal.
Thy love enfolds me;
Thy care protects me;
What need have I of aught but Thy blessed Presence and Thy unfailing love.

Salient Thought for the Day.

If you maintain contact with Infinitude, you will never be hurt or unhappy.

Lines to Memorize.

On the lonely trail of my life as I walk alone
How oft I feel distressed and desolate.
Stranded and helpless I look for my course.
Only the trailing light of Thy garment ever leads me on to follow Thee.

Lesson.

We want help, but we close the only avenue through which help can come. We have to be empty of self before higher influences can enter into us. Whenever we act according to our self-will we are thwarted. What people may say or do to you does not matter, if the contact with your Source is open and clear. Infinitude is an attribute of the soul. We perceive It through purity, through our fervor, through our power of discrimination.

Prayer.

O Thou Eternal One, do Thou reveal Thyself to me in Thy glory,
That I may learn to trust in Thee more fully,
And give myself up more wholly unto Thee.
May I never fail to hear Thy voice.
May I never close the door to Thy approach.
May I open my heart wide to Thy Divine influence,
And seek all my help from Thee alone.

NOVEMBER SEVENTH

Salient Thought for the Day.

Infuse your life with That which can be relied upon and trusted.

Lines to Memorize.

What hath chanced since Thou didst cast upon me Thy merciful glance and fill me with Thy Divine Being?
Naught is left of me, or what I thought was "I";
What remains of me is Thou and Thine.
The thought of self and "I", my desires and prayers, are all lost in Thee.

Lesson.

As we realize our higher Self, we have no longer any quarrel with life. It is a question of blending ourselves with the Great Power. We free ourselves by higher knowledge; and as we free ourselves, we manifest higher attributes. We must make room for every blessing. We must empty our heart before it can be filled.

Prayer.

O Thou Unchanging One, Source of my strength, my Support and Refuge,
I lay my life humbly at Thy blessed Feet;
Use it as Thou seest fit;
I am Thine own.
One thing alone I ask of Thee—
That Thou wilt inspire me with holy thought
And impel me to holy action.

Salient Thought for the Day.

Complete faith and surrender are perfectly practical in the spiritual life.

Lines to Memorize.

Anything or nothing,—I am content if it be Thy Will.
When Thou dost dwell in my heart feel no lack of things of this world.
Only one thing I ask of Thee—
That Thou dost abide with me always and evermore.

Lesson.

There is nothing impossible unto God. If we can only yield ourselves to His beneficent Will, no ill can touch us. It is through surrender that we know the Will of the Great One. What a pity it is when we forget the One who is always ready to guide us and protect us. When we have surrendered, all our troubles cease; not that they have been eliminated, but we have risen above them.

Prayer.

O Thou Giver of all strength, fill me with new strength and power;
Free me from all weakness and faltering.
May I never seek safety or protection apart from Thee;
Thou alone canst guide me and bring me fulfillment.

NOVEMBER NINTH

Salient Thought for the Day.

Through trust we approach nearer and nearer to the Supreme.

Lines to Memorize.

I will cling to Thee with all the might of my soul ;
I hold fast to Thy Hand which is full of saving,
With all the strength of my heart's devotion.
Do not look upon me and mine iniquities.
They will fly and have no place in me
If Thou wilt but cast upon me Thy merciful glance.

Lesson.

Spiritual trust gives us a conception of Divine Being. With calculation or mere intellectual grasp we can go only so far, but by spiritual surrender there is no limit to our progress. When a man has given up harsh, unkind feelings, he cleanses his own house and prepares for the Lord's coming. When we are in need, He will not fail to come.

Prayer.

O Thou Infinite Being, make me realize that I am part of Thy Infinitude.
Help me to forget my selfishness and limitation,
And become worthy to partake of Thy Divinity.
May I love all and serve all for Thy sake :
And seek no life or joy apart from Thee.

NOVEMBER TENTH

Salient Thought for the Day.

We live truly when we live in God. We walk steadily when we give our hand to Him.

Lines to Memorize.

Come hither, O friend, I shall tell thee the secret of this unknown land.
Let us shut the outer gates and the inner doors.
Have no fear or doubt, for the strange Guide to this unknown land is marvelous wise.
He knoweth our unacted acts; nay, even our unformed thoughts, our life's pulsation and every heartstring in His grasp.

Lesson.

We are all children of Divinity and we all have the same right to go to the Divine for help. We all belong equally to the Supreme Power. God takes us as we are. We must go to Him as His children. We must go to Him with the feeling that we are related to Him. Does a tender parent chide a child for falling down? He does not rebuke us for blundering; all He wants is that we do not give up.

Prayer.

Thou Effulgent Spirit, redeem and restore me.
May Thy light guide and protect me.
May It surround me and abide ever in my consciousness.
Thou art the Light of the Universe.
Thou art the Light of my life.
Shine with Thy full effulgence on my path,
That I may walk with Thee in peace and safety.

NOVEMBER ELEVENTH

Salient Thought for the Day.

By life in God we overcome all weakness.

Lines to Memorize.

When I hold Thy Hand and look on Thy smiling Face
My heart is filled with childish confidence
And I think that Thou couldst never hide from me again.
When Thou dost hide from me,
I am powerless to find Thee.

Lesson.

We do not grasp Infinitude by alertness of mind. It comes rather the opposite way. We resign, we surrender. When we do this, the true picture comes in the mind. Our hands and feet can work efficiently only when they are directed by a higher intelligence, so we accomplish very little unless we are under the guidance of a Higher Power. There is only one Doer, but we forget. It is He who is working through us. There is an unfailing Power that works in us. When we are in right avenues, nothing will be lacking.

Prayer.

Infinite Spirit! Thou art the Reality of my life;
Thou art the Storehouse from which I draw my strength;
Thou art the Source of all my power.
Without Thee I cannot speak or think or act.
I give myself unto Thee,
Do with me what Thou wilt.

Salient Thought for the Day.

When we trust wholly in the Infinite we cease to be small. Our blindness and our deafness are removed.

Lines to Memorize.

Strange way is this mystic way—
And more strange without a Guide.
Poor wayfarers oft are stranded and sit at its very gate, not knowing it is there.
One who leads thee through its mysterious doors is thy Spirit Friend.
Trust Him with all thy heart.

Lesson.

The point of contact with God can come only when we are in rhythm with the Divine. This being of ours can be tuned to such perfect unison with God that it will move at all times in harmony with Him. Also we can become so out of tune that all we do will be out of rhythm with everything in life. When we realize our true nature, we gain contact with Infinitude and the spirit of surrender awaken in our heart.

Prayer.

The Supreme is my Companion and Guide.
The Supreme is my Friend and Protector.
The Supreme is my Support and Helper.
I lift my heart and thought to Him in lowly trust,
Asking that He make me more and more one with Him in my life and action.

NOVEMBER THIRTEENTH

Salient Thought for the Day.

Remember that complete surrender alone makes us clear channels for the Supreme.

Lines to Memorize.

Since Thou hast given me refuge and taken me into Thy safe-keeping, I have lost all fear.
My long night of anxious waking is forever ended.
I sit now with contentment in my heart;
I walk with free spirit,
And I sleep with surrender in my soul.

Lesson.

We need Divine guidance from within. There are two wills, God's Will and self-will; both are active. The foolish man chooses self-will; the wise man chooses God's Will, because he does not feel safe to be separated from God and His guidance. This is wisdom, but this wisdom cannot be imposed. Life has its culmination when we learn to have a true sense of God as the Supreme Doer. When we acquire spiritual surrender, we rise above all our troubles.

Prayer.

I am only an instrument in Thy Hands, O Lord;
Make me an efficient instrument;
Help me never to forget that Thou art behind me in every act.
Take from me all egotism and self-importance.
May I always be a humble instrument, wholly submissive to Thy Will.

NOVEMBER FOURTEENTH

Salient Thought for the Day.

Because we refuse to let go, we bar our way to happiness.

Lines to Memorize.

What makes thee so lonely, friend?
One is always lonely in the crowd; yea, and more lonely alone, with thought of self.
But when one's thought is lost in the Beloved,
One is never lonely in crowd or alone.

Lesson.

To whom comes the light? Not to one who is aggressive, who puts himself first always. If we only can remember what we are, what our relation with the foundation of life is, we are safe. Then whatever we do will be in accord with our higher intuitions. Not by thinking of the world shall we solve the problems of the world. We must step aside. We must step out of ourselves. Man himself prevents the solution of his problems.

Prayer.

Unchanging Eternal Deity, lift my hands from changing things
And fasten them to Thy Eternal treasure.
Free my thought from attachment to the perishable
And tie it to the everlasting.
Cure me of the fever of struggle for the finite.
And teach me to find all my happiness and peace in Thy Infinitude.

NOVEMBER FIFTEENTH

Salient Thought for the Day.

We must have the courage to be led.

Lines to Memorize.

It is best that Thou dost hold my hand and lead me where'er Thou deemest.
I shall follow Thee now with unfaltering faith.
How oft in my searchings have I been distracted and delayed!
Do Thou hold me now by Thy gentle Hand,
I am always in Thy holy keeping.

Lesson.

There are moments in our life when we like to be led; but there are others when we are rebellious. A wise man always wants to be led and this desire does not spring from defeat. In our lack of wisdom and in our lack of the sense of proportion we resist the great Power that is behind the universe and we are broken by it. When we are ready to be led, what a solace it is to the soul!

Prayer.

Compassionate Deity, make my faith in Thy beneficence so unfaltering
That I shall lay whole life in Thy Hand
And feel unbroken trust in Thee even at the darkest hour.
Thou healest the wounds of the heart.
Thy Divine touch brings joy and peace.
Teach me complete surrender,
That I may drop from my grasp the fleeting objects of this world.

Salient Thought for the Day.

The way of wisdom is to surrender to the fundamental laws of life. No one is clever enough to change them.

Lines to Memorize.

When I place my hand of faith in Thy Hand of
 Grace,
I feel secure and walk with free spirit.
When I walk with Thee, mountains of obstacles
 melt before my feet.
I am always safe when Thou dost lead me by
 Thy Hand of Grace.

Lesson.

Fear is a strange element. It distorts. We must remove the cause of fear, and we do it by bringing in the light of understanding. It is a great solace to be reminded by circumstances of our relation with the Infinite. Shall we not inquire : Whence do I come? Whence are my blessings?

Prayer.

May I be ever a humble, faithful servant in
 the Lord's household;
May I never give way to rebellion or arrogance.
May I never obey the dictates of my little will,
May I overcome all egotistic sense;
And learn to say from my heart, "Not I, not I.
 Only Thou!"

NOVEMBER SEVENTEENTH

Salient Thought for the Day.

God gives us more than we ask for; we have only to leave ourselves in His loving, protecting Hands.

Lines to Memorize.

Thou and world, I and mine—
All these thoughts arise;
But when I am alone with Thee
And no thought hinders my soaring soul,
I find all and
All I find in Thee.

Lesson.

The Lord never fails toward His children. As long as we depend on our changeable lower nature we are constantly shifting and unstable. We cannot help matters by giving way to anxiety. Ours is to trust in God and do as well as we can. His care is untiring and always wisely given. He never fails to know our need and to meet it. Surrender to the Divine gives us something which we do not find in the ordinary walks of life.

Prayer.

O Thou All-blessed One, I am Thy servant;
I am Thy child;
I am nothing apart from Thee.
I can do or say nothing except as Thou makes me to speak or act,
I am only an instrument in Thy Hands.

NOVEMBER EIGHTEENTH

Salient Thought for the Day.

Until we learn to trust wholly in our Origin, we cannot express our highest.

Lines to Memorize.

I am always near thee.
Thou needst never call Me aloud,
I hear the silent whisper of thy soul.

Lesson.

When we are oppressed, we seek the remedy on the outside: but it is never found in the physical. We must seek our Source. Worry or anxiety is not caused by misfortune. It comes from lack of trust. It shows a need of spiritual unfoldment. Never let your mind be disturbed by outside happenings. Try to relax and be free from all anxiety. When we surrender wholly to Him, we can never come to grief in any way. When we understand our real being, Infinitude dawns in our heart and we become a mighty factor in the life of humanity.

Prayer.

Take my hands and feet, my heart and mind, O Lord;
Make what use of them Thou wilt.
I am but a lowly channel for Thy Divine power
Manifest that power in whatever way Thou deemest best.
Make me a conscious part of Thy Effulgent Being
And may I have no life separate from Thy Life.

NOVEMBER NINETEENTH

Salient Thought for the Day.

Self-consciousness is a very great obstacle in the path of trust and surrender.

Lines to Memorize.

Who art Thou that walkest before me and behind me.
And in the hour of sleep standest in watch beside me?
Wilt Thou not unveil Thy Face whose love hath already made me captive?

Lesson.

What does self-consciousness imply? It means that we are primarily conscious of our outer surroundings, our outer setting. People, things, incidents, objects are of minor importance. We should not give them first place. What is the most important thing for a worker to be conscious of? The task he is going to perform. What is the most important thing for a student to be conscious of? His study. If they are conscious of anything else, no matter what it is, it is an impediment to their success. Self-consciousness is always a drawback in life.

Prayer.

All-merciful One, grant me strength to cast off all self-love and self-will.
Help me to rise above all alien thoughts.
May I learn through Thy Grace to overcome all selfish impulses.
May I lose myself in unceasing devotion to Thee.
May I seek Thee at all times with ardor of spirit.

Salient Thought for the Day.

More childlike we are, more we have access to the Divine.

Lines to Memorize.

Thy blessing of protecting love
Ever riseth up in my heart
Like an unfailing spring.
I am washed, cleansed and made alive anew
By its sacred water.

Lesson.

If we can abandon our fears and anxieties, the Power within will not fail us. We all have Divine intelligence. It may burn dim; but that which burns dimly, by our own effort can be made to burn brightly. That Divine Power is ever with you to give you courage and make you strong. May It ever fill you with life and light and cheer.

Prayer.

May the All-loving Mother of the Universe, bestow on me Her tender blessing.
May She never withdraw from me Her loving care.
May I learn to be worthy of Her care and blessing.
May I never cease to be Her humble child,
Wholly dependent on Her Will
And looking to Her for all strength and protection.

NOVEMBER TWENTY-FIRST

Salient Thought for the Day.

The spirit of self-surrender and earnest prayer always brings true growth.

Lines to Memorize.

Sweet Comforter, my soul's abiding shelter,
Thou hast saved me by Thy look of boundless compassion.
Thy smile hath gladdened my whole being:
Touch of Thy Hand hath filled me with strength.

Lesson.

Peace and Divine blessings are always with you. May the Divine Mother ever protect you and surround you with Her love. Pray to Her always to make things clear to you. We are parts of that great unbounded Whole. Always keep your gaze on the fact that you are a child of Divine Mother. She will never fail you. When we have severed ourselves from the little self, we shall find that we are connected with a very deep Source of life.

Prayer.

May that One who is always a loving Mother, watching over every living thing,
May She grant me endurance and forbearance.
May a new zeal and a new sense of consecration awaken in my heart.
May I turn to the Great Mother in the hour of sorrow and in the hour of joy.
And seek all my consolation in Her alone.
May I have no life separate from Her Life.

NOVEMBER TWENTY-SECOND

Salient Thought for the Day.

It matters not how long we have to wait.

Lines to Memorize.

Why art Thou hiding from me?
How long wilt Thou remain hidden?
My hope will not bid me rest.
With desolate heart I seek;
With yearning heart I pray.
Wilt Thou not come once again
And receive my love?

Lesson.

We are many times stranded, when we need to hear the word of command, when we need to feel a guiding hand. The Lord alone knows His work, we can only try to make ourselves fitting instruments in His Hands. It is a great loss when we miss any opportunity to serve Him. We impoverish or enrich ourselves by the way we take advantage of our opportunities. Too often carelessness or indifference cheats us of our blessings and we give up in discouragement.

Prayer.

Grant me, O Lord, untiring patience and abiding perseverance.
May I seek Thee at all times with unswerving devotion.
May I never grow disheartened or give up my search.
May I never forget that those who pray humbly and earnestly, their prayers are answered.
Do Thou bestow on me Thy peace and Thy tender blessing.

NOVEMBER TWENTY-THIRD

Salient Thought for the Day.

Where shall we put our trust if not there where we find the light of perfect wisdom and perfect love ?

Lines to Memorize.

Forget I may at times when dark clouds gather,
But to have seen Thy Face of love
And known what is not known, save when Thou dost lift the veil,
Is joy forever and crowning glory of life !

Lesson.

There is no separation in the Divine spiritual realm. There can be no separation. Our lives, our actions, are not for our personal blessing. We are not to think of our own salvation. We are not to go anywhere for it. It is done once for all. God is using us to bless His countless children, to bring them to the light. He is doing His work. He knows where we should be placed. We are not here for a moment without His guidance.

Prayer.

O Thou Boundless One, may I never fail to turn to Thee ;
May I never feel Thy closeness
And learn to depend wholly on Thy love and wisdom.
Keep me mindful of Thy unfailing care.
Fill me with Thy blessing that I may carry that blessing to others.
May I always bear aloft the torch of wisdom
And radiate Thy light in my life.

NOVEMBER TWENTY-FOURTH

Salient Thought for the Day.

Be brave and do not have any anxiety about anything.

Lines to Memorize.

I know now that in storm or calm, in light or dark,
The passage of my life without Thee is ever fraught with danger.
I need Thy Hand of mercy to guide me every hour of day and night.

Lesson.

The sun penetrates the thickest cloud; so will it be with our spiritual consciousness, when we learn to turn to the Great Sun. The only man who can be called a superior man is the one who exhibits his spiritual nature. He stands out like a light. When a person realizes his Divine nature, he is free himself and he brings freedom to others. A man, who is ruled by his physical nature, casts himself off from his Source and closes the door to his rightful heritage.

Prayer.

All-Effulgent Spirit, may I walk in Thy light,
And feel safe and secure because of that light
Grant me Thy loving protection that my mind may be at rest.
May I trust wholly to Thee and take no step without Thy guidance.
Free me from self-bondage and make me strong and full of courage.

Salient Thought for the Day.

Constant leaning upon That which never changes, never fails, is the fulfilment of all joy.

Lines to Memorize.

I have nothing apart from Thee;
I am nothing apart from Thee;
I want nothing other than Thee.
Wilt Thou not stay with me who am so dependent on Thee?
Wilt Thou not take me who have no other than Thee?

Lesson.

Surrender is the greatest of all sources of security. We must not be frightened by it. Our imperfections may seem an insurmountable barrier, but they are nothing. When once we can open our hearts, when once we can bring ourselves before that Great Light which reveals everything, this little darkness of ours will seem only an insignificant momentary condition. We must have faith in the Divine. Those who have such faith, such real devoted yearning, they are not afraid to open themselves to that direct Divine guidance through surrender.

Prayer.

May the Eternal and Unchanging Deity,
Bestow on me a great sense of His Holy Presence.
May I lean upon His Divine strength;
And turn to Him only for help and inspiration.
May all my joy be found in contact with His Divine Being.

Salient Thought for the Day.

One who is mighty in the might of God, evil does not touch him.

Lines to Memorize.

When Thou dost withdraw from me, my heart grows faint with fear and loneliness.
Without Thy grace my life is an empty vessel that I carry day and night.
What joy have I when Thou, Source of my joy, art far from me?
What peace can I have when Thy absence rends my soul with anguish?

Lesson.

As long as we live confined to the physical, there is no getting away from evil and misfortune. The only way a man can escape from evil is to transcend bodily consciousness. What is evil? How can we have a point of contact with it unless we give it? If we have found our point of contact with God, no evil can overtake us. The man who makes the Supreme his source of supply will always flourish in this world.

Prayer.

Grant, O Thou Infinite One, that I may never place my faith in the perishable,
That I may never fix my heart on the ephemeral and fleeting.
May I never seek my comfort or happiness in the material world.
Help me to live my life wholly in Thy great Life
And merge my being in Thy Divine Being.

Salient Thought for the Day.

There must be a definite relationship with our Ideal.

Lines to Memorize.

Speak to me now in this hour of aloofness!
My soul cries out to Thee.
Wilt Thou not hear me and speak to my hungry ear?

Lesson.

Our tendency is to go outward for everything. When we are struck by pain, we seek the remedy outside. We need to turn within for our strength and solace. The path we follow is according to what we ourselves express more or less. We are all equally equipped. We all have the same avenues of expression, but our faculties are focused at different points. As spiritual beings we are inexhaustible, but our material resources are quickly exhausted.

Prayer.

O Thou Most Holy One, bestow on me the blessing of conscious kinship with Thee.
Thou art the Source of my existence;
Grant that I may never forget
That I live and move in Thee alone.
May my thought never be severed from Thee.
May I rest my mind ever on Thy glory.
And feel united with Thee in humility of spirit.

Salient Thought for the Day.

An act of surrender is an act of thanksgiving.

Lines to Memorize.

Bounty of this world only makes my heavy heart heavier.
Now I pray unto Thee with my naked soul, —hiding nothing from Thee,—
That Thou dost show me Thy tender mercy
And abide with me ever and forever.

Lesson.

We cannot help but lift our hearts in gratitude to the One who has given us so much. We revolve in His safe-keeping, whether we have much or little, in difficult moments or in moments of exuberance. In our dark moments we need most to maintain our association with God. We all have cause to be thankful to that One from whom our life flows, from whom we receive all blessings and inspiration. No man can have fullest measure of happiness until he has related himself with the Source of all. It is the fullest blessing to be able to remain in constant mindfulness of the Creator.

Prayer.

I lift my heart to the Divine Being in silent supplication.
May He fill it with thankfulness for all His blessings.
He is the Guiding Power of my soul.
May I learn to offer up my life to Him without reserve.
He is my shelter and unfailing protection.
May I look to Him for safe-keeping and guidance.

Salient Thought for the Day.

Service, worship and submission, these three form the foundation of the spiritual life.

Lines to Memorize.

The wound of separation from Thee remains ever fresh in my heart.
I pray not for its healing;
Its sacred pain doth sanctify my life every hour.
Thou art my unfailing blessing.

Lesson.

If we can learn to wait our turn with ungrudging patience and watchful vigil, we shall find to our amazement that the long hours of day and night, winter and spiring, autumn and summer, are pleasant pastimes for the soul, to renew and refresh it. Does not Nature hold before us the picture of restoration and renewal? We all possess within us the seed of spiritual fruition. Whether it is quickened depends upon us. If we neglect to water and care for it, it will shrivel and die. We must nurture and foster it, then it will grow and bear abundant fruit.

Prayer.

Supreme Being of the Universe, my entire being rests in Thee.
I offer up to Thee my prayer and my thought in humble worship.
Infuse my heart with a new sense of safety.
When Thou art absent from my thought, my soul suffers.
Stay Thou ever near me.

NOVEMBER THIRTIETH

Salient Thought for the Day.

When we gain the consciousness of a spiritual Presence within, a new sense of trust, security and surrender awaken in our heart.

Lines to Memorize.

Oft I sit by thee when thou dreamest thy fancies and seest me not.
I do not wake thee from the slumbering, but only watch thee with my eye of love.
Sweet child, when thy heart is ripe, thou wilt know there is no waste of time either waiting or watching for love.

Lesson.

An abiding sense of an inner Presence not only helps us, it enables us to help others. Amidst turmoil and confusion we seek outer remedies, but these are never lasting. We must go to the very root of our being and find our connection with the inner Source. Then alone shall we come in contact with that upon which we can lean and in which we can trust.

Prayer.

O Thou unfailing Source of life and power and love,
Thou art the sure protection in all affliction and trial,
Thou art my one safe Shelter,
I take refuge in Thee.
Draw me close to Thy Divine Heart
And may I live in constant communion with Thy Holy Spirit,

I seek no more for I have found Him, not by
seeking,—
He came to me when I was not looking,
Opening my soul's secret door.
Friend, how can I tell thee of this strange
mystery ?
He is seen unsought only through this, the soul's
secret door.

December

REDEEMING POWER WITHIN

He whose joy is within, whose pleasure is within, and whose light is within, that devotee, being well established in the Supreme, attains to absolute freedom.

Bhagavad-Gita

DECEMBER FIRST

Salient Thought for the Day.

Man is born Spirit. Primarily he is of God.

Lines to Memorize.

Thou art the fragrance of the flower,
Sweet taste of water,
Life breath of air;—
Verily Thou art the essence and substance of all!

Lesson.

It is a calamity to forget our Divine heritage. It means a voluntary acceptance of ignorance. When the mind is open to the radiant light of the soul, we feel exuberant, and inspiration rises in us; then whatever we perform becomes effective. We are constantly putting off the important things and giving our attention to the non-essential and the lesser. We must turn from the lesser to the greater and lay the chief emphasis on the spiritual and the essential. Life is as we produce it through our thoughts, our aspiration and our action.

Prayer.

Lift the veil from my soul that I may feel the presence of the Great Soul.
Fill me with joyousness, the sense of freedom and all the spiritual blessings my heart longs for.
May I keep my inner eyes ever fixed on the Ideal.
And may my perception of the Inward Presence never grow clouded.

Salient Thought for the Day.

The physical is only a garb. Man wears this at his pleasure and should not be thwarted by it.

Lines to Memorize.

Lord, I called unto Thee in agony of soul, but Thou didst not hear me.
I sought Thee with heavy heart, but Thou didst not come.
My child, I came, but thine eyes were blinded by grief—
Thou couldst not see Me;
And thy heart was senseless with sorrow,
Hence thou couldst not feel My touch.

Lesson.

There is a spiritual type of man. This is the type we admire and look up to. It is the type we find in seers, mystics, Saviours and prophets. How do they differ from us? They have a finer, more transparent quality. When a window is neglected, the glass becomes covered with dirt and dust and lacks transparency. But when the dust is removed, light comes through. So it is with us. When the dust of doubt, selfishness and self-bondage is wiped off, our heart and mind become clear and shining.

Prayer.

May the All-loving Deity pour His healing, strengthening influence on my life.
May He wash it clean and free it of all blemish.
May He help me to live in harmony with my spiritual nature.
And transcend all the limitation of mind and body.

DECEMBER THIRD

Salient Thought for the Day.

A radiant light fills every corner of our existence

Lines to Memorize.

Brilliance of the sun art Thou;
Veil of the twilight art Thou,
Heat of the fire art Thou.
Coolness of the earth Thou art,
Lustre of the moon Thou art,
Mystery of the dark Thou art.

Lesson.

There is no reason for us to dwell in darkness. An inextinguishable soul-light burns in every living being. This is the supreme blessing of God and it is given equally to all. It rests with us to make the medium, through which the light shines, so transparent, so devoid of everything that is alien, that it will shed its glow uncolored and unhindered. The light itself is unfailing; but we can block its radiance by selfish petty thoughts and unworthy actions, by pride, ambition and harshness.

Prayer.

Eternal Spirit, Thou art the Soul of my soul.
Thou art the Essence of my life.
It is Thy light which illumines my being,
May it shine without hindrance.
And drive out all gloom and darkness from my mind and heart.
Mayest Thou be glorified by my every word and action.

Salient Thought for the Day.

If we have a light, it must shine forth.

Lines to Memorize.

Let me read this holy script without the glare of mortal light,
For I see its subtle beauty more vividly by soul's softer glow.
Let me sing this unaccompanied by all other instruments of music,
For I can follow better the one unmingled note.

Lesson.

What the world needs is the inner light. Fulfilment of life does not come when a man carries a heavy weight of materialism. You cannot buy happiness ; you cannot buy peace. The greatest possession is this inner light. Reveal that in your daily living, in every expression of life ; then you will find unending happiness and will give something definite and real to the world. When you have cleansed your inner house, you will radiate something which will throw light upon everything in your path.

Prayer.

May the Supreme Being pour the light of His Divine radiance through my heart and soul.
May I shine with His glory
And shed forth His Divine Light.
May that Light brighten the path of the desolate and afflicted ;
May my whole life be a light to my fellow-men.

DECEMBER FIFTH

Salient Thought for the Day.

The man who knows his Divine heritage becomes like unto it in nature.

Lines to Memorize.

Hail to Thee, Thou who comest at morn with gentle raiment to open our sleep-worn eyes!
Not in dazzling splendor, but with soft white light dost Thou soothe our mortal sight.
Hail to Thee, Thou who comest at morn with fragrant breath.
Filling our mortal frame with vibrant life!

Lesson.

There is no power compelling us to the spiritual life or forcing us to live it. There can be no compulsion in the realm of spirituality. Spiritual living must be spontaneous. This comes in one way only,—when our higher intuition unfolds. This intuition brings us to a consciousness of something beyond this life. The call of the Spirit is ever asking us to go forward. Until we are able to respond to that call, we cannot do our part well as human beings, nor gain access to the spiritual realm.

Prayer.

Infinite Spirit, grant that the voices of this world may never drown Thy voice.
Grant that I may never fail to hear Thy call.
Thy silent word directs my steps.
Thy invisible Presence lights my path.
May I ever follow Thy guidance
And walk in Thy light.

DECEMBER SIXTH

Salient Thought for the Day.

Great souls are sensitive to the touch of the Divine.

Lines to Memorize.

It is not the wind alone that speaketh to our ears.
It is the voice of the Infinite that speaketh to our soul with many tongues.

Lesson.

A man fixes his thought on the great Immensity and at once he bursts out with inspiration. We touch this wholeness of God and immediately we are filled. Our hands become vibrant; our heart becomes vibrant; our mind becomes vibrant. No room is left for the little self. Spiritual intuition is a great aid in the life of spirit. It develops only in that heart in which there is no selfishness. It throws light on every subject and before it even the most insurmountable barriers dwindle away.

Prayer.

Giver of all life, make me more living and fervent in my spiritual striving.
Thou alone dost understand my deeper yearnings
And canst fulfil the longings of my heart.
Thou alone knowest what is needful for my inner growth.
Grant unto me greater inwardness and loftier aspiration.
I yield myself up wholly to Thy loving care,
And ask Thee for Thy blessing.

DECEMBER SEVENTH

Salient Thought for the Day.

If a man is really free and awakened, no one can interfere with his freedom or peace.

Lines to Memorize.

When soul's effulgent light shines forth
Troubles are no more.
Petty worries, fears and all our endless cares
Are no more, are no more,
When soul's effulgent light shines forth.

Lesson.

When we are loving and exuberant, we are not humiliated by anything. It is when our heart is full of harsh feelings that we feel humiliation. A man who is really free never feels harshness; he is never disturbed by outer conditions. What we have or what we have not makes very little difference. The foundation of our happiness rests upon our nobility, our strength and our aspiration. When all our mind and heart are in a state of tranquillity, evil will not find any place in our consciousness and we shall not strike any discordant note in our dealings with others.

Prayer.

Bestow upon me inward freedom, O Lord.
Thou art All-merciful,
May Thy mercy save me from the bondage of selfishness and ignorance.
Make my aspiration so earnest
That it will carry me to Thy blessed Feet.
May I never seek elsewhere my joy or peace or safety.

DECEMBER EIGHTH

Salient Thought for the Day.

As we go deeper within ourself, we are less inclined to notice outer happenings.

Lines to Memorize.

Drink, my soul! from life's perpetual spring,
Where eternity flows in rhythmic current;
Where finite and infinite play in unison their
  game of harmony.

Lesson.

A person who lives in the outside notices all things and all things are noticeable to him. He magnifies. He imagines that a person looks or acts with evil intent. We can magnify evil to such an extent that it becomes a tremendous burden to us. We find no peace even in a jungle. We must learn to conquer this. When a person lives inwardly, he loses contact with the world. When he has found his inner contact, he misses nothing.

Prayer.

May I never go outward for my help and
  protection,
But may I always live close to that inner Spirit
  who dwells in my heart.
May I find freedom through surrender
And gain peace through deeper trust.
May my strength and happiness rest wholly in
  the infinite Presence dwelling in my heart.

DECEMBER NINTH

Salient Thought for the Day.

The life within opens an immense vista.

Lines to Memorize.

I keep still;
Do Thou speak,
For Thou alone canst speak to my soul.

Lesson.

There is but one Saviour—that is the redeeming Spirit within us. The outer Redeemer points the way and the inner Redeemer carries us on it. He speaks to us in the silent solitude of our soul. Out of this inner stillness we often get the greatest refreshment. When our outer life is still, it opens up new avenues for unfoldment. That is why the practice of silence has so much value and helps so much toward spiritual development.

Prayer.

Infinite and Eternal One, help me to feel the need of Thy Presence at every hour of this day.
In each task may I unite my life with Thy Life;
May I live in unbroken communion with Thee.
I listen for Thy Voice:
May it direct my thoughts and words and acts.
I reach out for Thy Hand:
May it lead me ever in the path of wisdom.
Help me to forget my own littleness
And remember only Thy majesty and glory.

DECEMBER TENTH

Salient Thought for the Day.

The real soul of man is in the Cosmic.

Lines to Memorize.

I am the Spirit of eternal youth.
I am form in infinite space.
I am unchanging beauty.
I am undying life.

Lesson.

Our life, our consciousness, we draw from an infinite Source. We may not know it, but we cannot be severed from that Source. Suppose you had found a sure refuge from all misfortune; would it not give a feeling of safety? A wise man does not seek safety in outer riches or defences, he looks to quite another source for his safety—to the inner Spirit. The Spirit within always quickens in us new hope and a new sense of security.

Prayer.

May my life become more and more a part of the Universal Life.
May I lose all smallness of vision.
May my thought expand and heart grow wider in its love and sympathy.
May I seek all my strength and blessing from within,
And depend wholly on the inner Source of inspiration and power.
May the Infinitude or God encompass me,
And lift me out of the narrowness of the finite.

Salient Thought for the Day.

We need all of us to awaken within ourselves the sense of soul-life.

Lines to Memorize.

Thou art all, all ; yea, all in all !
Thou art this, the visible.
Thou art the audible.
All that is invisible and beyond the realm of sound art Thou.

Lesson.

Every soul carries with it its past and is constantly building its future. The soul is the index of the life. We go on evolving, shifting and changing until we find our fulfilment. And where do we find it ? Not in the physical or the material. We must look to another Source. Going within may mean a change for us, but it does not mean finding blankness. It gives man a fresh start. It is as if he were born again. When we have awakened, there comes to us spiritual grandeur born of the indwelling Spirit.

Prayer.

O Thou All-seeing Power within my soul,
Thou alone knowest my life in its many ways,
Thou alone knowest how to guide my destiny,
Do Thou guide my steps in the path of holiness
And keep my heart loving and peaceful.
In Thee alone shall I find rest and peace.

DECEMBER TWELFTH

Salient Thought for the Day.

Suffering bravely borne brings inner unfoldment.

Lines to Memorize.

Pain, Thou art always at work;
Thy hand is ever active, finishing our life's unfinishing structure.
Thou art like a Master-builder, trimming with Thy sharp adamantine tool.
Oft in our ignorance and childish fear we weep and groan.
But I know that Thou art my true and blessed friend.
Thy chisel hath shorn me of my self-delusion.

Lesson.

Are there two entities in the human body? Yes and No. They seem two, but they become one. Very few of us can sever ourselves from the eating, sleeping man; the man who is affected by heat and cold, pain and pleasure, jealousy and anger. This is the part of us which belongs to mortality; this is the part that suffers, changes and dies, because it is the product of the physical. It is good that it suffers, since through that suffering we are led to that other part of us, the eternal part, the selfless part.

Prayer.

Give unto me faith and wisdom, O Lord.
Make my yearning for Thee deeper and more sincere.
May I never seek the things of this world.
May I never give up striving until I have found that Holy One within my soul.

Salient Thought for the Day.

It is not on the outside we must seek our Source.

Lines to Memorize.

The Infinite speaketh to us through earth and water, rock and river, beast and bird, tree and flower;
Through all—Through all;
At dawn It speaketh to our soul
Through the rays of the rising sun.

Lesson.

We are like thirsty souls running away from a spring of fresh water. We run away from that which would bring us what we are seeking. We wonder why we have miseries. We blame others. But there cannot be any misery or discontent without an inner cause. The cause is always inward. Misery comes because we do not listen to the voice within. We must not be content with mere theory. We must find the way of carrying out our ideals.

Prayer.

May my heart be freed from all blemish of material desire,
May I cease all longing for the ephemeral and the changing.
May the Infinite and Eternal One fill my being with greater longing for union with Him.
May He help me to love and serve Him with humble, worthy spirit.

DECEMBER FOURTEENTH

Salient Thought for the Day.

A man is redeemed by knowledge of his innate Divine heritage.

Lines to Memorize.

Naught exists but the empty shadows and sounds of this material world,
That promiseth much, but beareth no fruit,
For it hath a barren heart.
I will not turn to it now that Thou hast opened my sight of understanding.

Lesson.

The remedy for outwardness is for man to learn from what he has come. Every man must have direct consciousness of his Source. A man is not redeemed when we remind him of his imperfections. Our life must always be unproductive so long as we turn our attention to outward things. The only way we can find the blending harmony in a harsh discordant world is by finding something else ; and that something is not outside, it is within.

Prayer.

Thou who art the Embodiment of all blessing,
Make my life fruitful and rich in blessing to others.
Help me never to seek happiness in the outward world.
But to turn within for all my joy and strength.
Open my eyes to the inward Beauty.
Open my ears to the inward Voice.

DECEMBER FIFTEENTH

Salient Thought for the Day.

It is through the inner that we govern our outer life.

Lines to Memorize.

Search in thine house;
Look again and yet again.
Why dost thou go about wandering,
Roaming like a wanton beggar from door to door?
Thou art not such;
Thy estate not so low.

Lesson.

What we see in outer life, whether it makes for success or failure, beauty or ugliness, is the result of what we evolve from within. We are responsible for it. We are preparing all the time for our blessing or for our misfortune. Whether our thought, our attitude, our interest, is incoming or outgoing will determine the whole question. We never find our fulfilment through the outer. A man cannot continue to live wholly in the outer life without breaking himself.

Prayer.

O Thou Infinite Spirit, I came to Thee in humble submission.
Thou art the Source of my life;
To live apart from Thee means death.
Thou art the Source of my power;
To act apart from Thee means weakness and defeat.
In supplication I lift my heart to Thee,
Fill it with new life and inner strength.

Salient Thought for the Day.

Only when we start from within do we attain the highest fulfilment.

Lines to Memorize.

One speck of this doubting dust lodged on our heart draws another and yet another,
Till no longer our vision is true.
We pray unto Thee, Thou destroyer of darkness,
Help us to keep our heart pure, clear and free from this veil of unknowing.

Lesson.

Failing and faltering must not discourage you. If you hold fast to your inner point of contact and keep your eyes fixed on it, it will clear away all imperfections. It will surely lift and redeem. Never lose your inward vision or turn away from the inner Guidance. Do not doubt or question it. Life to reach the highest fruition must find its expression from within. Do not forget that you are a little child. You may blunder, but so long as your heart is free from sordid thoughts and your inward vision is clear, you are safe. It is not merely a question of wanting the inner light, we must kindle it within ourselves; rather, we must uncover it, for it is always burning there unperceived.

Prayer.

May my vision grow clear and my inward sight far-reaching.
May I seek within for all my knowledge and inspiration.
May the inner Guidance always lead me.
May I walk always by my soul's hidden light.

DECEMBER SEVENTEENTH

Salient Thought for the Day.

If we can let our mind dwell even for a moment on Infinitude it will revive us.

Lines to Memorize.

Master Ferry-man, Thou hast saved this desperate and helpless wayfarer
From drowning in the black waters of misery.

Lesson.

We suffocate ourselves when we dwell on our outward limitations and material problems. If we can bring ourselves to self-forgetfulness, poise and peace will come. We must empty ourselves of these thoughts that weight us. If we do this, a sense of inner Presence will rise in our heart. We cannot feel this inward Presence without quite spontaneously gaining freedom from all our troubles and difficulties. To reveal it we must have fervor of feeling and steadfastness of purpose.

Prayer.

Thou In-dwelling Spirit, Thou art the Infinite Presence within my soul.
Make me conscious of Thy vastness and effulgence.
Pour out upon me Thy soothing influence.
Heal me and restore me.
May I forget myself utterly in thought of Thee.

Salient Thought for the Day.

When we know that we are a definite part of that mighty, indivisible Spirit, all petty thoughts vanish.

Lines to Memorize.

Art Thou finite?
Art Thou infinite?
I know not Thy vastness,
Nay, I crave not such knowledge.
This only I know through Thy grace,
That Thou art my all,—
Yea, my all-in-all.

Lesson.

We make ourselves over to God, then we become one. Freshness of faith, freshness of love, freshness of trust; these will all come. God is the whole of life, we are the part. No matter how vast God and the universe may be, we are still a part of them. Sometimes through our selfish whims we drift away from the Center of things, but we never cease to be a part of the Whole.

Prayer.

Loosen my hold on the objects of this world, O Lord,
And fasten it to Thy eternal Being.
Thou art full of infinite compassion:
Have mercy and grant unto me a new understanding.
Quicken in me a new sight.
Bestow upon me a closer touch with Thee.
May I never forget that Thou art the Source of my life and strength.

DECEMBER NINETEENTH

Salient Thought for the Day.

It rests with each one of us to set a standard for the world..

Lines to Memorize.

When I brought Thee my broken *vina* it was unstrung and dumb:
Music had it none,—
Discordant and harsh were the sounds in its desolate heart.
Now I know not whether this be the same that was once broken and mute,
Or a new one Thou hast given me to finish my life's unfinished song.

Lesson.

We must have definite standards in all our actions. These standards must rest upon our inner consciousness. There must be a definite point on which to focus, and through this we relate ourselves to all things. If we must neglect something, let it be the outer rather than the inner. An inner sense of proportion is absolutely necessary in spiritual life. We must measure all things by an inner soul-standard. We injure ourselves and our fellow-men when we grow careless and negligent in our inner life.

Prayer.

All-abiding Spirit, may I grow more conscious of Thy Reality.
Do Thou heal all my wounds,
And refresh my spirit.
Do Thou kindle a new flame in my heart;
And help me to keep it burning with steady glow.

Salient Thought for the Day.

The great safety and power of man lies in the consciousness of his Source.

Lines to Memorize.

In solitude's inmost stillness there is a sacred shrine.
Divine harmony sings there,....,
Pure gladness shines there,
Sweet fragrance permeates the air.

Lesson.

When we have our hands and brain and heart all working as a whole, there is no limit to our power. How much more is this the case if we become united with the wholeness of life. When this comes, the entire being is radiant. When we do not do our part according to inner guidance, we always feel a void ; and it is that sense of void which brings unhappiness. The outgoing person finds nothing but trouble.

Prayer.

May I realize more and more that the blessings of the Supreme
Flow through my life in fullness at every hour ;
That He abides within me unceasingly
And perceive my innermost thoughts and feelings.
He knows my difficulties and trials.
He also knows their remedy.
May I take shelter in His Divine Being
And dwell ever with Him in the inner shrine.

DECEMBER TWENTY-FIRST

Salient Thought for the Day.

Life is never safe unless we walk in the soul-light.

Lines to Memorize.

Pure thought is more precious far than all the diamonds and the rubies of this world,
For it brightens our inner life
And sheds upon us its precious peace.

Lesson.

If we fix our whole interest on the exterior, we see nothing but confusion and disorder; and there is little possibility of bringing about an ordered state of mind. That is why we need to go within. There would be no calamity if every individual took time to go within. In our life now we seem to think and feel and seek more outwardly than inwardly, and that is the reason we are so often distressed in mind and body.

Prayer.

All-protecting One, Thou art my only defense and source of safety.
Do Thou guide my thoughts and actions
That they may be illumined by Thy inner light.
May that light shine in my life
And make it radiant with joy and holiness.
Grant me Thy blessing and bestow upon me Thy loving protection.

Salient Thought for the Day.

The inner Light is always there shining with gentle glow even when we lose our contact with it.

Lines to Memorize.

Perchance the flame of thy life burns dim
Or flickers in the wind of this world.
Fear not its extinction.
Hold fast with all thy faith.
No power in gale or storm,
Nay, naught in heaven or earth,
Can rob thee of thine immortal flame.

Lesson.

We must let God hold our hand and guide us. He will heal all our wounds and quicken our higher aspirations. He will fill the lamp of our soul with fresh oil. Life is not burdensome, if we enter deeply into its spirit. If we keep the light burning, it becomes beautiful. We cannot force our access to the Divine. We gain access to It by a loving heart and a guileless mind. It is deep within that we find our connection with Divinity ; and we cannot enter that inner Holy of Holies until we lose our outward habits of mind and cultivate the habit of looking inward.

Prayer.

May I learn to turn inward for all my help.
May I never fail to perceive Thy indwelling
  Presence.
May my eyes never be blind to its radiance,
And may I live and act always conscious of that
  glowing light burning in my soul.

DECEMBER TWENTY-THIRD

Salient Thought for the Day.

The great in-dwelling Mother always takes care of us.

Lines to Memorize.

Gracious Mother look to us, look to us awhile.
These mountain-like obstacles will vanish,
If Thou wilt but for a moment turn Thy gentle face to us, Thy helpless children.

Lesson.

Too often we try to solve our spiritual problems by material means. We seek on the outside and never gain any satisfaction. Wise men search within. There they find a Power which answers all their questions and solves all their problems. A loving Mother dwells in every heart, safeguarding, protecting and guiding. If we would have peace, we must learn to depend on Her never-failing love, and surrender to Her all-wise Will.

Prayer.

O Thou Infinite and Effulgent one,
I pray unto Thee that Thou wilt dispel all deadness from my heart,
That I may sense Thy protecting, watchful love abiding there.
Drive out from my mind the darkness of doubt and ignorance.
Make my vision clear and my faith unfaltering,
That I may lean upon Thee and look to Thee for all my needs.

Salient Thought for the Day.

We turn a deaf ear to the inner Voice that is pleading lovingly to redeem us.

Lines to Memorize.

But none can find access to this holy sanctuary
Whose inner eyes are closed;
Nor can one enter there
Whose footsteps are heavy and hard.

Lesson.

If we realize our inefficiency, our helplessness, let us try to find that part of our being which will bring us assistance. The soul cries out for freedom, freedom from the outer self. The greatest struggle is with the outward self. One who has conquered this self is devoid of self-bondage that when he asserts himself all he can assert is the Divine part. One who has blended his life with the Divine, he is master.

Prayer.

Thou redeeming Power within my soul,
Quicken my inward senses,
That I may hear and see Thee
And follow Thy path.
Make my ears so alert that they may always catch the sound of Thy Voice.
Make my sight so keen that it will perceive Thy silent approach.
Make my heart so pure that it will be ready to receive Thee.

Salient Thought for the Day.

Let there be Christmas in our hearts every day, renewing us, bringing us a new birth.

Lines to Memorize.

What need have I of aught else,
When Thou dost fill me and surround me
With Thy inexhaustible and all-filling love?

Lesson.

The Christ is a great Spirit of universal significance. We clothe Him in the garment which is familiar to us. The Christ-Spirit is a universal avenue through which flows Divine blessing. Jesus was an Oriental. In order to understanding the pathos of His life and soul, we must enter into the Oriental consciousness. The true Christ is not the dogmatic Christ, but a Light shining from a lofty height shedding beneficence on all humanity. It is for each one of us to bring this Christ-Light into our soul.

Prayer.

O Thou Saviour of men, make my heart a fitting sanctuary,
Where Thy saving Presence can find Its dwelling.
Create in me a new openness to Thy supreme blessing.
Rouse in me a new yearning for Thy redeeming grace.
May my soul become Thy abiding-place.
Thou bringest joy: fill me with Thy holy joy.
Thou bringest peace; bestow on me Thy unbroken peace.

Salient Thought for the Day.

The real redemption is innate. The door must be opened from within.

Lines to Memorize.

Glance of Thine eyes hath given me new sight of hope;
Fragrance of Thy being hath awakened in me pure love.
Verily Thou art the breath of my life,
Strength of my limbs,
Solace of my soul!

Lesson.

There is only one thing which either helps or hinders, it is the application of our Ideal in our life. When we miss the higher inspiration of the inner Power, we miss everything. That which is vital in our life and that which cannot be separated from our life is inborn. How do we carry it? As the flower carries fragrance—unconsciously. All our higher thoughts and aspirations are ours by innate right. When we forget this, our vision becomes distorted. Forget yourself and you will be lifted up to state of inspiration and become a mouth-piece for the Highest.

Prayer.

Abiding Spirit within my heart!
Keep me ever mindful of my sacred heritage.
Make me so steadfast that I shall never forget that Eternal One from whom I have descended.
Help me to live my life in close communion with that Holy One
And prove worthy of His saving grace.

DECEMBER TWENTY-SEVENTH

Salient Thought for the Day.

Man becomes his own redeemer when he turns within.

Lines to Memorize.

The warring sea of life hath torn my garment in its wild fury;
It tossed me by its mighty waves into a whirlpool of despair;
But Thy thread of love like a life-line fell over me,
Wind Thou this single thread of love all about me;
I need no other shielding for my life.

Lesson.

Even God cannot help us, a Saviour cannot save us, unless we are awakened and willing. If One should come with all the power of healing and restoring, who will receive that One but those who are awakened? That is why great teachers tell us again and again that riches, perfect health or happiness can have no lasting quality unless they are based on our soul-heritage within.

Prayer.

O Thou Infinite and All-wise Being,
Awaken in me a consciousness of Thy unbounded love.
Thy love is the redeeming power in my soul;
May I be fortified by Thy love,
And may I carry Thy love into the world.
Thou art the embodiment of all blessedness.
Bestow upon me Thy loving blessing
And enfold me in Thy abiding peace.

DECEMBER TWENTY-EIGHTH

Salient Thought for the Day.

A man opens or closes his own inner door.

Lines to Memorize.

Behold how the sky of our fair heart is darkened by the rising mist of jealousy and anger, suspicion and doubt.
These powers of blackness by their quick alliance, form this veil of unknowing.
Shall we not keep the sky of our heart clear and fair like a polished mirror, to reflect the truer image of our inmost soul?

Lesson.

We must not find fault with the Supreme and call Him partial. We must look to ourselves to find out in what way we fail to be perfect channels for His power. Not a Saviour, not a prophet or a saint, can pour salvation on our heads; we ourselves open the door to receive it. We also shut the avenue of the Spirit, when it is closed. The Spirit flows through us all equally; according to the avenues through which it flows is it colored.

Prayer.

All-merciful One, do not let me close the door of my heart to Thy mercy.
Do not let me bar the current of Thy love.
Thou seest my innermost depths;
Thou knowest that I long to love and serve Thee.
Grant unto me the power to be a worthy channel for Thy work.

Salient Thought for the Day.

Man possesses the power of Divinity within him.

Lines to Memorize.

Get thee gone, thou foul disease of mind!
Doubt is thy name; thou dweller in darkness.
Pestilent thoughts are thy creation.
Thou dost cloud our mind and by strange distortion hide our soul's effulgent light.

Lesson.

If we allow doubt of the inner Power to linger in our mind it clouds our spiritual vision and destroys our peace. When we doubt the reality of our inner being, we lay the foundation for all misery and unhappiness. As long as we dwell in the outer, we cannot escape from limitations and inperfections. But the outer is a very small part of man. We all have the power of God within us. To disbelieve this is to cheat ourselves of our true heritage. It is better to believe in our higher nature. When we have faith in that we break the power of the lower nature.

Prayer.

Thou who art the Ruler of the Universe,
In Thee I seek my resting-place.
In Thee alone can I find safety.
Thou art the one eternal refuge.
In Thee I seek my shelter.
To Thee I surrender my all.
Thou alone canst fulfil my desires,
And Thou alone canst free me from desires.
I give myself up wholly unto Thee.

DECEMBER THIRTIETH

Salient Thought for the Day.

Turning within is the sum and substance of all spiritual life.

Lines to Memorize.

In serene and silent contemplation
I feel Thy infinite Being.
It is ever smoothing to my soul.

Lesson.

We cannot afford to be careless in our inner life. We help ourselves and other just in proportion as we exhibit our inner soul qualities. We devote ourselves eagerly to outer nonessentials and they color our mind. It is not that God gives more power to one than to another. He equips all equally; but man does not always take advantage of His blessings. True efficiency must come from within. It springs from spiritual ardour. We cannot have power without inner wisdom. Our salvation lies in the practice of inwardness.

Prayer.

Thou Infinite and Eternal Deity, teach me to seek Thee always in my inner striving.
May I never go without to find Thee.
Thou art the soul of my soul;
Thou art the Heart of my heart.
Thou art the Life of my life,
May I ever seek Thee where alone Thou canst be found.

DECEMBER THIRTY-FIRST

Salient Thought for the Day.

If we keep our inner lamp burning, it will transmit to the world its radiant glow.

Lines to Memorize.

Awakener, Thy robe of many hues
Hath transformed the dull sky into a lustre of loveliness.
I never tire of Thy wondrous light;
I am never sated by Thy ever-fresh beauty.

Lesson.

In order to find our point of contact with God, we must find our point of contact within. All ideals are first conceived in that inner being; and as they are applied in the life, our life becomes fruitful or unfruitful. Every one has some ideal, but all do not live up to it. We must work it out. Those who from the outset deny their power to do this, they accomplish little; but those who strive for it, their life is productive. We must not leave our ideal indefinite.

Prayer.

All-radiant Light of the Universe!
Make my heart so harmonious, so free from alien and unworthy impulses,
That I may ever feel Thy infinite and all-loving Presence within me.
Sun, moon, stars, all express Thy Divine radiance
Thou art my life; Thou art the Light of my soul.
Shine brightly within me
And may I never veil Thy glory.

NOTES

Food which increase life-force, energy, strength, health, joy and cheerfulness and which are savory, soothing, substantial and agreeable are liked by one of finer nature.

The over-active nature likes food which are bitter, sour, saline, over-hot, pungent, dry, burning and which produce grief, pain and disease.

That which is stale, insipid, putrid, cooked overnight, even leavings or unclean food, are liked by the dense, heavy nature.

Bhagavad-Gita